D0714062

Discourse and Organization

edited by

David Grant, Tom Keenoy and Cliff Oswick

WITHDRAWN

SAGE Publications

London • Thousand Oaks • New Delhi

Acknowledgements

Our thanks go to Rosemary Nixon, Hans Lock and their colleagues at Sage for their advice, encouragement and patience.

Introduction and editorial arrangement © David Grant, Tom Keenoy and Cliff Oswick 1998
Chapter 1 © Robert J. Marshak 1998
Chapter 2 © Jill Woodilla 1998
Chapter 3 © Iain L. Mangham 1998
Chapter 4 © Cynthia Hardy, Thomas B. Lawrence and Nelson Phillips 1998
Chapter 5 © Yiannis Gabriel 1998
Chapter 6 © Miriam Salzer-Mörling 1998
Chapter 7 © Anne Wallemacq and David Sims 1998
Chapter 8 © Gibson Burrell 1998
Chapter 9 © Gerrit Broekstra 1998
Chapter 10 © Didier Cazal and Dawn Inns 1998
Chapter 11 © Mike Reed 1998
Chapter 12 © Richard Dunford and Ian Palmer 1998

First published 1998

All rights reserved. No part of this publication may be reproduced, stored in a retrieval system, transmitted or utilized in any form or by any means, electronic, mechanical, photocopying, recording or otherwise, without permission in writing from the Publishers.

SAGE Publications Ltd
6 Bonhill Street
London EC2A 4PU

SAGE Publications Inc.
2455 Teller Road
Thousand Oaks, California 91320

SAGE Publications India Pvt Ltd
32, M-Block Market
Greater Kailash – 1
New Delhi 110 048

British Library Cataloguing in Publication data

A catalogue record for this book is available from the British Library

ISBN 0 7619 5670 0
ISBN 0 7619 5671 9 (pbk)

Library of Congress catalog card number 98–61095

Typeset by Photoprint, Torquay, Devon
Printed in Great Britain by Redwood Books, Trowbridge, Wiltshire

Contents

List of Tables and Figures

Tables

Figures

Notes on Contributors

Gerrit Broekstra is Professor of Management and Systems Sciences at the Netherlands Business School, Nijenrode University, The Netherlands. He is also Director of CORE, the Nijenrode Centre for Corporate Renewal. He was formerly a professor at Erasmus University, Rotterdam. He holds a PhD in physics and has been President of the Dutch Systems Society and President of the International Federation for Systems Research. He was also a visiting Professor of Organization Behaviour at the Kellogg Graduate School of Management, Northwestern University, Chicago. His research interests include applying cybernetics and systems thinking, and specifically complexity theory, to problems of organizational change and renewal.

Gibson Burrell is Professor of Organizational Behaviour at the University of Warwick, UK, and joint editor (with Mike Reed) of the journal *Organization*. He is author of *Pandemonium* (1997) and co-author (with Gareth Morgan) of *Sociological Paradigms and Organizational Analysis* (1979). He has published on issues of sexuality and postmodernism.

Didier Cazal is currently Maître de Conférences at Université Lille I, France. He served as an assistant cultural attaché in the French Embassy in Seoul and as an invited lecturer at Seoul National University in Korea. He has been an Associate Professor at ESC Marseille for nine years. He has published various articles and book chapters (some in English) and two books (in French). He is now completing a book on the social construction of organizations and their boundaries (in English). His research interests focus on discourse and action in organizations and international comparisons of management and organizations. He is a member of the board of the French-speaking Human Resource Management Association.

Richard Dunford is Associate Professor of Management at the Macquarie Graduate School of Management, Macquarie University, Sydney, Australia. He has spent most of the last twenty years as an academic within a number of universities in Australia and New Zealand, but has also spent periods outside universities, both in the private (oil industry) and public (technology policy) sectors. His teaching, consulting and research interests span corporate strategy, organizational discourse and organizational behaviour. His current research is on corporate restructuring. He has published in a range of journals, including *Administrative Science Quarterly*, *Academy of Management Review*, *Social Studies of Science*, *Organization Studies* and the *Journal of Organizational Behaviour*.

Yiannis Gabriel is a Lecturer in Organizational Studies at Bath University, UK. He is the author of *Freud and Society*, *Working Lives in Catering*, joint author of *Organizing and Organizations*, *Experiencing Organizations* and *The Unmanageable Consumer*, and author of various articles on social psychology, organizational culture and symbolism. His research interests lie mainly in the areas of organizational and psychoanalytic theory and focus on issues such as organizational storytelling and folklore, contemporary consumption and the concepts of the unmanaged and unmanageable. He is joint editor of the journal *Management Learning*.

David Grant is a Senior Lecturer in Human Resource Management at the Management Centre, King's College, University of London, UK. His current research interests include analysis of the language, ideology and beliefs surrounding human resource management. He has published in a range of journals. This includes recent contributions to *Personnel Review, Organization, Journal of Applied Management Studies, Industrial Relations Journal* and *Employee Relations*. He has also co-edited *Metaphor and Organizations* (1996, with Cliff Oswick) and *Organization Development: Metaphorical Explorations* (1996, with Cliff Oswick).

Cynthia Hardy has recently moved to the Department of Management at Melbourne University in Australia after sixteen years as a Professor in Strategy and Organization in the Faculty of Management at McGill University, Canada. She received her PhD from Warwick University in the UK. Her research interests focus on the role of power and politics in organizations, especially with regard to interorganizational collaboration and strategy making. She has published articles in, among others, the *Academy of Management Journal, Organization Studies, Journal of Management Studies, California Management Review* and *Journal of Applied Behavioural Studies*. She has also published eight books and edited volumes including (with Stewart Clegg and Walter Nord) the *Handbook of Organization Studies* (1996), which won the 1997 George R. Terry Book Award at the Academy of Management.

Dawn Inns is Senior Lecturer in Organizational Behaviour at the University of Westminster, UK. She obtained an MA in Organizational Analysis and Behaviour (International Variant) from Lancaster University. Previous to this she worked at INSEAD in France, organizing management education seminars. Her current research interests include: metaphor and organizational language; literature and organizational analysis, and cross-cultural comparisons (France/England). She is a doctoral candidate at the Centre for Social Theory and Technology, Keele University. Her PhD is on the topic of 'identity'.

Tom Keenoy is a Reader in Management at the Management Centre, King's College, University of London, UK. His research interests include human resource management, metaphor, managerial discourses and industrial relations.

Thomas B. Lawrence is an Associate Professor at the University of Victoria, Canada. His research interests centre on the manner in which interested actors work to shape their institutional context. For the past four years, he has been involved in an intensive examination of the relationship between interorganizational collaboration and the domains in which it occurs.

Iain L. Mangham is Emeritus Professor of Management at Bath University and Senior Research Fellow at the Management Centre, King's College, London, UK. His publications have been largely concerned with dramaturgical perspectives on social and organizational life, and with power, performance and organizational change. He is currently researching and writing about similar issues, but has recently developed an interest in emotions, morality and character. Presently, he is seeking to address some of these subjects through the medium of fiction.

Robert J. Marshak is an organizational consultant affiliated with universities and institutes around the world. He is President of Marshak Associates, Adjunct Professor in Residence at the School of Public Affairs, American University, Washington, DC, Visiting Senior Research Fellow at the Management Centre, King's College, University of London, visiting faculty at the Behavioral Science Institute, Korea University, Seoul, and a professional member, NTL Institute for Applied Behavioural Science, USA. His consultancy and research focuses on strategic organizational change, the use of metaphors and symbolic data in organizational diagnosis and intervention, East Asian culturally based models of change, and the covert or hidden dimensions of groups and organizations. He has published in a range of journals, including *Journal of Applied Behavioural Science, Organizational Dynamics, Organization Development Practitioner, The Annual Handbook on Developing Human Resources* and *Training and Development Journal.*

Cliff Oswick is a Senior Lecturer in Organization Theory and Development at the Management Centre, King's College, University of London, UK. He has ongoing research interests in metaphor, rhetoric and other discursive aspects of organizing. At present he is exploring the role and cognitive status of irony, paradox and anomaly in the study of organizations. He has contributed chapters to several edited books and published in a range of journals, including recent contributions to *Industrial Relations Journal, Journal of Applied Management Studies, Organization* and *Personnel Review*. He has also co-edited *Metaphor and Organizations* (1996, with David Grant) and *Organization Development: Metaphorical Explorations* (1996, with David Grant).

Ian Palmer is an Associate Professor in the School of Management at the University of Technology, Sydney, Australia. He teaches and researches in the field of organizational analysis. He has recently held visiting positions at Cornell University and the University of Virginia. He has published in a range of national and international journals, including *Sociology, Journal of Industrial Relations, Academy of Management Review, Asia Pacific Journal of Human Resources, Labour and Industry* and *Journal of Management Education*. His current research interests concern collaboration, new forms of organizing and the discourse of change.

Nelson Phillips is an Associate Professor in the Faculty of Management at McGill University, Canada. His research interests include organizational collaboration, corporate reputation and the intersection of management and cultural studies. Much of his work has involved the application of semiotic and discursive approaches to organizational research. He has published articles in the *Academy of Management Journal, Organization Science, Organization* and *Organization Studies.*

Mike Reed is Professor of Organization Theory in the Department of Behaviour in Organizations at Lancaster University, UK. His research interests include theoretical development in organizational analysis, changes to the expert division of labour and their implications for organizational forms, and the emergence of 'disorganized organizations' in high/postmodernity. His previous publications include *Redirections in Organizational Analysis* (1985), *The Sociology of Management* (1989), *The Sociology of Organizations* (1992), *Rethinking Organization* (1992, co-edited with

M. Hughes) and *Organizing Modernity* (1994, co-edited with L. Ray). A book provisionally entitled *Beyond the Iron Cage?* is forthcoming, and he is joint editor with Gibson Burrell of the journal *Organization*.

Miriam Salzer-Mörling works half-time as an Assistant Professor at the School of Business, Stockholm University, Sweden, and half-time as a consultant in the areas of corporate communications and change. She received her PhD in 1994 at Linköping University with a dissertation on organizational identity across borders, in which she focused on the construction of meanings in an international corporate setting. Inspired by anthropologists' works, she has carried out ethnographic studies at Ikea and Sweden Post (the Swedish Post Office). Her writings centre on culture, story-telling, the production of texts, and sense-making.

David Sims is Professor of Management Studies at Brunel University, UK. He has a background in operational research and organizational behaviour. His research interests have been in management thinking and learning, particularly where it concerns agenda shaping and problem construction and the links between these topics and organizational change. An additional recent emphasis has been on approaches from narrative psychology and viewing the managerial world as story-telling. He is joint editor of *Management Learning*, and is author or co-author of some sixty books and articles and a further forty or so international conference papers.

Anne Wallemacq is Assistant Professor at the University of Namur, Belgium. She has published a number of studies on the perception of time. From this she has developed a research interest in sense-making in organizations, in particular 'anomical' situations, that is, crises of perception and interpretation. She currently leads an interdisciplinary research group on the development of language and logic in organizational life.

Jill Woodilla recently completed her PhD in Organization Studies at the University of Massachusetts, Amherst, USA. Her dissertation focuses on sense-making around changing work practices during organizational change. Her other research interests include exploring how organizing is accomplished through conversing, and ways in which times – as multiple concepts and unique individual experiences – influence organizational behaviour.

Introduction: Organizational Discourse: Of Diversity, Dichotomy and Multi-disciplinarity

David Grant, Tom Keenoy and Cliff Oswick

The analysis of organizations, as they struggle to survive and expand within the context of globalizing market forces, presents us with a bewildering diversity of managerial strategies, policies and practices. In order to make sense of progressively uncertain, inconsistent and fluctuating managerial behaviour, commentators have increasingly turned to the identification and analysis of the language and symbolic media we employ to describe, represent, interpret and theorize what we take to be the facticity of organizational life. In many instances this has enabled them to move to new levels of understanding in the analysis of contemporary organizational issues. These developments lead to two broad assertions. First, that it is difficult to deny the importance of discourse analysis in the study of organizations; and, second, that 'organizational discourse' is an emerging focus of interest in current management literature and thinking.

However, organizational discourse is poorly defined. Despite numerous theoretical antecedents, it has few clear parameters and, as a field of study, it incorporates a variety of diverse perspectives and methodologies reflecting its multi-disciplinary origins. This collection represents an attempt to both illustrate the range of possible approaches to discourse and demonstrate its analytical purchase in the study of organization. The book's title, *Discourse and Organization*, reflects the contributors' central concerns with both the discursive aspects of the behaviour of organizations and their members and how discourse is embodied in the *process* of organizing. The book is divided into four parts. The chapters in Part I, 'Talk and Action', explore the relationship between discourse, action and interaction and their impact on organizational structure and behaviour. Part II, 'Stories and Sense-Making', focuses on the analytical potential of the 'story' as a means of illuminating the ways in which organizational members make sense of their experience of organization. Part III, 'Discourse and Social Theory', includes contributions which demonstrate the fundamental significance of linguistic usage and discursive construction to the ontologies of 'organization'. The final part, 'A Concluding Discourse', explores the claims and limitations of organizational discourse as a means of enriching our understanding of organization.

Discourse in Perspective

Defining discourse is no mean feat. Language, talk, stories and conversations are the very stuff of organizational interaction and, of course, discourse is an inevitable feature of social life in general. The definitions in use are heavily influenced by the theories and concepts underpinning the type of analysis being pursued and, given the multi-disciplinary roots of discourse analysis, this is both a strength and a weakness. On the one hand, the array of sociological, psychological, anthropological, linguistic, philosophical, media and literary approaches have given discourse analysis credibility and status (Brown and Yule, 1983; Fairclough, 1995; Gumperz, 1982; Potter and Wetherell, 1987; Schiffrin, 1987; Silverman, 1993; van Dijk, 1997a). On the other, such variegated disciplinary roots might suggest that discourse analysis is 'all things to all people'. As Fairclough remarks, 'discourse is a difficult concept, largely because there are so many conflicting and over-lapping definitions formulated from various theoretical and disciplinary standpoints' (1995: 3). Similarly, Potter and Wetherell identify it as an 'area in which terminological confusions abound' (1987: 6), while van Dijk suggests that the 'ubiquitous presence of the term "discourse" in the humanities, the social sciences and even the mass media' makes it a rather "fuzzy" notion' (1997b: 1).

The strict view of discourse confines it to spoken dialogue (Sinclair and Coulthard, 1975). More conventionally, it refers to the combination of both spoken and written text (Gilbert and Mulkay, 1984), and one widely accepted definition of discourse is 'all forms of spoken interaction, formal and informal, and written texts of all kinds' (Potter and Wetherell, 1987: 7). However, with the emergence of 'social semiotics' (Hodge and Kress, 1988; Kress and van Leeuwen, 1990), it has been argued that the definition of 'text' can be broadened to include cultural artefacts such as music, art and architecture. Fairclough, although concerned that this pushes the concept of text into undue ambiguity, acknowledges that the increasing social sig-nificance of discursive media such as television means that 'texts in society are increasingly multi-semiotic; texts whose primary semiotic form is language increasingly combine language with other semiotic forms' (1995: 4).

At a more general level, some regard discourse not simply as a linguistic or semiotic mechanism, but as a mode of thinking. Van Dijk, for example, suggests that ' "the discourse of neo-liberalism" refers not merely to the language of neo-liberal thinkers or politicians, but also to the ideas or philosophies propagated by them' (1997b: 2). Significantly, such an inter-pretation directly implicates discourse in the social construction of reality. Everyday attitudes and behaviour, along with our perceptions of what we believe to be reality, are shaped and influenced by the discursive practices and interactions we engage in and are exposed or subjected to (Berger and Luckmann, 1967; Searle, 1995). This view of discourse also informs the analyses of critical theorists, such as Foucault (1972, 1980) on power/

knowledge, Gramsci (1971) on ideology and hegemony, and Habermas (1984, 1987) on communicative action. All three stress the empirical contiguity of power and discourse, for, as Potter and Wetherell point out, discursive practices 'do not just describe things; they *do* things. And being active they have social and political implications' (1987: 6).

Perhaps unsurprisingly, the more influential approaches to discourse analysis are those which situate discourse within a social context (Fairclough, 1992, 1995; van Dijk, 1997a, 1997b). For Fairclough, discursive events are 'simultaneously a piece of text, an instance of discursive practice, and an instance of social practice' (1992: 4). Consequently, their analysis requires: (i) examination of the language in use (*text dimension*); (ii) identification of textual production and interpretation (*discursive practice dimension*); and (iii) consideration of institutional and organizational factors surrounding the discursive event and how they might shape the discourse(s) in question (*social practice dimension*). Similarly, van Dijk, drawing on linguistics, psychology and the social sciences, argues for: (i) analysis of the form and content of the text in use (*language use*); (ii) an appreciation of the ways in which people use language in order to communicate ideas and beliefs (*communication of beliefs*); and (iii) an examination of the social event by which the communication takes place (*interaction in social situations*). Thus it is possible to move beyond textual examination to explore '*who* uses language, *how*, *why* and *when*' (van Dijk, 1997b: 2) through 'intertextual analysis' (Bakhtin, 1986; Fairclough, 1992, 1995; Kress and Threadgold, 1988; Thibault, 1991). Intertextual analysis 'crucially mediates the connection between language and social context and facilitates more satisfactory bridging of the gap between text and contexts' (Fairclough, 1995: 189).

The Scope of Organizational Discourse

As a field of study, organizational discourse is comprised of diverse perspectives and approaches; and few have attempted to delineate its scope. Mumby and Clair (1997) suggest that the general focus is on the ways in which organization members utilize a variety of discursive activities and resources in order to perform and coordinate their roles. Moreover,

> when we speak of organizational discourse, we do not simply mean discourse that occurs *in* organizations. Rather, we suggest that organizations exist only in so far as their members create them through discourse. This is not to claim that organizations are 'nothing but' discourse, but rather that discourse is the principal means by which organization members create a coherent social reality that frames their sense of who they are. (Mumby and Clair, 1997: 181)

Hence, they see discourse as 'both an expression and a creation of organizational structure' (Mumby and Clair, 1997: 181). Seen in this light, organizational discourse encompasses a wide range of research which illuminates the ways in which discursive practices are deeply implicated in daily organizational processes and the routines of organizational behaviour. These include studies of the role and impact of *metaphor* (Deetz and Mumby, 1985; Grant and Oswick, 1996; Koch and Deetz, 1984; Morgan, 1980, 1983, 1996, 1997; Oswick and Grant, 1996; Tsoukas, 1991), *stories, narratives* and *novels* (Barry and Elmes, 1997; Boje, 1991, 1994, 1995; Case, 1995; Clair, 1993; Downing, 1997; Gabriel, 1991a, 1991b, 1991c; Hay, 1996; Helmer, 1993; Mumby, 1987; Phillips, 1995), *rituals* (Rosen, 1984, 1985a, 1985b; Trice and Beyer, 1984), *rhetoric* (Keenoy and Anthony, 1992; Legge, 1995; Watson, 1994, 1995), *language games* (Mauws and Phillips, 1995), *texts* (Czarniawska-Joerges, 1992; O'Connor, 1995), *drama* (Clark and Salaman, 1996b; Goffman, 1990; Mangham and Overington, 1987), *conversations* (Crouch and Basch, 1997; Ford and Ford, 1995; Perren and Atkin, 1997; Yeung 1997), *emotion* (Fineman, 1993, 1996a, 1996b; Fineman and Gabriel, 1996; Hopfl and Linstead, 1997) and *sense-making* (Feldman, 1989; Mangham, 1986; Sims et al., 1993; Weick, 1993, 1995).

In recent years, there has been a growing research interest in all these aspects of organization. Nevertheless, as noted elsewhere,

> discourse has rarely been a primary focus of management research. For many writers, discursive processes and outcomes have remained an unacknowledged and taken for granted aspect of managerial work rather than as being integral to effectiveness; and, when it has been included, it is usually addressed in a limited, indirect or implicit way. (Oswick et al., 1997: 8)

There seem to be at least four reasons why this is so. First, it reflects the continued dominance in the literature of managerialist concerns with effectiveness and efficiency. With such a focus, organizational discourse appears as a mere epiphenomenon, an intellectual luxury with no measurable or marketable pay-off (see Wallemacq and Sims, this volume). Second, it reflects what are mistakenly perceived to be the preferred methodologies within discourse analysis – qualitative and interpretative techniques. In practice, organizational discourse is characterized by a wide range of quantitative and qualitative methodologies (van Dijk, 1997a, 1997b). These encompass lexical and content analyses (Dunphy et al., 1989; Spence and Owens, 1990; Weber, 1990) and studies of institutional dialogue (Drew and Sorjonen, 1997) as well as metaphorical analysis (Morgan, 1980), rhetorical analysis (Hamilton, 1997) and conversation analysis (Boden, 1994). Third, it reflects a simplistic association which appears to have been drawn between discourse analysis and certain forms of postmodernist deconstruction. However, the work of Derrida, Baudrillard, Foucault, Lyotard, Lacan and others does not provide the dominant perspectives within the field. That said, the 'postmodern turn' has certainly stimulated an increasing interest in organizational discourse and sensitized researchers to complexity, contradiction and the inherent indeterminacy of organizational meanings as well as raised fundamental philosophical questions about 'organization' *per se* (Burrell,

1997; Cooper and Burrell, 1988; Hassard 1994; Hassard and Parker, 1993). Fourth, and perhaps most importantly, the most formidable barrier to the legitimacy of discourse analysis is the deeply rooted cultural preference for action over mere talk. This point merits further elaboration.

Acting Talk

Underlying the present marginal status of organizational discourse lies a conviction that action is preferable to talk. Such commonplace notions as 'actions speak louder than words', 'talk is cheap' and that things are 'easier said than done' reflect the cultural privileging of action over discourse in Western culture. And, more specifically within organizations, dialogue, discussion and debate are usually portrayed as being of secondary import- ance to action. In consequence, we suggest, three common mistaken assumptions lie submerged within organizational thinking. First, discourse is generally depicted as being of less value than action. Second, discourse is seen as a passive activity while 'doing' something is seen as active and purposive with a tangible outcome. Third, 'talking' and 'doing' are invariably assumed to be consecutive rather than concurrent or mutually implicated activities.

Austin's (1962) general theory of speech acts provides the rationale for rejecting these three assumptions as untenable. He concluded that language is not only descriptive, but invariably carries an action component; in short, the distinction between talk and action is unsustainable. While his primary concern was with what might be termed 'pure' speech, his findings have important implications for understanding organizational *behaviours*. In effect, he demonstrated how discourse plays an 'active' role in the routine social accomplishment of 'organization'.

Indeed, such a conception lies in the sub-text of the discourses about 'good management'. For example, Mary Parker Follett's (1941) iconic definition of management, 'the art of getting things done through people', while clearly emphasizing action, implicitly acknowledges that the 'art' in question entails the effective deployment of the managers' discursive skills. Similarly, in the conventional identification of managerial roles in terms of putative 'actions' such as leading, organizing, planning, motivating, con- trolling and coordinating (Brech, 1953; Fayol, 1949; Koontz et al., 1955; Mintzberg, 1973; Mullins, 1985; Stewart, 1963), it is simply assumed that the critical discursive aspects of all such activities will be effected success- fully. The subtextual nature of this is underlined by the invariable inclusion of a separate chapter on 'communication', which is thus projected as a discreet 'activity' (see also Oswick et al., 1997).

In Part I, 'Talk and Action', each chapter illustrates vividly why it is inappropriate and, potentially, deeply misleading to separate talk from action in organizational analysis. Robert Marshak highlights the analytical priority accorded to action over talk within management and organizational literature. He argues this predilection has arisen out of a 'folk' tradition which construes talk as worthless 'inactivity'; as non-work. Such unproductive passivity needs to stop before the 'real' work, that is, action, can begin. Marshak concludes that organizations must 'redeem the meaning of talk' and appreciate its economic value, for, otherwise, organizations will be ill equipped to cope with the rapidly changing economic environment and remain competitive.

Jill Woodilla's analysis of conversation also draws attention to the potentially negative consequences for business if organizations do not allow sufficient conversational space for all organizational members to genuinely critique the dominant discourse. She, too, is concerned that talk is devalued in organizations and that researchers tend to dwell on the outcomes of talk rather than utilize it to explore its contribution to organizational processes. Her chapter develops a theory of *workplace conversation* to encapsulate the fundamental importance of conversation to meaning-making, and proceeds to illustrate how this can be used to analyse an empirical example. She shows in detail how the medium of conversation – 'language-based inter-actions' – permits shared meanings to emerge, how it facilitates the formation of relationships and occupational identities, and how differences of interpretation arise and are resolved. One key question for Woodilla is ' "whose" conversations am I writing about?', and this leads her to explore how, through conversation, a dominant rational discourse (while it may secure consent from all) may be used to subjugate competing viewpoints. Her chapter concludes with a call for the promotion of greater openness, enriched communication and for a more moral discourse in organizations.

The subtext of Iain Mangham's concern with emotional discourse is also about the neglect of moral order in organizations. For Mangham, the critical feature of talk which has been relegated to the analytical undergrowth through conventional organizational analysis is emotion. In a broad-ranging discussion he explores the nature of emotions and emotional discourse in organizational interaction and establishes that 'emotions are *embodied* and conveyed in discursive acts'. Thus, for example, he argues that apparently rational managerial discourse is employed to cloak what are, in reality, decisions springing from an emotive engagement with the issues. At the core of his analysis is a plea that we acknowledge how emotion pervades management and organization, since 'practical reasoning unaccompanied by emotion is not sufficient for practical wisdom'.

The final contribution in this section examines the processual interdependency of talk and action in the context of interorganizational collaboration between members of a service organization. Cynthia Hardy, Thomas Lawrence and Nelson Phillips develop an approach which combines micro-sociological conversation analysis with discourse theory. Thus they are able to illuminate the processes through which participants utilize 'talk-action' to analyse and reconstitute organizational 'reality'; in effect, they are able to identify how talk is translated into actions and how actions inform talk. A significant strength of their approach is that it teases out how conversations generate and, intersubjectively, create identity, skills and emotion. In the process, they suggest ways in which organizations might use discursive activities in order to facilitate collaborative action.

Monologues and Dialogues

Despite the diversity of ontological assumptions and methodological practices which inform discourse analysis, there appear to be 'two overarching analytical positions or "meta-discourses" within organizational discourse' (Keenoy et al., 1997). Researchers tend to approach organizations as either 'monological' or 'dialogical' entities (Eisenberg and Goodall, 1993); the former reflects a modernist and the latter a social constructionist epistemology.

Monological approaches tend to contract a coherent story of the organization and one which, usually, represents the perspectives of one actor or group of actors (Boje, 1995). This is not to say that such accounts invariably assume the view of the dominant actors; nor that discordant, alternative and interacting discourse are excluded. What distinguishes a monological account is the attempt to combine all such elements to construct a singular, coherent discourse or narrative. Mumby and Clair term this the 'cultural/ interpretative' approach, which

> tends to operate at a largely descriptive level, and focuses on the ways in which organization members' discursive practices contribute to the development of shared meaning. As such, the principal goal of this research is to demonstrate the connection between the shared norms and values of an organization on the one hand, and the means by which these norms and values are expressed on the other. (1997: 182–3)

Among others, Potter and Wetherell (1987) have questioned the validity of monological accounts for, perhaps inadvertently, adopting a selective reading of their data and constructing a reified, rhetorical analysis. This can be avoided, they suggest, by utilizing more dialogical forms of analysis.

Dialogical analyses explicitly acknowledge that 'organization' is comprised of a multiplicity of discourses which reflect the 'plurivocal' meanings brought to bear by the participants. Potentially, this permits a multitude of 'organizational realities' which, although relatively autonomous discourses, may overlap and permeate each other. Similarly, actors who are 'locked into' particular discourses may experience and interpret the same discursive event – such as a conversation – differently. This means that we can never construct a singular account. For Boje (1995), researchers are implicated in the 'research object' and their frames of reference shape what they 'see'. Accordingly, Boje's analysis is a powerful exposition of how discourses can *co-exist* within organization and underlines the frailties of a monological approach to organizational discourse.

However, his central argument – that there is little value in trying to identify coherent, dominant discourses within organizations – is challenged by those dialogical approaches which assume organization involves socio-economic dependency relations between the actors (Phillips and Hardy, 1997; Reed, 1997). Such analyses suggest that plurivocality reflects an overt or covert struggle for discursive dominance within, between or among organizations and is indicative of the structurally endemic struggle for power and control. In this respect, discourse itself is construed as a power resource (Clegg, 1975; Deetz, 1995; Giddens, 1979; Mumby and Stohl, 1991; Rosen, 1985a). Mumby and Clair (1997) term this the 'critical approach' to organizational discourse.

Such 'dialogical struggles' are represented in Part II, 'Stories and Sense-Making'. Each chapter illustrates the intimate relationship between discourse, discursive activities and what has been termed 'sense-making' (Alvesson, 1994; Feldman 1989; Gowler and Legge, 1983; Louis, 1983; Sackmann, 1992; Weick, 1993, 1995). All three contributions focus on that most influential discursive medium – the story. As Weick has remarked, an organizational story is

> something that preserves plausibility and coherence, something that is reasonable and memorable, something that embodies past experience and expectations, something that resonates with other people, something that can be constructed retrospectively, but can also be used prospectively, something that captures both feeling and thought, something that allows for embellishment to fit current oddities, something that is fun to construct. A good story holds disparate elements together long enough to energise and guide action, plausibly enough to allow people to make retrospective sense of whatever happens, and engagingly enough that others will contribute their own inputs in the interests of sensemaking. (1995: 160–1)

Yiannis Gabriel is concerned that discursive distinctiveness of 'the story' is being undermined by the postmodern predilection for treating almost any phenomenal form as a 'narrative'. In his chapter, he reviews or, perhaps, deconstructs the usages of 'the story' within contemporary organizational discourse. Having noted that the truth of a story does not reside in 'the facts', but in its meaning for organizational members, he observes that, recently, virtually anything that is not a fact has been portrayed as 'story'. In consequence, 'stories' are losing their power to generate and sustain meaning. He argues that 'only by treating stories as distinctive types of narrative, claiming special privileges and subject to special constraints, can we use them as windows into organizational life'. In the process of arriving at this conclusion Gabriel details the differences between modernist, inter-pretativist and postmodern accounts of stories, re-evaluates what might constitute 'a story', and illustrates this with some empirical examples.

Miriam Salzer-Mörling's contribution is a highly personalized account and evaluation of the Ikea story, but that is its strength not its weakness. The design of her contribution is intended to give the reader a 'sense' of how the 'emotional pull' of the story contributes to making the Ikea organization what it is today. She argues that, as sense-making media, stories provide a powerful means of constructing and understanding organizational identities. While undertaking an ethnographic study at Ikea, she was, necessarily, exposed to the evocative story underpinning the creation and evolution of the company. Within the 'saga' of Ikea, the idealized achievements of the past inform and infuse the organization's present purposes and activities. For Salzer-Mörling, the Ikea story is 'a saga that makes sense'; one that simultaneously contextualizes and shapes the organizational reality for those who work there. Yet, as she points out, although the story is replete with pre-defined meanings and seeks to provide homogeneity within Ikea, it also takes on heterogeneous properties: not all involved with Ikea engage in the folkloric reality. Because the story worked for her does not mean it works for all. Thus, she concludes that organizations such as Ikea might best be understood as trying to create a management monologue, while succumbing to a dialogue, or what she describes as a polyphony.

Anne Wallemacq and David Sims explore the nature of organizational 'non-sense'. First, they suggest that most organizational members experience an uneasy relationship between sense and non-sense, a phenomenon they describe as 'the struggle with sense'. It is a perennial struggle, one that is epitomized by the way in which the sense-making process in organizations is often articulated around the non-sensical elements of organizational reality. These features are reflected in narratives about episodes, events and practices which can be read as the organization behaving in a 'senseless' fashion; and are celebrated by signs declaring 'You don't have to be mad to work here, but it helps'. While such 'non-sense' may fuel feelings of senselessness – for no one story seems to quite resonate with what is perceived to be the immediate organizational reality – they may, para-doxically, also permit participants in one locale to 'make sense' of what appears to be happening in other, less visible locales with which they have little or no direct experience.

But, secondly, there is another significant variety of 'non-sense' which is associated with organizational change processes. It emerges when organizational actors' taken-for-granted assumptions about the nature of organizational reality cease to reflect their 'experienced reality'. Utilizing a phenomenological approach, Wallemacq and Sims detail an example of organizational intervention which demonstrates how organizational actors break down stories inducing non-sense and replace them with new stories which make sense of their changed situation.

As examples of the dialogical approach to organizational discourse, all three contributions in Part II of this volume illustrate the way in which stories vie for dominance within organizations. Moreover, they highlight the limitations of monological accounts.

From Modernism to Postmodernism?

Each of the four chapters in Part III, 'Discourse and Social Theory', is concerned with various ontologies of organization and their associated epistemological assumptions about the nature of organizational discourse. In this respect, each provides a rich articulation of the fundamental para-digmatic schism which has long pervaded the social theories of organization and which, these days, is usually signified by the 'debate' between modern-ists and postmodernists. However, as Alvesson observes:

> A problem with the term 'postmodernism', as well as its shadow 'modernism', is that it refers to a wide range of different issues. The more texts about modernism and postmodernism I come across, the more I doubt that there is any particular point in using their terms or wisdom in trying to capture the 'totalities' to which these terms are usually directed. Due to the number of various and slippery meanings – not all of them compatible – ascribed to the terms, contradictions and confusions are created making it difficult to express something 'meaningful'. (1995: 1047)

In short, both terms are gruesomely overgeneralized categories which should regarded as no more than metaphors for a multiplicity of discrete per-spectives which, at best, are differentiated by the extent to which they assume a realist or a contructionist social ontology.

It is, of course, no mere coincidence that as 'postmodernism' has gained momentum, so too has interest in organizational discourse. As noted elsewhere, 'contemporary organizational analysis is confronted, if not con-founded, by increasingly paradoxical, fluid and contradictory accounts of organizational realities' (Keenoy et al., 1997: 147). This scenario is reflect-ive of the putative iconic transformation of 'organization' from 'modernist bureaucracy' to 'postmodernist virtual network' – a process which appears to have been accompanied by the 'death of reason' (Power 1990: 110) and a crisis of re-presentation for managers and academics alike (Keenoy et al., 1997). For some, this means 'the world is basically self-referential, it is neither pro-human nor anti-human; it just is' (Cooper and Burrell, 1988: 94): organizational discourses are merely arbitrary narratives within the un-bounded plurivocality of social realities. For others, such realities are reflexively constituted from within the confines of power/knowledge dis-courses (Foucault, 1972, 1980). But ambiguity and uncertainty reign supreme: for language itself has been deconstructed to the point where it can no longer 'mirror the reality 'out there'' (Alvesson, 1995: 1057). So what remains to be said and what are we left with?

Drawing on the work of Deleuze and Guattari (1984, 1986, 1988), Gibson Burrell explores some alternatives in his chapter on the effects of modernist production and its discursive linearity. He argues that the dominant dis-course of Western modernism is linearity. This refers not merely to the production lines of alienation and the singular achievement of the twentieth century in perfecting the machinery of mass destruction, but also to modernist knowledge-forming 'texts' which, through their insistence on coherence, order, regularity, prediction and linguistic certainty, achieve a parallel effect. In short, linearity kills; and, moreover, our chances of escaping linearity are rather limited. As Burrell notes, Deleuze and Guattari's work, though extremely valuable, has its limitations, and discursive deconstruction – even when constituted through the inherent ambiguity of non-linear texts (see Burrell, 1997) – ultimately merely perpetuates linearity. In the meantime, then, organizations will remain, by their very nature – even when thriving on chaos and re-engineering – incorrigible creators of linear discourses which inevitably lead us, blinkered, down the path of destruction. It is a bleak prospect.

But not everyone agrees. Alongside the 'nihilistic turn' of some postmodern accounts, we have also seen a comparable growth of interest in organizational discourse from those operating from, in particular, social constructivist, critical modernist and critical realist epistemologies. One among these is Gerrit Broekstra.

His contribution draws on the same historical linearities as Burrell but, in a contrasting intellectual reading, we are offered the potential of what might be called 'circularity'. Broekstra's analytical touchstones are a combination of cybernetic systems theory and discourse analysis. He urges us to consider organization as a conversation and demonstrates how organization emerges out of processes of dialogue and discussion among and between the constituent parts and individual members of the company: organization is a day-to-day social accomplishment arising out of a network of micro-conversations. Thus, any attempt by management to exercise 'control' over such a multiplicity of dialogues is not only doomed to fail but is also a fundamental source of ineffectiveness. To flourish in contemporary times, management need to harness the potential flexibility arising out of micro-conversations and promote the values of self organization and self reference. Management must practise what Broekstra calls 'unmanagement' if they are to capitalize on the reflexive circularity of institutionalized participation.

Didier Cazal and Dawn Inns contribute a cautionary overview of the use (and abuse) of metaphor within organizational analysis. At the root of their analysis is an acknowledgement of the instability of language and, from this base, they detail the contingent epistemological limitations and methodological ambiguities associated with metaphorical analyses. Their review of the empirical status of metaphor draws on and responds to both 'modernist' and 'postmodernist' critiques of metaphor. In particular, they explore the fundamental issues of 'meaning' raised by Jacques Lacan's analysis of metaphor. Echoing Burrell (see above), they warn against allowing particular metaphors to dominate organizational discourses. While, for example, the organismic metaphor may permit us to construct a rational and plausible account of organization, it is only an imprecise analogy which captures elements of 'reality'. More generally, they celebrate the theoretical potential of metaphor to create and evaluate discourses that organize, describe and interpret organization and organizational behaviour. However, if we over-interpret metaphor, it is likely to become little more than a 'rhetorical ornament'.

In the only contribution which is distinctly unsympathetic to organizational discourse, Mike Reed insists that any account of organization must be based on an appreciation of the structural context of action (and discourse), an approach which prioritizes the constitutive role of social power. From this critical realist perspective, he develops a richly detailed critique of Foucault's formulation of power/knowledge discourse. Having outlined the major ontological and analytical features of a Foucauldian approach, Reed explores the way in which it has been used to analyse three contemporary organizational issues: organizational identities; organizational surveillance and control; and organizational change. This provides the basis for arguing that, despite the insights which the power/knowledge approach generates at the micro level, it is ill equipped to account for the more deeply embedded structural props of domination *within* which the power/knowledge discourse is 'played out' by organizational actors. Somewhat ironically, it seems that, despite his focus on the discursive construction of social power, Foucault's framework cannot explain the historical and material roots of power.

Concluding Remarks

In our view, the various contributions to this volume demonstrate the analytical salience of organizational discourse to understanding contemporary organization. Each illustrates how the varieties of discourse and discursive forms both shape and constitute our perceptions of organizational reality; and, in the process, they offer the potential for innovative interpretations of organization.

More specifically, the various chapters indicate clearly that organizational discourse is not simply about the analysis of 'text', 'emotion', 'stories' or 'conversations' in and about organization. Discourse analysis is not to be equated with the mere reportage and analysis of socially constructed *accounts* of 'reality'. What is illustrated throughout this book is the significance of discourse in constructing, situating, facilitating and communicating the diverse cultural, institutional, political and socio-economic parameters of 'organizational being'. Thus, discourse not only shapes and directs organizational behaviours but also *constitutes* actors' contested and contestable meanings. With such a reading, 'organization' can be seen as a continuous process of social accomplishment which, in both senses of the term, is *articulated* by and through the deployment of discursive resources.

However, as demonstrated by most contributors, the articulation, delivery and interpretation of discourse remains open-ended. And any focus on discourse not only exposes the probability – we would say certainty – of multiple readings, but also encourages us to examine underprivileged discourses and alternative 'realities'. Discourse analysis prioritizes subjectivity, acknowledges instrumentalism, explores rhetoric, values multiplicity and celebrates uncertainty. Hence, while we interrogate discourse as a means of generating meaning and constructing reality, simultaneously, it draws our attention to the intrinsic ambiguity of the various modes of re-presentation. We would describe this as the *discursive paradox*.

We contend that this discursive paradox compels us to take a reflexive approach to 'doing organizational discourse'. Moreover, in contrast to conventional disciplinary habits, the paradox suggests we avoid attempts to 'define' organizational discourse in anything other than the very general terms offered in this introduction. As the contributions to this volume indicate, the 'field' is a multi-disciplinary, many layered project informed by a diversity of ontological and epistemological positions. Whatever the approach – be it lexical, semiotic, inter-textual, monological, dialogical, modernist, critical realist or postmodern – the 'field' of organizational discourse mirrors the multiple realities, the intrinsic indeterminacy and the perpetual uncertainties which it seeks to 'uncover'.

In the final part of the book, 'A Concluding Discourse', Richard Dunford and Ian Palmer elaborate various elements of this discursive paradox. In their summary chapter, they identify six sources of paradox within our 'text' which, more generally, seem to resonate with the epistemological plurivocality of the 'field'. Rather than identifying them as a source of weakness, they are presented as issues which demonstrate the inherently reflexive nature of discourse analysis and as analytical issues which have to be addressed as a matter of routine. In order to assist in this process, Dunford and Palmer outline six alternative (but not mutually exclusive) methodological possibilities or 'strategies of engagement' to accommodate these seemingly uncomfortable features of social and organizational 'reality'. What they allude to is the conundrum which preoccupied Gary Zukov:

> 'Reality' is what we take to be true. What we take to be true is what we believe. What we believe is based upon our perceptions. What we perceive depends upon what we look for. What we look for depends upon what we think. What we think depends upon what we perceive. What we perceive determines what we believe. What we believe determines what we take to be true. What we take to be true determines our reality. (Zukov, 1980: 328)

Part I

TALK AND ACTION

---

1   A Discourse on Discourse: Redeeming the Meaning of Talk

Robert J. Marshak

What happens when we think about thought and talk about talk?

Bruner and Feldman, 1990: 237

The end of the twentieth century is witnessing a rapidly growing movement of ideas away from the traditional, objectivist conception of reality towards a still not fully defined, but more subjective, constructionist ontology. Although the objectivist view has been a central part of the privileged dogma of Western philosophy and science since Plato (Finocchario, 1990; Soyland, 1994), in the last few decades there has been an impressive outpouring of alternative and ultimately constructionist views. As Laughlin et al. observe:

> There have emerged at least two principal themes from this revolutionary readjustment of view: (1) a shift away from a fragmented, mechanical, non-purposive conception of the world toward a holistic, organic, and purposive conception . . .; and (2) a shift away from a concern with objectivity toward a concern with subjectivity – that is, with the role of perception and cognition in the process of scientific inquiry. . . . (1992: 5)

A central aspect of this shift has been increased inquiry into the role of language in the ongoing creation of 'reality'. For example, according to Hall and Ames:

> The transition from modern to postmodern perspectives is not merely a theoretical shift. It entails a vast network which has drawn together in a single mix movements as seemingly diverse as deconstruction, the new historicism, cultural studies, and feminist criticism – all of which at one level or another are rooted in the critique of the rationality of language. (1995: 145–6)

The growing interest in, and indeed legitimacy conferred upon, metaphor in recent years is another clear and specific indicator of this shift (Johnson, 1987; Lakoff, 1987; Lakoff and Johnson, 1980; Leary, 1990; Ortony, 1993). In the administrative sciences, despite attempts to uphold the objectivist view (Bourgeois and Pinder, 1983; Pinder and Bourgeois, 1982; Tsoukas, 1992), metaphor has become an area of legitimate and serious inquiry (Grant and Oswick, 1996; Marshak, 1996; Morgan, 1980, 1983, 1997; Oswick and Grant, 1996; Palmer and Dunford, 1996). The emerging outlines of a field or school of inquiry more broadly focused on 'organizational discourse', marked in part by the publication of this book, is another indicator of this trend. There is now a growing, if still quite eclectic, group of scholars actively asking questions, doing research and communicating their ideas about the impacts of linguistically mediated experience in management and organizational settings (Combes et al., 1996). For this group of people talk is more than simply a means to communicate, report or, through sophistry, manipulate information. Instead, talk is one, if not the primary, means of socially constructing reality; privileging some stories, narratives or accounts of that reality over others; and generating alternative conceptions of both proper questions and their answers (Berger and Luckmann, 1967; Bergquist, 1993; Schön, 1993). Put simply, the real action is in the talk.

This perspective, however, runs counter to not only the objectivist views of other social scientists, but the embedded 'folk models' or 'folk theories' of many managers in organizations in the United States, and possibly many other countries as well. According to Lakoff:

> Ordinary people without any technical expertise have theories, either implicit or explicit, about every important aspect of their lives. Cognitive anthropologists refer to such theories as *folk theories* or *folk models*. (1987: 118)

If one listens with an ethnographer's ear to day-to-day management discussions, notes the terminology of popular management terms and theories, and reflects on broader cultural themes, a very different assessment of talk and its relationship to action is revealed. Implicit in most discourses, and the broader culture, are assumptions that signal the paramount importance of action over talk. There is, in short, a strong 'bias for action' (for example, Peters and Waterman, 1982). Characteristics of 'action', such as being observable, measurable, concrete, practical and specific, are routinely lauded over those associated with 'talk', which is considered to be more contextual, interpretative, elusive, abstract and emotional. The traditional American cultural icon is the 'strong, silent type', exemplified in popular culture by the action-adventure hero (for example, Eastwood, Schwarzenegger, Stallone) who says little, but gets things done by letting his 'fists do the talking'. This contrasts with another icon, 'the loquacious type', best exemplified in popular culture by the talk show host/hostess whose role is to amuse, empathize and/or entertain. That the bias for action over talk may also extend to a bias for the masculine over the feminine should be obvious.

The remainder of this chapter will explore in more detail the everyday discourse and implicit folk model(s) about 'talk' and 'action', articulate a broader conception of talk to include three types of talk and an alternative folk model, and conclude with a discussion of some of the implications for organizations and the emerging field of organizational discourse.

The Rhetoric About Talk and Action

As implied by the opening discussion, developing and legitimating a field of inquiry based on the importance of organizational discourse ('talk') may have more than a few difficulties to surmount. These include the weight of a Western philosophical tradition that cautions against the illusion of sophist rhetoric, as well as an objectivist scientific tradition that prefers literal or mathematical statements to anything that might reflect subjective, mediated experience. Talk is the province of the poet not the philosopher-scientist. Talk is more about rhyme than reason; emotion not fact.

The legitimacy and importance of organizational discourse as a field of inquiry is also challenged by the embedded folk model(s) about 'talk' and 'action' expressed in the daily rhetoric of most (American) organizations. In these implicit models talk is routinely demeaned and devalued, with potentially serious, but unacknowledged consequences. Action, on the other hand, is highly lauded and valued. Not only is action valued over talk, but talk is implicitly considered as an impediment to action; something that must be 'gotten over', 'gone through' or 'finished with' before there can be any action. It is instructive to take a closer look at some of this rhetoric and the model(s) it implies.

First, *talk is worthless*. Expressions conveying a sense that talk has no real value are commonplace. How often have we heard: 'talk is cheap'; 'it's just empty words'; 'idle talk, idle chatter'; or that 'talk is a waste of time'? And, because everyone knows that 'time is money', if talk is a waste of time, it must also be a waste of money. Remember, 'silence is golden'.

On the other hand, *action counts*; *action is valued*. We are routinely reminded that 'it's deeds that count, not words', or that one should 'watch what we do, not what we say'. People in organizations are admonished to 'walk the talk', guard against 'too much talk and not enough action', engage in 'less talk and more action', and to avoid being seen as 'all talk and no action'.

Not only is action valued over talk, but *talk must stop for action to start*. We are frequently told in meetings and discussions that we need to 'stop talking and start doing something' or that 'it's time to stop all the talk and get down to business'. Finally, we all know that 'if everyone would just stop talking, maybe we could get something done'.

The bias for action is also demonstrated by such commonplace terms in the workplace as: 'action lists', 'actionable issues' and 'to do lists'. The professional literature is not exempt from a bias for action either, at least in nomenclature, for example 'action science', 'action research' and 'action learning'. Consequently it would not be unusual to attend a management meeting where after the participants engaged in some 'action research' or 'action learning' they proved the event was not a waste of time by developing a detailed 'to do list' with specific 'action items' assigned to accountable persons so that everyone would know 'who was to do what by when'. Meetings that fail to generate any or enough specific action items are routinely dismissed as having been 'all talk and a waste of time'.

Underlying Folk Model(s) About Talk and Action

Underlying these common expressions would appear to be implicit conceptions about the nature and interrelationship of talk and action. These implicit constructs, or folk theories/folk model(s), have powerful influences over everyday experience. The critical question, then, becomes: what conceptions or folk model(s) related to talk and action would lead to the conclusions that talk is worthless, action counts, talk must stop for action to start, and, consequently, to a strong bias for action over talk?

First, we note that talk and action are conceived of as disjoint entities. There is something called talk and something else called action with no apparent overlap between them. Either one talks, which is worthless, or acts, which really matters. In no cases do the everyday expressions imply that talk and action occur simultaneously in the same time and place, for example 'if everyone would stop talking maybe we could start doing something'. At any point in time the expressions imply you either have the one or the other. Furthermore, not only are talk and action disjoint entities, but they are separated in time as well as space. Talk precedes action; action follows talk. They also occur in a linear sequence: from talk to action. Finally, the sequence is uni-directional, with talk always preceding and sometimes leading to action. The reverse direction is mostly or totally absent in everyday workplace conversations. We simply do not hear people being told to 'stop getting things done so we can start talking', or that 'we should stop all the action so we can have a good discussion'. On the few occasions when people are asked to 'stop working so we can talk things over', the purpose of the talk is to (again) lead to *doing* things better. In sum, the constructs underlying many of our everyday expressions imply a folk theory where talk and action are separate entities, disjoint in time, space and value. Furthermore, the preferred sequence of events over time is to quickly move from, or through, talk in order to get on to the more valuable action. Talk can also be an implicit impediment or barrier preventing action, for example: 'getting stuck in too much talk', 'spinning our wheels in endless debate' or 'getting sidetracked in long-winded discussions'.

The Path–Goal Image Schematic

At this point it is hard not to notice the similarities between these constructs and the path–goal image schematic extensively discussed in the research of the cognitive linguists Lakoff and Johnson (see, for example, Johnson, 1987; Lakoff, 1987; Lakoff and Johnson, 1980). An 'image schematic' is essentially a pre-conscious, cognitive analogue that functions as a 'template' to order experience. According to Johnson:

> Image schemata exist at a level of generality and abstraction that allows them to serve repeatedly as identifying patterns in an indefinitely large number of experiences, perceptions, and image formations for objects or events that are similarly structured in relevant ways. Their most important feature is that they have a few basic elements or components that are related by definite structures, and yet they have a certain flexibility. As a result of this simple structure, they are a chief means for achieving order in our experience so that we can comprehend and reason about it. (1987: 28)

The path–goal image schematic always has the same pattern or structure: there is (i) a source or starting point, (ii) a destination or goal, and (iii) a path of contiguous locations connecting the starting point to the destination. Moreover, the further along the path you go, the more time has passed since starting (see Johnson, 1987: 113–17). This particular image schematic is ubiquitous, especially in the analogy *life is a journey* which helps explain why such terms as *forks* in the road (choice), getting *over* traumatic events (obstacles on the path), *mapping* out one's life (setting the course), and so on, can make analogical if not logical sense.

Reviewing how talk and action are described in everyday expressions against the path–goal image schematic reveals a great deal of correspondence and coherence. While inaction may be the source or starting point, talk is certainly at an early point on the path towards the destination or goal of action. After all, isn't talk supposed to lead to action? As a location(s) along the path to action, talk can take on several analogical or metaphorical characteristics. For example, talk can be a necessary stage or state that one must pass through in order to get to action; or an impediment or obstacle that can bog things down or get you stuck; or where you can get side-tracked or lost. Because the goal, or what is valued, is the destination of action, one should not waste too much time along the way 'in talk'. Thus many of our most common expressions and implicit valuations of talk and action seem rooted in an underlying folk model based on the path–goal image schematic. This folk model implicitly structures talk and action as: (i) separate states, disjoint in time and space, (ii) where talk is an initial or earlier location(s) on a path or journey (iii) to the goal or destination of action, and (iv) where talk must be gone through, gotten over or finished before one is able to move on to the goal of action. In this folk model talk at best helps lead to action and at worse can block or prevent one from getting to action.

Expanding the Folk Model

Once revealed, it is easy to see how this folk model or image schematic may structure the rhetoric about talk and action as well as the implicit and explicit

A. Talk ——→ Action

B. Talk ——→ Conclusion ——→ Action

C. Discuss ——→ Decide ——→ Do ——→ Deed

FIGURE 1.1 *Linear paths of talk and action*

language and metaphors used in that rhetoric. This becomes even clearer as we add in some other aspects of the folk model. One is the role of 'conclusion' as the transition 'point', 'state' or 'bridge' between talk and action. Conventionally, conclusions are where the talking stops and action begins. First we talk, then we 'reach' a conclusion, and after that we begin action. Reaching a conclusion is usually considered to be the last 'step' before starting to act. When all the talk has ended and a conclusion has been reached, it is then time to 'get on' to action. Thus a conclusion must be reached as a key milestone along the way to achieving the action destination. This is shown in Figure 1.1 (A and B).

When only talk, conclusions and action are considered, talk tends to be located as an early or beginning point leading to a conclusion, followed immediately by action. This linear sequencing places action at the end of the path as the final destination or goal of the journey. The end result we want is action, not a return to more talk. So strong is this orientation that action can literally become an end unto itself. 'We don't care what you do, just stop talking about it and do something!' 'Just get on with it!' This tends to obscure some other everyday injunctions about not making action the goal of the journey. We are also reminded to avoid aimless or meaningless action. When these injunctions are added to the folk model of talk and action they imply that action, too, is a point or location along a path leading to a desired goal or outcome. Thus our actions lead to our outcomes.

The expanded folk model suggests a linear sequence moving from talk to a conclusion, followed by action(s) that leads to an outcome. Modifying our descriptors for purposes of alliteration we now have the implicit folk model of Discuss–Decide–Do–Deed. This is shown in Figure 1.1 (C).

This sequence occurs in time and space with each step along the way bringing us closer to our goal. Because the outcome or goal is what is valued, the steps along the way also connote gradations of worth. Action(s) that leads directly to our desired outcomes is most valuable; aimless action(s) is not. Talk, which is at the beginning or an earlier point of the journey, farthest away from the desired outcome, is hardly worth anything at all.

Based on this analysis it appears clear that many of our everyday discussions at work reflect an implicit theory about talk and action wherein action is exalted and prized, while talk is routinely demeaned as worthless or an impediment to action. The rhetoric reveals not only the strong bias for action, but a powerful folk model implicitly at work in many organizations.

This has implications in the work setting, as will be discussed later, but also for the emerging field of organizational discourse.

Redeeming the Meaning of Talk

As long as the rhetoric about talk and action, as well as conclusions and outcomes, is implicitly ordered by an underlying path–goal image schematic, or folk model, talk will continue to be demeaned. Unless, or until, an alternative model comes into use, talk in most organizations may continue to be, implicitly at least, not much more than idle chatter. This, of course, impacts on the nascent field of organizational discourse. Put simply, given the folk model described so far, can a field devoted to organizational 'talk' ever be taken seriously? It seems hard to escape the conclusion that without another folk or formal model it will be difficult to legitimate organizational discourse as an important field of inquiry, especially as compared to anything related to addressing organizational action(s). Maybe the field will need to be marketed as 'action discourse' or 'discursive action' to imply it is part of the 'real' action and therefore worthwhile.

Towards Another Model

As we have seen, in an implicit path–goal folk model where action is considered to be the goal or leading directly to the goal, talk will be devalued and demeaned. We have also noted that although action in general is highly valued, aimless or meaningless action can also be disparaged. This suggests a two-part approach to redeeming the value of talk. The first part is to reassert the function of talk in providing meaning, and specifically imbuing action with meaning. The second is to link such a theory of meaningful action with an image schematic different from the path–goal one.

In the first part, we will need to side with the constructionists and assert that actions are behaviours devoid of meaning until redeemed by talk. Talk, in the form of narratives, stories, accounts, and so on, interprets what actions mean and thereby performs an evaluative function. To be meaningful an action(s) must be evaluated as producing a 'significant outcome'. Such interpretative evaluations are created and applied through 'talk'. In essence talk makes action meaningful by turning behaviours and outcomes into 'deeds' worthy of recognition and commentary (Starbuck, 1985; Weick, 1995). Actions may or may not be purely objective, empirical events. What those actions mean and how worthwhile they are, however, is inherently subjective and based on what we say about them.

Types of Talk

To advance this proposition further requires the development of a way of talking about 'talk'. We must be able to distinguish several types of talk, including talk that leads to action, and talk that makes action(s) meaningful. Three types of talk are proposed with labels intended to convey their primary function.

The first type is *tool-talk*. Tool-talk includes all instrumental communications required to discuss, conclude, act and evaluate outcomes. It is utilitarian, that is, used to accomplish some purpose. Tool-talk is usually literal, conscious and intentionally objective.

The second type is *frame-talk*. Frame-talk provides the interpretative frameworks and symbols that generate and evaluate the meaning of discussions, conclusions, actions and outcomes (for example, Donnellon, 1996; Fairhurst and Sarr, 1996; Goffman, 1974; Schön, 1993). By providing context, frame-talk enables implicit and explicit assessments while also conveying subjective meaning and accomplishment. Frame-talk usually includes symbolic, conscious, pre-conscious and contextually subjective dimensions.

The third type is *mythopoetic-talk*. Mythopoetic-talk conveys the ideogenic ideas and images (for example, myths, cosmologies, *logos*) that create and communicate the nature of reality within which frameworks and symbols are applied. It creates and communicates the privileged narratives that guide frame-talk and tool-talk within a particular culture or society. Mythopoetic-talk is usually mythic and metaphorical; conscious, pre-conscious, and unconscious; and intuitive and mystical.

This three-part typology is not intended to imply rigid categorization of types of talk. Rather it is more a fuzzy delineation or gradation intended to distinguish the different functional contributions of what would otherwise be the undifferentiated term 'talk' (Lakoff, 1987: 21–2; Zadeh, 1965). Talk, of course, in this context implies both oral and written forms of communication, discourse, narrative, account, and so on. It should also be noted that two-part delineations between talk and 'meta-talk' have been made by others concerned with the practical aspects of discourse (for example, Nierenberg and Calero, 1973; Tannen, 1986, 1990). In their usage, meta-talk is the hidden meaning beyond or behind the literal words. Meta-talk involves paying attention to or listening for unarticulated assumptions, contextual relationships, symbolism, and so forth. While by no means equivalent to the formulation presented here, meta-talk is more like frame-talk, with some possible overlap with mythopoetic-talk. What is clearly consistent in both typologies, however, is the desire to invent a special form of the word 'talk' that conveys the power to create and convey meaning beyond literal, instrumental language.

Cycles and Containers of Meaning

As somewhat implied by their names, tool-talk is contained or framed by frame-talk, and frame-talk is contained or informed by mythopoetic-talk. This is shown in Figure 1.2. Furthermore, not only are the three types of talk related to each other through containment, but they also re-create and

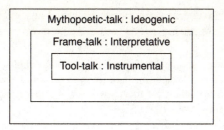

FIGURE 1.2   *Types of talk*

reinforce each other in ongoing cycles of meaning, interpretation and events. This is shown in Figure 1.3. Mythopoetic-talk creates the fundamental ground of ideas which are then selectively used through frame-talk to set the context or interpretation within which tool-talk occurs. The outcomes or deeds resulting from tool-talk are then interpreted or evaluated through further frame-talk in terms of how well they do or do not meet the fundamental premises established by mythopoetic-talk. To the degree that frame-talk can successfully interpret or provide meaning to the outcomes or deeds, it will also reinforce and uphold the legitimacy and validity of the

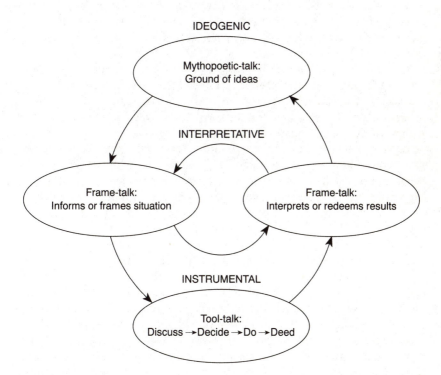

FIGURE 1.3   *Containers of talk and cycles of meaning*

ideogenic ideas conveyed by mythopoetic-talk. Thus we have a system of talk that has self-referencing cycles and containers of meaning:

> Cosmological understanding is depicted in symbolic dramas that in turn lead to individual experiences, which are then interpreted within the framework of the cosmology that first produced the experience – thus completing a 'cycle of meaning'. (Laughlin et al., 1992: 335)

There are two aspects of this model of talk and action that importantly, for our purposes, distinguish it from the previously discussed path–goal folk model of talk and action.

First, talk and action are not conceived of as separate, independent entities. Instead talk *contains* action. Following the container metaphor (Johnson, 1987; Lakoff, 1987), the action is *in* the talk. Frame-talk and mythopoetic-talk form containers of meaning within which action occurs and takes on significance. Actions themselves are meaningless until interpreted in the context of the frame and foundations provided by frame-talk and mythopoetic-talk. In that sense all action is bound, contained and embedded within the 'cage' of language (Wittgenstein, 1968). Because, metaphorically, buildings are a form of container (Lakoff and Johnson, 1980), frame-talk about social *constructionism* (Foucault, 1972) or *deconstructionism* (Derrida, 1978, 1982) is coherent within the mythopoetic-talk of constructionist philosophy and science. Thus a shift to a containment image-schematic regarding talk and action seems also to be a prerequisite for most postmodern perspectives.

Second, talk and action do not form a linear sequence ending in action or some outcome(s). Rather they are linked in self-referencing cycles of meaning and experience. Mythopoetic-talk establishes the fundamental set of ideas that frame-talk applies selectively to form the interpretative context within which tool-talk addresses a particular issue. Any resulting actions and outcomes are then evaluated through further frame-talk in terms of how well the actions and outcomes fit/support a prevailing set of fundamental ideas. When actions and outcomes are interpreted by frame-talk as fitting or supporting the fundamental ideas, the cycle of meaning is reinforced, thereby continuing the cycle of self-referencing talk, meaning and action. A cyclical image schematic, wherein linked entities or events form circular relationships, is also clearly part of most postmodern perspectives in all the sciences (Capra, 1982, 1996; Maturana and Varela, 1980, 1987).

The proposition of this argument, then, is that a shift from an implicit path–goal, linear folk model of talk and action to a formal and/or folk model(s) based on cyclical and container image schematics will be a necessary condition for the redemption of talk in comparison to action. Such a shift will also be required to help establish and support the appropriate formal and informal theoretical constructs upon which to build a meaningful field of organizational discourse (for example, see Munro, 1988, for a discussion of the crucial importance of metaphorical or structural images in

Chinese philosophy). Talk would thereby be re-located from a position implicitly distant, removed and secondary to action to a more immediate, encompassing and meaningful relationship with action.

An Illustration: The Great Chain of Being

At this point it is perhaps appropriate to attempt to provide greater elucidation to the discussion of types of talk and containers and cycles of meaning. This will be done through a brief exposition of a set of mythopoetic concepts that are collectively known as 'the Great Chain of Being':

> We shall first discriminate not, indeed, a single and simple idea, but three ideas which have, throughout the greater part of the history of the West, been so closely and constantly associated that they have often operated as a unit, and have, when thus taken together, produced a conception – one of the major conceptions of Occidental thought – which came to be expressed by a single term: 'the Great Chain of Being'. (Lovejoy, 1936: 20–1)

According to Lovejoy and others, 'the Great Chain of Being is rooted in Platonic and Neoplatonic thinking, though adopted by Christians for most of their history in order to relate perfect spirit to imperfect matter' (Hardy, 1987: 112). The image of the concept is simple, powerful and implicitly familiar to almost any Western reader. There is a transcendent perfect good, or perfect God, at the apex of the universe and the most imperfect, most mutable, primitive matter (or devil) at the bottom. In between, arranged in descending order of perfection, is everything in the universe: angels, humans, animals, plants, slugs, and so on. From saints to sinners, 'higher' to 'lower' forms of life, the ideal to the gross and base, everything has its place in the Great Chain of Being.

This image is created and supported by three principal ideas set in the context of the assumption of a transcendent, perfect, ideal good or God. Those three ideas are: (i) plenitude, (ii) continuity and (iii) unilinear gradation. As Lovejoy explains, plenitude is the concept that everything that is possible exists; continuity, that everything is contiguous without gaps, empty spaces or vacuums; unilinear gradation, that everything is ordered in a hierarchy from most to least perfect, ideal, spiritual, good. Taken together, these concepts easily engage and evoke such ascent–descent image schematics and metaphors as great chains, ladders, levels and staircases.

Thus the ideogenic conception of the Great Chain of Being provides us with a universe ordered in levels from top to bottom, where one's place denotes degrees of goodness, perfection and/or accomplishment. As Lovejoy richly documents, this set of ideas permeates the mythopoetic-talk of the Western tradition. Examples include the perfect creator who filled the universe with everything possible in Plato's *Timaeus and Critias*, and Dante's precise demarcation of the rings and levels between the lowest and highest parts of the universe, from the depths of Hell to the pinnacle of the Godhead in the *Divine Comedy*.

The mythopoetic-talk that creates and re-creates the primal image of the Great Chain of Being also provides the context or ground for how frame-talk positions problems and possibilities. This will be demonstrated through two examples: one biological, the other organizational. First, for the biological example:

> No history of the biological sciences in the eighteenth century can be adequate which fails to keep in view the fact that, for most men of science throughout that period, the theorems implicit in the concept of the Chain of Being continued to constitute essential presuppositions in the *framing* of scientific hypotheses. (Lovejoy, 1936: 227; emphasis added)

Hence, the mythopoetic-talk that first creates a chain of being provides implicit legitimacy and coherence to frame-talk that might 'set naturalists to looking for forms which would fill up the apparently "missing links" in the chain' (Lovejoy, 1936: 231). This would then be followed by the appropriate tool-talk required to instrumentally search for new and/or missing species. The act of discovering a previously unknown life form might then be interpreted through frame-talk as finding a *missing link*, thereby reinforcing the original conception that there is a Great Chain of Being encompassing all possible beings. As Lovejoy points out,

> Every discovery of a new form could be regarded, not as the disclosure of an additional fact in nature, but as a step towards the completion of a systemic structure of which the general plan was known in advance, an additional bit of empirical evidence of the truth of the generally accepted and cherished scheme of things. (1936: 232)

Support for the primal conception would then provide encouragement for the continued framing of situations, experiences and hypotheses in terms of hierarchical forms, missing links and the like. Furthermore, little or none of this would occur explicitly; instead the concepts would be implicitly embedded in how people talked, literally and figuratively, about the universe. A schematic showing the pattern of containers and cycles of meaning for this and the next example is provided in Figure 1.4.

Staying within the container provided by the mythopoetic image of the Great Chain of Being, but switching focus from biology to organizational behaviour, reveals similar types of talk and containers and cycles of meaning. Take, for example, the metaphorical framing of personal organizational success in terms of 'climbing a ladder'. There are job ladders, career ladders and corporate ladders of success. One attempts to avoid getting stuck at too low a level, or otherwise plateaued or topped-out. Instead, success is measured by how fast and how far you climb the ladder. The fast track is not horizontal, it's vertical. Those at the top are presumed to be somehow wiser, smarter, better and/or more talented than those at successively lower levels.

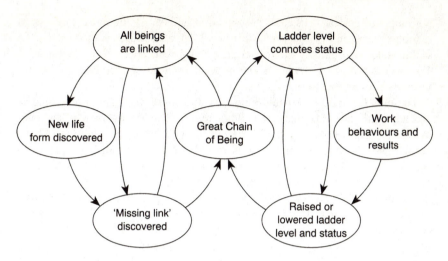

FIGURE 1.4   *The Great Chain of Being: missing links and ladder levels*

An exception is when you didn't advance on your own but were 'kicked upstairs'. Where one is stationed in the organizational hierarchy matters, therefore, as an indicator not only of role and responsibility, but of existential and status levels as well. Tool-talk about how to succeed – what actions to pursue to achieve desired outcomes – is implicitly formulated within this framework. The resulting actions and outcomes are then interpreted by frame-talk within the context of movement up or down the ladder.

For example, a negative evaluation might lead to a person being characterized as having been knocked down a peg or two, having fallen off the fast track, or having his or her position lowered in the overall scheme of things. Alternatively, a favourable evaluation might be described in terms of someone being elevated, raised up, moved up, advanced a few rungs, or otherwise headed to the top. All of these evaluative framings serve to confer varying degrees of power and status on individuals, thereby reinforcing and reminding people of the importance of location on the Great Ladder of Corporate Success.

The Bias for Action: Some Organizational Implications

The discussion so far has argued that the conventional path–goal folk model of talk and action supports an implicit, but pervasive, bias for action, at least in the United States. A shift to a 'containers and cycles of meaning' folk or formal model(s) would reveal another relationship between action and different types of talk. This relationship would help demonstrate the critical importance of talk in creating meaningful action. It would also be consistent with a paradigmatic shift from an objectivist, linear, reductionist philosophy to one that is more constructionist, cyclical and relationship-oriented. A viable field of organizational discourse could well depend on such a shift. This would require a change in the mythopoetic- and frame-talk used in the discourses of the administrative sciences.

The bias for action over talk, however, has more than mere philosophical and academic consequences. It also has real consequences for what happens in real organizations. In today's organizations the foci of attention, what's valued, what's rewarded and, therefore, what's done are all biased towards action and away from talk. At first this may seem appropriate, even necessary. After all, aren't organizations created to foster collective action, to do things? The answer, of course, is yes, . . . but. The 'but' serves as a marker to note that there may be some unintended implications, some consequences to privileging action at the expense of talk. One, which we have already noted, is the potential to value and pursue any action, even meaningless or aimless action, to 'spinning our wheels in endless talk *that goes nowhere*'. Another is the potential gender bias created by a folk discourse that implicitly favours strong, silent, linearly oriented action to reciprocal, relationship, and emotionally oriented conversation. When talk is demeaned as relatively worthless, and, if, as it is for some, 'talk is women's work', then the consequences are obvious for women in the workplace. Even the most cursory review of feminist or gender-oriented literature reveals the central importance of how language is constructed and framed for how women (and men) are treated in the workplace (for example, Acker, 1992; Cameron, 1990; Gherardi, 1995; Tannen, 1994b). Other gender and cross-cultural implications should also be considered, including the possibility that the path–goal image schematic is more a preference of Western men than women or people raised in the context of alternative mythopoetic ideas and images (see, for example, Hall and Ames, 1995; Marshak, 1993b, 1994).

The last area of potential consequence to be addressed here has to do with change in contemporary organizations. The transition from the Industrial Age to the Information Age is compelling organizations to pursue new management and organization paradigms and possibilities (Marshak, 1995). The nature of the required changes to established patterns and practices is more transformational or revolutionary in nature than simply maintaining or developing existing capabilities and competencies (Marshak, 1993a). This is forcing organizations and their leaders to rethink fundamental assumptions, theories and practices in the pursuit of competitive success in a global economy. Rethinking, however, demands time on reflection and contemplation, to *talking* to oneself and others to discover the implicit frameworks that may be constraining innovation and adaptation. Rethinking, reflection and contemplation are therefore analogically and metaphorically related to 'talk', at least first-cousins if not siblings. The same or similar folk stigmas also seem to apply, whether the talk is with others or oneself through 'talk-in-the-mind'. For example, psychology is nothing more than 'mind games'; theorizing is 'fine in the abstract, but not in practice'; thinking and rethinking run the risk of 'analysing too much'; reflection is 'navel gazing'; and contemplation is just 'staring at the ceiling'. None are described as *doing* anything worthwhile, and most as valueless, *inactive*, wastes of time and therefore money.

At the same time, the professional and popular literatures related to organizations and organizational change have reflected an increasing interest in theories and techniques related to rethinking, reflection, contemplation and learning in organizations. These include theories and concepts related to single-loop, double-loop and triple-loop learning (Argyris, 1982, 1990, 1993; Argyris and Schön, 1974, 1978; Nielsen, 1993); reflective practice (Schön, 1983); sense-making (Weick, 1995); learning organizations (Senge, 1990); and dialogue as 'a process for transforming the quality of conversation and, in particular, the thinking that lies beneath it' (Isaacs, 1993a: 25; also see Bohm, 1989; Isaacs, 1993b; Schein, 1993). All of these approaches are more consistent with a containers and cycles of meaning model of talk and action rather than a linear, path–goal model. All must also deal with the countervailing managerial folk wisdom that such concepts are perhaps interesting or entertaining in theory, but in reality only action counts. Thus, in the United States at least, while having their adherents and places of application, few or none of these approaches have acquired the same status of centrality as the theories and methods that promise or promote tangible actions in pursuit of a goal. Interestingly, and possibly as a result of competing with the 'only action counts' folk wisdom, many of the promoters of these concepts have packaged or framed them with action, not talk, as the central reference point. Presumably, talk, by itself, doesn't sell. For example, there is action-learning, knowledge-in-action, action-reflection-learning, reflection-in-action, and the promise that 'dialogue . . . is at the root of *all* effective group action' (Schein, 1993: 42).

The paradox facing many leaders and organizations, then, is that there is a clear and compelling need to talk about, think about and confront the prevailing assumptions and taken-for-granted practices that are constraining organizational success in the Information Age. This requires reflection about the containers and cycles of meaning that restrict current thinking and action, including the frame-talk and mythopoetic-talk that are keeping management thinking 'in-the-box'. At the same time, there has been a profusion of formal theories and techniques to help leaders and managers address fundamental ways of thinking and knowing. Nonetheless, such approaches are still not considered mainstream, and it is difficult to get most managers to spend much time in reflective discourse. Instead, they are usually anxious and agitated to 'get on with it', to 'stop talking and move into action', because 'there is no time to waste'. They are, after all, responsible, 'action-oriented' managers.

The analysis here suggests that one culprit behind this apparent paradox may be the folk model that talk is worthless, action counts, and talk must stop for action to start. In short, the power of this culturally based folk model may covertly undermine the overt logic of the formal theories and competitive challenges (Marshak and Katz, 1997). *Your* formal theory may claim that talk is critical, but *my* folk model keeps telling me that 'talk is cheap and only action counts'.

Closing Comments

The primary purpose of this discussion has been to highlight the dimensions and impacts of the implicit folk models about talk and action. Moreover, the chapter has argued that a viable field of organizational discourse is timely, needed and not open to serious debate. When all is said and done, however, the viability of organizational discourse may well rest on whether or not we are able to leave the action trail and redeem the meaning of talk – for as we have seen, the everyday talk about talk is not favourable, leaving it with a tarnished and questionable reputation. All of this presents a major challenge for the nascent field of organizational discourse. Clearly there are many folk prejudices that will need to be overcome in order to establish discourse as a serious and central part of contemporary management and organizational narratives.

2 Workplace Conversations: The Text of Organizing

Jill Woodilla

Talk is everywhere in organizations, as members take for granted communication, information and decisions that are all based in interaction and language use. Talk also documents and constitutes worklife as members make sense of past events or anticipate future actions. Such talk becomes fundamental data for organizational research: ethnographic studies quote language-in-use to demonstrate particular meanings, survey researchers present statements assuming similar understanding by researcher and respondents, while critical scholars re-examine meanings within texts already 'written'.

Conversation, implying two people talking directly to each other to share information, ideas and feelings, is the most taken-for-granted process of social talking. Conversation appears as fragmented managerial interactions, or during meetings forming the backbone of organizational work, or labelled as gossip essential to a network of office relationships. Through conversation, relationships between individuals are established, shared meanings are developed, and contested meanings are made visible. But, before using such conversations for academic purposes, we need to first ask: What should we take into account to study organizing from the raw data of conversing? How can workplace conversations be represented as text to be analysed by researchers and then presented to others? At the same time, what may be excluded from such a perspective?

In this chapter, I assume that, within organizational settings, socially constructed meaning is created in language-based interactions (Berger and Luckmann, 1967), with 'conversation' as the most common, taken-for-granted practice. Using work from a number of disciplines, I develop a theory and practice of the *workplace conversation* and show it to be fundamental to meaning-making. I then go on to illustrate this with an empirical example.

Towards a Theory and Practice of Workplace Conversations

Typically for organizational theorists, the actual process of conversing is less important than the outcomes of the exchange. 'Talk' as the outcome of conversation has instrumental value for coordinating actions, establishing

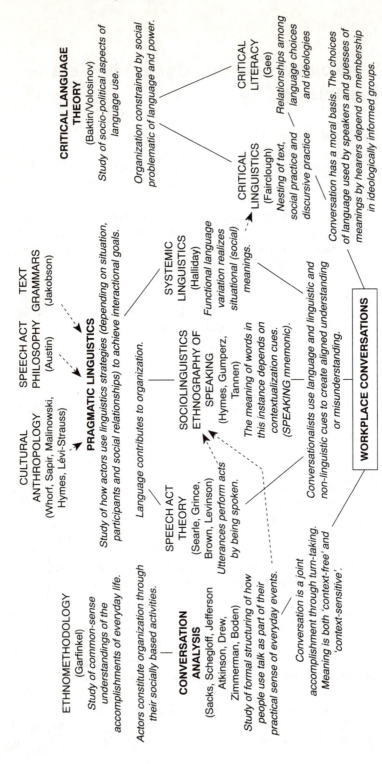

FIGURE 2.1 *Theoretical contributions to a description of workplace conversations*

control or motivating others. Indeed, some say talk *is* the work of managers (Gronn, 1983; Mintzberg, 1973). But, only infrequently do organizational researchers dwell on ways in which conversation is initiated, maintained, closed and maybe subsequently reopened. Ways in which personal and occupational identities are constituted and revealed through this process are seldom explored. Similarly, while we may be aware of different 'languages' in use in organizational settings (Daft and Wiginton, 1979), ways in which individuals use or misuse linguistic cues to overcome or sustain mis-understandings are rarely the basis for theorizing. Employing a multi-disciplinary approach, however, allows our taken-for-granted understandings of conversations to be replaced by a theory and method applicable to organizational contexts.

Three informing fields contribute to theorizing 'workplace conversation' (this term is introduced to focus attention on language-based interactions of individuals within organizations). These are conversation analysis (as a sub-discipline of ethnomethodological sociology), pragmatic linguistics (as a sub-discipline of linguistics) and critical language/literacy theory. Each discipline considers meanings as socially constructed through language use, yet each takes a different perspective on ways in which these meanings emerge. Each contributes in part, and they also work together to position workplace conversation as fundamental to ways in which organizational actors construct meanings.

The major theoretical contributions to a description of workplace con-versations can be represented diagrammatically (see Figure 2.1 and Table 2.1). The informing fields, schools of thought and major theorists are presented in Figure 2.1, and a synthesis of the specific contributions from each field is contained in Table 2.1. In practice, many disciplines are related, as the work of major theorists influences others.

Ethnomethodological Conversation Analysis

In sociology, ethnomethodology examines ways in which actors make sense of their ongoing experiences, where actors' understandings are separate from scholars' interest in how they come to this understanding (Bittner, 1965; Garfinkel, 1974; Weick, 1995). Ethnomethodological conversation analysis considers the formal structuring of ways people use talk to make sense of the minutiae of everyday events (Garfinkel, 1967). Scholars focus on how participants 'know' they are having a conversation, and how they are able to distinguish among different types of conversational interactions.

According to these scholars, conversation is the joint accomplishment of participants which is possible only because 'everyone' unconsciously attends to the basic rules of its 'common-sense' turn-taking structure (Sacks et al., 1974; Schegloff and Sacks, 1973).[1] In order to be able to take a turn at talk, each participant must have attended to, and 'understood', what hap-pened in the previous utterance in the sequence, implying a link between cognition and interaction (Schegloff, 1991). Conversation is context-free, in

TABLE 2.1　Summary of contributions to understanding workplace conversations

About conversations	Conversation analysis	Pragmatic linguistics	Critical language theory
What kinds of questions are asked?	How do actors know they are having a conversation? How do actors distinguish one kind of conversation from another?	How do actors use language and linguistic and non-linguistic cues to understand each other?	Why do actors make particular language choices when speaking, and specific guesses about meaning when listening?
What kinds of answers?	'Everyone' uses certain 'turn-taking rules'. Actors understand this conversation only as it unfolds – they must 'understand' the previous turn in order to make the next one. Actors use ambiguity to construct identity and meaning. Specialized conversations differ from mundane ones by looking at ways 'turn-taking rules' are both similar and different.	We can infer how actors are negotiating meaning from their language and contextualization cues. Speech act theory: utterances perform actions by being spoken. Sociolinguistics: meaning of words used in this instance depends on contextualization cues. Ethnography: SPEAKING mnemonic. Systemic linguistics – functional language variation realizes situational (social) meanings.	Choices and guesses are informed by tacit assumptions of 'normal conversational behaviours'. All language use constrained by structuring of institutional discourse and/or moral obligations of membership in cultural groups. Distinction among text as linguistic artefact, discourse as actual practice, and social discursive practices (see note 4).
Issues studied within discipline	How turn-taking rules are used differently in different social settings and by different classes of people. How important the wider context is to the social setting (return to a broader ethnomethodological focus).	How language used indicates meaning and associated behaviour. How mis/understanding develops and the reasons for this. How spoken and written language form a continuum ('the text'). Difficulties connecting language-level analysis to social situations.	Reflection on societal practices involving acquisition and use of language. Analysis uncovers linguistic-discursive forms of domination and exploitation.
Methodologies	Transcript in standardized format. Punctuation indicates prosody. Look for pairs of turns (adjacency pairs). Examine utterance meaning within these turns, then between one pair and the next.	Transcript presented according to level of language studied. Ethnographic detail added as relevant for analysis. Issues of how researcher gathers and presents data. Analysis depends on theoretical focus.	Researcher identifies problematic moments which reveal contested meanings. Analysis links levels of discourse. Less emphasis on transcript and more on argument.

that anyone can speak to anyone else, anywhere, about anything, because meaning is achieved through sequential ordering and commitment to the reciprocity of the process. At the same time, meaning is context-sensitive, in that a particular context is necessary for the current topics being understood within this situation. Researchers track meanings through conversationalists' use of 'adjacency pairs', such that the structure of one turn (for example, as a question, statement or greeting) requires a particular response (that is, an answer, an acknowledgement or follow-up greeting), while the content of the response reveals the unfolding sense in context. For example, individual identities are constructed and maintained when one speaker uses his/her own turn to create ambiguity such that the second speaker responds according to the meaning he/she attaches to the first speaker's utterance after assuming it was spoken by that person with a specific identity (Drew and Heritage, 1992). Participants organize the unfolding conversation according to their own agenda, and provide an optimal display of their self through presentation of preferred roles and relationships (Schenkein, 1978).

Since the original research on turn-taking rules was conducted with white, English-speaking, mostly male, dyads, this is the foundation on which most of the theoretical work rests (Watson and Seiler, 1992). However, conversational turn-taking has been shown to be based on different rules in other cultures (Dunne and Ng, 1994; Moerman, 1988) and when women are predominantly involved (Edelsky, 1981; Fishman, 1983; West and Zimmerman, 1985). More than one person may talk at the same time in order to collaborate on constructing the conversational turn, periods of silence may be accepted, or 'turn-taking' may be considered to have a broader implication than just the opportunity to speak (see examples in Boden and Zimmerman, 1991; Watson and Seiler, 1992).

In organizational studies, conversation analysis allows researchers to ask what is distinctive about conversational exchanges within institutional settings by comparisons with other examples of conversations, and hence to focus on ways in which participants are making sense in the particular organizational setting. Interviews, oral reports and meetings, for example, are each structured through particular turn-taking patterns which are attended to by participants (cf. Atkinson and Heritage, 1984; Boden, 1994; Bogen, 1992; Schegloff, 1988/9). Identifiable turn-taking patterns also structure workplace tasks, including ways in which information is gathered and a decision-making process unfolds (Boden, 1994). Meanings embedded in turn-taking practices allow actors to know what conversational behaviours are expected in each situation, and to anticipate interactional patterns so they can pay attention to potential meanings from language use.

Methodological Issues in Conversation Analysis Conversation is structured in all settings, so that it becomes visible to the analyst, and since the nature of the structuring differs from context to context, analysis is useful for particular research settings. The researcher presents a particular instance of conversation, and shows that the reader can understand the meaning that conversationalists achieved by following the ordering of pairs of utterances ('turn-taking'). This requires attending to turns within turns, and the particular strategies conversationalists use for achieving the meaning that they desire within the context of the particular interaction. By constant reference to a transcript of the recorded exchange which uses punctuation marks unconventionally to indicate pauses, intonation and overlap of speakers (cf. Button and Lee, 1987), the researcher identifies regularities in the patterning of talk and corresponding meanings ascribed by the participants. Analysis first marks groups of utterances that function together as units in a turn. Next, drawing on the context of the conversation, the researcher shows how the participants seem to understand each other, and just what this understanding is, based on the phrases and sentences that make up each utterance. Often an earlier turn is pointed out as important for establishing this particular meaning, or the reader may be alerted to upcoming sequences since they are already present in the transcript. Analysis is extremely detailed, since at each step the underlying assumptions and artful practices of the speakers are unravelled, and it is shown why they are this way and not some other. Validity is established by moving back and forth between hypotheses for understanding the data and realization of the hypothesis by comparison of one sequence of conversation to another. Then, through analysing many exchanges, results in the particular instance are generalized to the larger case.

Pragmatic Linguistics

In contrast to ethnomethodological conversation analysis' foundation in the structuring aspects of turn-taking, pragmatic linguistics, as a sub-field of linguistics, focuses on situated language practices through which meaning is derived by the language user (van Dijk, 1981). Individuals expect their verbal interactions to accomplish conversational goals, and pursue linguistic strategies which vary as a function of the situation, the other participants, and social relations among participants. Conversation involves the use of language (that is, syntax, lexicon, phonology) and contextual linguistic and non-linguistic cues to indicate underlying meanings, which impact on actions. Pragmatics highlights the discrepancy between what is said and what is meant and examines how those involved work out what is meant (Putnam, 1992). Pragmatic linguists focus on the 'utterance' and 'situated' or 'natural' language use to distinguish a pragmatic approach from the more formal study of grammars or written text, and their constant attention to understanding emphasizes language as a meaning system rather than a sign system. The emphasis is not on *performance/competence* (Chomsky, 1957), or *parole* as opposed to *langue* (Saussure, 1960), but on ignoring these divisions, just as everyday users of language do. Pragmatics incorporates a variety of theories, rather than a single school of thought, since the extreme elasticity of language-in-use makes a simple definition impossible (Levinson, 1983).

The three main roots of pragmatics provide theoretical links between language and social action: (1) the philosophy of Austin (1962) links language as abstract linguistic objects and utterances as forms of action; (2) anthropology applies real language use in a socio-cultural context (Hymes, 1974; Lévi-Strauss, 1964; Malinowski, 1923; Sapir, 1921; Whorf, 1956); and (3) 'text-grammars' provide the functional analysis of sentence and discourse structure (Halliday, 1978; Waugh and Monville-Burston, 1990). Contemporary scholars use different linguistic features as the unit of analysis and show how these link to meaning in context, drawing on one or a combination of these theories to provide a systematic link between actors' intentions, language used and observed actions.

Speech act theory develops a typology of actions that utterances perform just by being spoken (Austin, 1962; Bach and Harnish, 1979; Searle, 1969). According to this perspective, actions such as requesting, demanding, apologizing and asserting occur through the form and rules of language use rather than in the context of the interaction. Meaning is defined as mutual knowledge, in which the sender knows that the hearer knows the sender's intention of a particular utterance as a result of communication (Grice, 1957). Analysis identifies the different aspects of the speech act and relationships between acts, documenting the basis for each in terms of the speaker's intention and the extent to which 'hearer uptake' realizes that intention.

In organizational studies, focusing on speech acts indicates ways in which language can be used to gain compliance of subordinates (Drake and Moberg, 1986), especially during periods of organizational change (Ford and Ford, 1995), and how power is implicated in politeness (Brown and Levinson, 1987; Wasson, 1995) and silence (Jaworski, 1993). However, attention is generally directed to the speaker, while the contributions of the hearer and the dynamics of evolving conversation are ignored (Levinson, 1983).

Building from observations that children learn language and meaning simultaneously, a systemic linguistics approach (Halliday, 1978, 1985; Halliday and Hasan, 1989) theorizes parts of speech according to their 'meaning function' rather than their syntactic function of conventional grammar. A 'text', representing anything that may be spoken or written, may be described by the various meaning functions that language performs in this context. Using the clause as the unit of analysis, the researcher system-atically charts linguistic features (for example, transitivity, mood, theme, cohesion, and so on) in terms of contextual observations (for example field, tenor, mode) to show how, and why, the text means what it does because of the functions that language performs in this situation, without invoking any cognitive capabilities of the language user.

Although considered an important branch of pragmatics, since Halliday's approach developed through his application of linguistic theory to educational questions, it has been used predominantly in studies of the development of children's and students' language capabilities, and issues related to curriculum reform (Halliday, 1993). It has had fewer applications in organization studies. In one, Kim Morouney (1995) demonstrated how subject positions of male and female managers are constructed as the dominant discourse.

The branch of pragmatics most familiar to organizational analysts is that of sociolinguistics. Here the focus is on the speech community – whose members share knowledge of rules for the conduct and interpretation of speech – rather than the individual speakers of the language or their linguistic competence (Gumperz, 1982). Most work in an organizational setting is based on Dell Hymes's (1974) work on the ethnography of speaking, using the mnemonic SPEAKING[2] as the empirical method for observing and recording data. For a speech event such as a meeting, the researcher identifies the particular components (for example participants, speech styles, norms of interpretation, and so on), using various speech acts occurring within the event. Speech acts, such as a joke, an exact description or a formal request, are minimal units for understanding, and include not only the grammatical form of what is said, but also knowledge of the way in which it is usually uttered and interpreted. For the most part, the research interest is in how meaning is constituted within the community, and how talk accomplishes this.

Important research in organizational situations includes studies on counselling interviews, on use of different linguistic styles in the workplace, and on groups involved in meetings and teams. In each case empirical analysis follows an interpretative approach by making an in-depth study of selected instances of interaction, observing whether or not actors appear to understand one another, then eliciting participants' interpretations.

Studies of cross-cultural interviews (Erickson and Shultz, 1982; Gumperz, 1992; Roberts et al., 1992) show how misunderstandings develop because participants interpret contextual cues differently according to membership in different speech communities. Individuals who are fluent in interpreting cues in familiar contexts may fail in unfamiliar organizational settings.

Other misunderstandings have been shown to occur when conversationalists attend to different patterns of linguistic interaction, such as reoccurring patterns of sounds, hence making sense in different ways (Tannen, 1989, 1994a, 1995). Following Muriel Saville-Troike (cf. Tannen and Saville-Troike, 1985), other studies invert silence and sound, emphasizing its complex nature as a cultural phenomenon, especially when indicating politeness or agreement.

Conversational involvement in work-groups has been explored in meetings, functional-task and team-talking situations. For example, Helen Schwartzman (1989) shows how meetings are a place for individuals to negotiate as well as to learn about their place in the organizational hierarchy.

Anne Donnellon (1994) shows how, linguistically, team members go about negotiating differences amongst themselves in order to integrate their various skills, knowledge and experience as needed to complete the team-task. She suggests that responsible team members can use 'talk' to reshape team dynamics, by using a 'team talk audit' and focusing on instances of conflict and decision-making (Donnellon, 1996).

Methodological Issues in Pragmatics   Empirical research centres on developing a written text (a transcript) of naturally occurring conversation, where the level of detail of prosody and non-linguistic cues and inclusion of ethnographic observations depends on the specific research question.[3] Usually the transcript is prepared from an audio or video recording, which is dependent on the fidelity, number and placement of recording devices, as well as invasive effects due to the presence of strangers and equipment. The written transcription may be of selected portions, assuming the conversation begins with the first speaker presented, and focusing on utterances in sequence, with few details of non-verbal cues of everyone present. How the transcriber assigns punctuation to any utterance affects all subsequent readings and hence meanings, and how the order of speaking is presented may perpetuate hierarchical biases (Ochs, 1979; West, 1996). The researcher provides an interpretation of the transcript as it unfolds, drawing the reader's attention to particular language use, and inferred meaning, by participants.

Depending on the research question, a number of examples may be used to build the 'general case', as representative of conversationalists' inferred meanings and subsequent behaviours based on their use of language; alternatively, a single 'telling case' may provide a particular insight. Such analysis provides a criterion against which to appraise participants' own explanations and conceptualizations of their behaviour, or to provide insights into a particular organizational theory.

Critical Language Theory

In pragmatics, the researcher assumes a common basis of understanding with both actors and readers. In a critical approach, the researcher makes visible such underlying social assumptions, and investigates multiple layers of meanings in what is being spoken. On one level, meaning is the effect of interaction between listener and speaker, because each word is said in a particular way. But meaning also depends on reflections of the listener on all the other instances in which the word has been used (Volosinov, 1973). What each person says, feels, thinks and does is always indebted to the social groups to which s/he belongs (Gee, 1990).

Critical language theory is concerned with the social problematic of language and power. Critical linguistics (Fairclough, 1992; Hodge and Kress, 1993) seeks to uncover linguistic-discursive forms of domination and exploitation through a combination of linguistic analysis and textual analysis. One particular project concerns the need to establish critical language awareness as a part of language education. Critical literacy theory (Gee, 1990) promotes an agenda for educational practices which provide access to multiple discourses as a crucial prerequisite to critical literacies.

Critical approaches examine how language intersects with ideology – the espoused social theory which involves generalizations about the ways 'goods' are distributed in society (Gee, 1990) – at points where speakers express their own viewpoints. Scholars point out what one needs to assume in order to understand or 'read' a particular text in a particular way, linking forms of language use with assumptions underlying particular meanings. By representing the socio-political affiliations of conversationalists, researchers also encourage readers to engage in self-critical examination of their own conversations.

For a critical reading, discourse[4] analysis examines how linguistic and contextualization features place each speaker within her or his networks of status (privilege) and solidarity (with like others) and how interpretations of the spoken or written text are affected by the position of those making the interpretation. Actual practices of talking and writing are seen to be constrained by broader social practices with structural and cultural implications. Each person belongs to many different groups – or Discourses with a capital D (Gee, 1990) – each indicating particular social ways of behaving, thinking, speaking and valuing that are accepted as instances of particular roles by specific groups of people. Conflicts arise when words chosen by the speaker to be understood in one Discourse are interpreted by the listener from within the ideology of another Discourse.

Methodologically, the text as a linguistic artefact is taken as the object of analysis, where interest is in how the text constitutes discourse. For some scholars, the object of understanding is a particular social discursive practice (cf. Escobar, 1995). By highlighting modes of reproduction, researchers point out modes of transformation, with the aim of producing lasting social change. With workplace conversations, a critical reading of the text of the transcript examines processes of local production and interpretation of meaning, and ways in which these are indebted to broader institutional practices. Uncovering these connections reveals how language used in everyday interactions enacts dominant structural and cultural organizational arrangements.

Critical language studies in educational or medical contexts are relevant for their organizational implications (cf. Fairclough, 1995). By analysing speeches at a company breakfast supposedly to inform and praise employees, Michael Rosen (1985a) identifies relationships of domination that exist throughout the company. Georg von Krogh and Johan Roos (1996) demonstrate how, when managers notice ways in which rules of 'authority', 'intimidation' and 'closure' are expressed differently on different types of conversations, they can initiate conversations aimed at promoting dialogue for understanding rather than advocacy for agreement. Then, innovation in language can be used to develop new concepts and new meanings around existing strategic issues, making conversations a vehicle for organizational knowledge development.

Methodological Issues in Critical Approaches Research projects tend to be defined in terms of a social practice, which in an organizational context may refer to broadly defined management practices. Analysis usually focuses on a 'moment of crisis', indicating a point during a conversation where there is a communicative problem which requires particular attention from participants, or which they may ignore. The language used is related to how 'texts' may be differently constructed or understood by others in the same situation, so that these moments make visible aspects of practice that might normally be neglected or normalized.

During analysis attention shifts constantly between the particularity of the text of the conversation and the discourses which inform it. Analysis is a combination of articulating precisely how participants produce and understand their unfolding interaction according to their own use of language, and the nature of language use in terms of discourse membership. The actual use of language is vital to articulating different underlying values. Rhetorical strategies of the researcher are instrumental in directing attention of the reader to instances of domination.

Workplace Conversations

From the above discussion of relevant literature, it is possible to locate the social construction of meaning and enactment of organizing through accomplishments of workplace conversations. Moreover, we can define workplace conversation as: involving the joint accomplishment of participants through 'turn-taking', where contingent meaning evolves only in the context of interaction. Language and linguistic and non-linguistic cues are used to create aligned understanding, which is never complete, where the choices of language used by speakers and guesses of meanings by hearers depend on the discourses each belongs to.

This approach places analysis as textual analysis within the arena of discourse analysis (Fairclough, 1995). Such analysis entails going beyond the natural attitude towards language to examine the social and cultural aspects of the interaction. Researchers represent the actual text of prolonged conversational interactions, and use a combination of linguistically informed theories to demonstrate how emergent meanings are essential to organizing.

Organizational Meanings through Workplace Conversations

Focusing on conversations draws attention to the dynamic linguistic interactions necessary for organizing and accomplishing tasks in a cooperative or collusional manner. Actors constitute organization through their socially based actions, which include talking with each other. Taken-for-granted structuring aspects of conversational practices constrain actors to enact different organizational arrangements of 'interactional orders' (Goffman, 1967, 1983), for purposes of information sharing, decision-making, or task-accomplishment. These include dyadic (one-to-one), 'platform' (one-to-many/many-to-one) or small-group (many to many) arrangements. In general workplace experience, these three types of connections may be understood as interviews, lectures or leadership situations, and meetings. In production-based organizations, these structures are realized through appraisals, briefings and work-groups, while in universities they involve advising students or consulting with peers, teaching and committees. In every workplace conversation, actors are constructing their occupational selves and the roles that they enact, which socially constructs 'their organization'. At the same time, conversation itself is socially determined, since actual conversations can happen only within institutional practices of pre-existing organization (Fairclough, 1992). Within conversational structuring, everyday language is used to attain shared and contested meanings – all the understandings, misunderstandings, ambiguities and ideologies that enable and hinder everyday actions among cooperative and conflicting actors with unique human experiences.

Arguably, the most common talk-based institutional practice of (Western) organizing is 'the meeting'. Many studies focus on meetings as tools for accomplishing administrative tasks, providing various definitions and typologies (Schwartzman, 1989; Volkema and Niederman, 1995). Distinctive features of meeting-talk, such as beginnings and endings, placing items on the agenda, and accepting the 'proper' control of talk, are maintained through the collaborative work of those present (Anderson et al., 1978; Cuff and Sharrock, 1985). Within this framework, specific agenda items, or segments within the agenda, may be in one-to-one format as two members negotiate particular understanding, while others present are privy to this conversation; one-to many/many-to-one as a report is presented for informational purposes; or many-to-many as decisions are made. Linguistic strategies indicate how those present go about negotiating differences among themselves in order to integrate their various skills, knowledge and experience as needed to complete the group-task (Donnellon, 1994), while determining their own role within the work expected of this and other meetings (Schwartzman, 1989). Conversational work during meetings shows how the apparently fragmented processes of information gathering, transmission and very local assimilation are transformed into the goals, agendas and decisions of organizations (Boden, 1994).

The following example demonstrates how organizing is constituted through conversing at the same time as participants are establishing aligned meanings around a specific task. Data are drawn from an exploratory study at a health maintenance organization in the United States. As part of a planned change to total quality management (TQM) practices, a Quality

Council was established to oversee and guide various TQM initiatives. Quality Council members were senior administrators, chiefs of medical specialties, and representatives of allied health professionals (about 15 members). They met monthly, for two to three hours, in a large conference room, and meetings were usually chaired by the organization's Director. Over a period of two years, I attended and audiotaped several meetings. This example, from one meeting, is representative of many conversations in my corpus of data.

A transcript of an audio-tape of the meeting becomes my text. Analysis is extremely detailed, as I isolate each utterance, identify cues from turn-taking, linguistic strategies or intertext links, and interpret meanings, both around the task at hand, and in the micro-processes of organizing. Establishing a plausible explanation takes considerable space, so here I analyse just a few turns. There are three main segments to the discussion. First, I provide a 'gloss' – the context and normalized meanings – to situate the conversation. Second, I analyse the transcript in Figure 2.2, which has been prepared according to sociolinguistic conventions.[5] Finally, a discussion of the meanings that have been established is undertaken.

```
 1 Jack:   ((introduces and explains goal)) maybe Cindy could you =
 2 Cindy:  = sure =
 3 Jack:   = (inaud) =
 4 Cindy:  = sure the only thing going to talk about that tomorrow partly the
 5            idea system generates points for prizes yeah and I wonder whether that
 6            might be tied in that might be (inaud) reward for that as well goal
 7            (inaud) have to think what concept rating too because number of ideas
 8 Jack:   /(inaud)/
 9 Cindy:  /tying into/ ideas that might be rewards be added (inaud) goal I don't
10            know what to think (inaud) have difficulty separating the two because
11            the number (inaud) part of the (inaud) programme someone might want to
12            mention that =
13 Bill:   = creates the potential for perhaps to this goal to /(inaud)/
14 ?       /yeah/ ((close to microphone))
15 Bill:   how well the team incentive was tied into our goals and how well you do
16            against these goals and then you have have the opportunity for earning
17            these points for ideas I don't know whether that's a problem
18 Mark:   it doesn't sound like a problem because the person who came up with the
19            idea is the only one who came up with the idea is going to put it into
20            place (inaud) you know not everybody you know presumably you know that
21            there's probably a lot of extra work I don't know if there's enough
22            extra work for everybody to profit around here
23            ((3-second pause))
24 Jack:   yeah (soft laugh) I there probably is enough (inaud) yeah to the degree
25            that somebody comes up with an idea that is related to eliminating
26            unnecessary work they can earn points and we determine at the end of
27            ninety-six that this goal is met that's positive towards the incentive
28            programme (.) I don't have a problem with that ((continues))
```

FIGURE 2.2 *Transcript of a workplace conversation*

A Gloss

The conversation is embedded in a Quality Council meeting agenda item to approve a number of organizational goals prepared by sub-groups. Here, as members focus on how they will achieve a proposed goal to eliminate unnecessary work, Jack, Cindy, Bill and Mark talk about how they will measure it. Jack, a doctor, is the organization's Director and meeting chair; Cindy, as the Chief Quality Administrator, is responsible for coordinating goal development and implementation. This position was established on the implementation of total quality management. Bill is a Physician Assistant, who works in direct-patient care, and Mark is a doctor, who, as Chief of a Medical Service, spends the majority of his time administrating and consulting with other physicians, rather than with patients.

Jack introduces the topic by referring to copies of the goal worksheet which give its full title as 'Goal to increase employee satisfaction by eliminating unnecessary work'. He explains that the goal is to eliminate unnecessary work, such as paperwork, for new approaches to managed health care, cost reduction efforts, or ideas related to patients or providers. He states that the concern is how to achieve the goal, and that the sub-group which developed the goal has suggested that measurement should be by the number of ideas proposed, using the idea system that is already in place. Cindy, who works with the sub-group, initiates a conversation around the proposal to use the idea-points system as a measure. What does this 'mean'? Meanings emerge through the conversation in Figure 2.2, in which Bill and Mark state what they already understand, and are not sure about, so that Jack is able to state what he believes to be the meaning shared by Council members. Then (not in the transcript), the conversation continues. Another Council member suggests, and others agree, that any individual who proposes an idea that truly eliminates unnecessary work will be awarded two points in the previously established incentive system. Also, exactly what constitutes unnecessary work will be decided by a special state-wide steering committee. The Director is pleased with these decisions.

The Analysis of a Workplace Conversation

Cindy takes the floor in line 4 (refer to line numbers in Figure 2.2), without waiting for Jack to finish his request for her to do so. Maybe she is eager to speak, but the grammatical incoherence of the beginning of her turn suggests that she is unprepared or unclear of what is expected of her. As she continues, her voice fluctuates in volume, suggesting a lack of confidence, and inaudible words on the tape make interpretation of the transcript difficult. Cindy may be insecure in her role as leader of the discussion about the goal. She is relatively new in her position, and the task of developing organizational goals in this form has been instituted with the TQM programme. In speaking, Cindy is making sense for herself. First, in an utterance punctuated by 'yeah' as confirmation (back-channelling) she remembers that at the sub-group meeting tomorrow they will talk about how the idea system generates points for prizes, then continues: 'I wonder if we can link both points for prizes, and points to measure the goal' (my paraphrase). This speech act both conveys her doubt, and is the act of 'wondering about meaning'. Cindy continues to explore the points concept, ignoring Jack's attempt to speak (line 8–9), which may be an attempt at clarification. In line 9 she begins a rhetorical question, 'I don't know what to think', then makes a request, 'someone might want to mention that' (line 11–12).

Bill begins talking (line 13) without waiting for Cindy to finish her turn, interpreting her last utterances as signals for a change of speaker, but his first few words do not link directly to her turn. He starts in the middle of a sentence 'creates the potential for perhaps', then backtracks to provide a subject 'this goal'. Bill was probably waiting for an opportunity to take the floor to state his opinion. He wants to establish his identity as a knowledge-able member of the Council, since many other members are his professional superiors.

When I fill in 'show' for the word that was masked on the tape by someone's 'yeah' (line 14), guessing as we all do when we miss a word during conversations, I can normalize Bill's utterance as 'the goal creates the potential to show how well the team incentive was tied into our goals and how well you do against these goals'. Here he links '*our* goals' with 'how well *you* do' (line 15). This may be colloquial grammar, or he may be deliberately identifying himself with those who formulate the goals, who are different from those who achieve them.

Bill states where meaning is unclear for him, repeating 'have' while he thinks, 'then you have the opportunity for earning these points.' He ends with either a statement or a rhetorical question, 'I don't know if this is a problem' (line 16–17). Bill's turn begins with his own understanding of the goal, then he tries to make sense of Cindy's statements.

Bill has signalled for someone else to speak, and Mark's turn indicates that he paid attention to Bill's last utterance as a question, since he answers with, 'it doesn't sound like a problem' (line 18), although he is not explicit about which part of Bill's utterance he assumes is the problem. Mark continues with, 'the person who came up with the idea is the only one who came up with the idea is going to put it into place' (line 18–20). Here Mark gives his understanding of Bill's 'you have the opportunity for earning these points.' For Mark, individuals are clearly responsible for both ideas and tasks, and since he does not use the word 'goal', he may be voicing an opinion for many situations. Mark's clear response to the prior question reveals his identity as someone comfortable with solving problems.

Then Mark hesitates, using the filler of 'you know' several times as he continues with 'you know not everybody you know presumably you know that there's probably a lot of extra work' (line 20–1). He is grappling with the concept of 'unnecessary work', which is 'extra work' in his meaning system. Mark is unable to connect 'extra work' to his professional experi-ence, so is explicit, 'I don't know if there's enough extra work for everyone to profit around here' (line 21–2). His choices of 'everyone' and 'profit' show he understands the goal to apply to the whole organization, and points are monetary-like rewards. The form of the utterance signals for someone else to take a turn.

There is a pause (line 23). It would be logical for Bill to take another turn here, to check his understanding of Mark's response to his utterance, but he does not do so. Since no-one responds quickly, perhaps others are thinking about Mark's question – how much unnecessary work is there? Jack takes the next turn, as a longer transcript would show he often does when there is a long pause. He begins with his own opinion 'I', then states categorically, 'there probably is enough (inaudible word)'. His 'yeah' at either end of the statement gives it emphasis, but his laugh suggests he is a little surprised or embarrassed to be saying so. Jack is showing he is the Director; he gives leadership, knows answers, and acknowledges that the organization is not as efficient as he would like it to be.

Jack then states his understanding, that an individual who comes up with an idea related to eliminating unnecessary work can earn points – this has been developed through Bill and Mark's turns. Jack continues, connecting meeting this goal and the incentive programme – apparently crediting the incentive programme with providing motivation for achieving goals, 'we determine . . . that this goal is met that's a positive towards the incentive programme' (line 26–8). Jack reinforces his understanding with 'I don't have a problem with that.' Jack's use of the word 'problem' connects his utterance with the two previous speakers. He then uses the privilege of the meeting chair to take longer turns than most other speakers, keeping the conversation open with a direct question about points.

Synthesis and Discussion

If space permitted, this analysis would be extended, carefully following and interpreting cues in a longer transcript. Insights from this conversation would be compared with those in other sequences, allowing interpretations to be generalized. Here I discuss how results from this transcript may be extended to contribute to organizational research.

Turn-taking   Turn-taking revealed how individual identities were woven into emerging roles as Quality Council members. An extended analysis would examine connections between displays of identity, construction of roles, and constraining effects of established organizational structures. In this example Jack extended his role as Director to 'leader' of the Council. As meeting chair he took the first turn, established the task, and stated his expectations for the work of the council. He usually took the next turn after any noticeable pause, to provide additional information or to summarize emerging, collective meanings. He then connected this summary to his own understanding of the task or process, revealing how he expected TQM to work. Even though Jack attempted to voice leadership for new practices (cf.

Pondy, 1978), he promoted established meeting rules (Cuff and Sharrock, 1985). He used the organizational agenda (Boden, 1994) of implementing a new management philosophy to include his individual agenda of validating organizational goals.

Fragments of three different 'member-roles' were apparent in this example and may be explored in other transcripts. Bill, an active participant in all meetings, took his first turn early in the conversation, to display his knowledge of the topic that had just been introduced, and to link his understanding of employee behaviours to the work of the Council. He seldom took a second (follow-up) turn to clarify or augment particular statements, suggesting his reluctance to promote his identity as an 'expert'. Mark (and other doctors) linked his turns to others', and spoke about established practices, sedimenting an identity based in accepted knowledge. Cindy (and others, mainly women, in administrative positions) tended to respond only when called upon directly, or when she had some unique knowledge about the process or task.

Most participants revealed identities already accepted within both the organizational hierarchy and within their professions. At least one person was attempting to use membership in the Quality Council as an opportunity to create an identity which augmented his professional role. Since the process of establishing a stable identity requires the collaborative effort of conversational partners, following the interactions would demonstrate how fragile the process is within an organization with a strong medical-professional hierarchy (Drew and Heritage, 1992).

Linguistic Cues   In this example, participants' speech showed similar linguistic patterns. The hypothesis that these strategies were common to all competent speakers in this organization as a speech community would be tested by examining many other speech events.

Repeated words and ellipses (missing words) marked utterances where the speaker articulated his or her emerging understanding, while coherent, simple syntax indicated a statement of internalized understanding. Speakers frequently juxtaposed personal pronouns with use of the passive tense to link personal experience with abstractions of 'the organization', indicating unfamiliarity with constructing such a connection. Rhetorical questions (for example, 'I don't know if . . .') were used more often than a direct question (for example, 'Do you know if . . .') when meaning was unclear to the speaker. Such linguistic patterns, which members used to signal understanding to each other, showed how organizational members were collectively making sense. All the while that conversationalists were making sense of immediate tasks, roles and events, they were constructing a *generic subjective* and a referent to a shared experience which existed independently of the individuals involved in this particular conversation (Weick, 1995). Bill, Mark and Jack (together with other meeting attendees who are silent witnesses to the conversation) were collectively engaged in making sense of what constitutes a member of the organization – as people whose work directly impacts on achieving organizational goals, and also people with responsibility for establishing and monitoring these goals.

Intertext Links Even in this short transcript, manifest links chained individual meanings to a summary. Uncovering such patterns forms the basis for a critical interpretation of language use. Speakers referred to the text of earlier speakers, ensuring that 'symptoms of problems with meanings' were preserved. The summary was assumed to be the collective meaning because it was spoken by an authority. In the example here, authority was vested in the organization's Director. In other examples the authority figure might be a medical specialist or functional administrator, depending on the context. Such conversations were clear-cut, event-based and linked authority to expertise. Conversations were aimed at advocacy for agreement rather than at promoting dialogue for understanding (von Krogh and Roos, 1996).

If members want to create and sustain new ways of working, involving truly new management philosophies, they must find a way of revisiting meanings that are unclear to any one person, providing a dynamic framework for advancing collective meaning within the context of any particular application. For example, either Bill or another person might initiate a turn around the meaning of 'team incentive' and how this was linked to the way the goal would be achieved. Here, however, the dominant discourse prevailed, valuing established ways of working and rewarding individually.

Meanings that emerged and were apparently accepted during this conversation were not only about the task at hand – a decision about giving points for ideas; they were also about the process of making meaning. Turn-taking patterns reflected individual identities (who is doing meaning), linguistic cues indicated expectations for communicative competence (how to do meaning), and intertext links revealed how the dominant discourse was being constructed (values that are assumed in order to accomplish meaning). Organizing was evident in these micro-interactions, as identities in relation to the group constructed roles, as expectations for behaviours constructed generic subjectivities, and as hierarchies were perpetuated.

Conclusions: 'Meanings' for Organizational Research

I have placed *workplace conversations* as fundamental to the social construction of meaning within organizational settings, and demonstrated how meanings around topics and around organizing are simultaneously created. My point is not that workplace conversations exist, but how organization scholars can move beyond the natural attitude to take advantage of a systematic interdisciplinary approach.

I have shown how actors are constantly constructing their discourse of organizing. Since it takes far longer to study a conversation with the detail presented here than the original act took, however, further research should establish how this methodology can be incorporated into any research question. This includes discussing ways of selecting conversations around a particular topic or amongst prominent actors, and how results of these micro-processes can be connected to more macro research interests.

What I have presented in this chapter glosses over many of the concerns of those working in the underlying fields; to compensate, I recommend reading current literature within these areas of study. I also ask, 'whose' conversations am I writing about? The ephemeral nature of 'talk' is such that meaning changes each time the words are revisited following their original utterance. As a researcher I attempt to uncover meanings of organizational actors and present these to other academics, so the locus of conversation changes from between actors to between scholars. Just as a transcript can never capture an actual unfolding situation, so meanings can never be completely isolated or fully articulated. We must be mindful of making actors' conversations into our own tools.

Implications for organizational practice follow from taken-for-granted assumptions about the nature of workplace conversations. When participants assume that the purpose of conversation is only to create aligned under-standings, they set aside problematic moments, when underlying meanings are contested. In particular, hierarchical arrangements dominate, without thought as to how these influence the creation of meaning. For new practices to emerge, dominant discourses must be expanded to facilitate the creation of new discourses, where members are able to critique their current workplace conversations as part of creating new ones.

Notes

1 For example, one speaker speaks at a time, the number and order of speakers varies freely, turn size varies, turns are not allocated in advance but change when either the current speaker selects the next or the next speaker self-selects, turn-transition is frequent and quick, topics may change with the speaker, or the current speaker may continue, but with a change in topic.

2 *SITUATION* = setting and scene; *PARTICIPANTS* = personalities, roles, relations; *ENDS* = 'ends in view' or goals from a community standpoint, and ends as outcomes for individuals, which are not necessarily the same; *ACTS* = act sequences, or message content and form; *KEY* = tone or manner of speaking, which may be signalled verbally or non-verbally; *INSTRUMENTALITY* = channels and forms of speech; *NORMS* = of and for interaction and interpretation; *GENRE* = formally recognized characteristics (Hymes, 1974: 62).

3 For examples of different approaches for variously oriented linguistic analyses of the same event, see the description of the 'Multiple Analysis Project' in Grimshaw, 1989; Grimshaw et al., 1994).

4 Critical approaches acknowledge the slipperiness of the word *discourse*. In general, *text* refers to a linguistic artefact, *discourse* refers to actual practices of talking and writing (or discursive practice as the production, consumption and distribution of texts), and *social discourse practices* refer to constraining (taken-for-granted) institutional structures as *orders of discourse* (Fairclough, 1992, 1995) or moral obligations due to membership in particular *Discourses* (Gee, 1990), where each level of linguistic-discursive practice interdetermines the others.

5 **Flow** *Slashes* (A: I don't/know/ B: /You/ don't) indicate that the portions of utterances so encased are simultaneous. *Equal signs* (A: what I said= B: =but you didn't) mean that the next speaker starts at precisely the end of a current speaker's utterance. **Prosody** *Punctuation* denotes intonation (! is rising, ? is falling). **Pauses** The *period encased in parentheses* (.) denotes a pause of about one tenth of second. (1.3) *Numbers* indicate seconds and tenths of seconds. **Descriptions** *Double parentheses* ((very slowly)) enclose descriptions, not transcribed utterances. **Omissions** *Single parentheses* (inaud) indicate that something was heard but the transcriber is not sure what it was. See West, 1996.

3   Emotional Discourse in Organizations

Iain L. Mangham

In recent years there has been a welcome awakening of interest in the role of emotions in organizations. A number of scholars and commentators have rubbed the sleep out of their eyes and stretched a little and one or two have gone as far as pushing back the bedcovers. The general neglect of emotions by contemporary writers on behaviour in organizations seems largely due to an acceptance of the common managerial perception that 'feelings' (a term often used pejoratively) have no place in institutions that are committed to considered judgement and rational action. They get in the way and cloud the issues. They may overwhelm us if left unchecked and indulging them will probably divert us from our purposes.

A central aim of this chapter is to present a limited number of largely philosophical perspectives on emotional discourse in organizations, but a secondary and important purpose is to call into question the managerial view of rational action. I wish to suggest that practical reasoning unaccompanied by emotion is not sufficient for practical wisdom. The discerning reader will note that my thoughts on these issues are inspired by Aristotle's claim that to be a good person, one must have the right emotions. This goes well beyond holding that emotions help make a good life because of the pleasure and pain that they involve. Aristotle is very clear that having the right emotions is necessary for being a good person, for knowing what to do and how to live. My assumption – perhaps foolish – is that all of us are interested in how one should live. My belief is that managers, as heroes of our times, ought to be interested in setting an example of the good life. I recognize, however, that in suggesting a role for morality as well as emotion in organizations I am pushing my luck.

Before I go very much further with these themes I must acknowledge my sources. In what follows I have indicated in the usual manner the contributions to my argument made by a number of authors. In putting together pieces such as this, however, I find myself strongly attracted to and heavily influenced by a number of texts. Three books have been particularly important for me and inform much of what I have written: the first is *Perception, Empathy, and Judgement* (1994) by Arne Johan Vetlesen, a closely argued text which focuses on the relation between reason and emotion; the second an altogether shorter and more succinct volume, is *How Should One Live?* (1996), edited by Roger Crisp (particularly the paper by

Michael Stocker); and the third is Justin Oakley's *Morality and the Emotions* (1991), which, as the cover states, is 'a wonderfully clear and readable book'. Interested readers should repair to them forthwith for a much fuller account of many of the matters touched upon below.

To begin, I offer an example of what I take to be an emotional interchange in an anonymous organization (Mangham, 1997) and outline a number of perspectives that may be taken upon it. You are invited to adopt the role of Katz's empathizer (ugh!), someone who 'is transported, becomes full of, is pervaded by, is attuned to, abandons himself in, is caught up with, is immersed in, shares, participates in, responds to, merges with, forgets himself in, is absorbed by' the actors in this little drama from real life (Baumann, 1975: 11).

Up Yours – A Drama in Two Scenes

Scene One. An exchange between three senior managers within Johnson's. An argument is developing about who has responsibility for certain large customers. Some months ago the organization has been restructured by Harry. Part of what was then Dick's division was handed to Tom, who had recently sold his business to Johnson's

Tom: It's not true. You and your people . . .
Dick: It is and you know it . . .
Tom: You and your people are not willing to concede anything!
Dick: Come on. Come on . . . we gave on the Jenkins contract.
Tom: Jenkins? Which Jenkins contract are we talking about?
Dick: See! See! You don't even know what is going on do you. You don't know what is going on in your own business. We gave on that and on the Blunt stuff in Ireland.
Tom: We are still talking on that.
Harry: Let's stick to the issue shall we.
Dick: I am sticking to it. That's what I am saying. We are still talking . . . still arguing . . . amongst ourselves. That *is* the issue. A year ago it would have been sorted, not an issue.
Tom: There is no need to argue now. Just accept our price or pass the contract over to us.
Dick: Admit it Tom. You haven't a clue what is going on.
Harry: Let's drop this. We can sort it out later.
Dick: Not a bloody clue.
Harry: Enough. Let's move on.

Tom raises his arm behind the back of Harry, his immediate superior, and extends two fingers to Dick. Dick laughs.

Body and Soul

Reading this piece, a number of you may sympathize with Harry. You may well argue that there is a danger that 'feelings' may get out of hand and could well prejudice the outcome of the discussion. It is possible that if you think about it, you would hold that emotions are bodily feelings. It is a view of emotion that appeals to common sense. We may feel our hearts racing in circumstances such as this one and we may note the onset of irregular breathing. William James and some of his contemporaries held a similar view and argued that an emotion is the feeling of certain bodily changes, mainly of a visceral nature, which are produced by our perception of the world. If Tom perceives himself to be under attack he will experience the emotion of irritation, or mild anger in his gut or some other part of his anatomy. James was unequivocal: 'My thesis is that the bodily changes follow directly the *perception* of the exciting fact, and that our feeling of the same changes as they occur *is* the emotion' (cited in Oakley, 1991: 120).

It is also possible that someone who reflects upon Tom's growing irritation will adopt a different but related theory of emotion. You may well assert that the emotion that Tom feels arises from non-bodily feelings. Again the theory appeals to common sense. We are often unaware of any bodily disturbance and yet we clearly are *feeling* emotional. Again, should you take this option you would be in distinguished company. David Hume, arguably the most important philosopher ever to have written in English, attempted to rescue the passions from the *ad hoc* explanations of his predecessors. From the time of Plato and the Stoics, the passions had been routinely characterized as irrational, inexplicable and unnatural elements which, 'given their head, will undermine and enslave reason, the essential and defining characteristic of humans' (Hume cited in Norton, 1993: 26). *Plus ça change*. Hume assumes that they are integral to human nature and can be treated as 'simple unanalysable impressions of a non-bodily variety, or in other words, a type of psychic feeling' (cited in Oakley, 1991: 124). They are no less powerful for being produced by the mind: 'When I am angry, I am actually possessed with the passion, and in that emotion have no more reference to any other object, than when I am thirsty, or sick, or more than five foot high' (Hume cited in Baier, 1991: 63).

Of course, few proponents of affective theories of emotion would deny the important role of perceptions, thoughts, beliefs and desires as causal factors that may produce and be produced by emotion. Few would dispute that Tom's perception of Dick's behaviour is likely to influence Tom's, feelings and behaviour. But what all affective theories of emotion have in common is a denial that these causal antecedents and effects of feelings or affects are an essential part of the definition of emotion. All such theorists are as dogmatic as Hume. As the latter put it in the *Treatise*, the pleasant sensation of pride and the painful sensation of humility 'constitute their very being and essence. . . . Of this our very feeling convinces us; and beyond our feeling, 'tis in vain to reason or dispute' (cited in Baier, 1991: 55).

These theories of emotions are based on the idea that emotions are felt reactions to environmental stimuli. For those broadly of James's persuasion this means that any explanations of the genesis and pattern of emotions could be sought in physiology. Unfortunately the physiological theory of emotions appears to suffer from a serious weakness. The emotions cannot be simply various kinds of feelings or affects, because it can be shown that different emotions can have the same feelings or affects. It has been shown repeatedly that we may undergo the same kind of bodily changes in having what are clearly different emotions. Tom is as likely to find his heart racing and his breathing becoming irregular when he is frightened as when he is angry. Indeed, as it has been rather wickedly pointed out by one critic of this view, he is as likely to experience these bodily changes when he is clearly in a non-emotional state, such as hypoglycaemia or fever (Oakley, 1991).

A parallel objection confronts the view that emotions are psychic feelings. Pride may be accompanied by psychic feelings of affection and warmth, but these psychic feelings also attend emotions more commonly labelled 'benevolence' and 'gratitude'. If one emotion feels like another, different emotion, then the distinction between emotions cannot always be drawn in terms of feelings. We must conclude that, however strongly stated, Hume and numerous less distinguished others may be collectively barking up the wrong tree.

Rom Harré and Grant Gillett, recent commentators on emotion, note that in such theories the felt physiological state is diffuse and indeterminate, 'while the display of emotion is precise and sharply distinguished' (1994: 27). Put another way, we can say that it is not a necessary truth that the bodily feelings one experiences when a certain emotion is undergone are experienced only when that emotion, and not any other emotion, is undergone. Furthermore, an emotion such as pride is rarely accompanied by any sense of bodily changes. It would appear that there is no requirement that if someone is to experience a particular emotion that someone must also experience a particular set of bodily feelings. Indeed, as Budd (1995) concludes, it is not clear that there are any emotions that are such that their experience necessarily and essentially involves the experience of bodily feelings. Harré and Gillett are equally unequivocal in claiming that the old theory is 'simply wrong, wrong in the way that the phlogiston theory of combustion or creationist theories of the origin of the species are wrong' (1994: 30). For them the old theory fundamentally misconstrues the nature of emotions and their nature in human life. James Averill also is clearly in the mainstream of opinion when he concludes his exploration of the role of bodily disturbances in emotion with the statement that 'romantic references to sudden floods of feeling that go straight to the heart' should not blind us to the probability that emotions are 'as much a product of complex cognitive processes as are such other cultural products as religion, science and the like' (1982: 148).

Strategic Cognition

In any group of readers one or two are bound to be smarter than the rest, and if you are one of them you may well consider that Tom and/or Dick is/are using a display of irritation (a mild form of anger) to achieve his/their own ends. You, too, would be in distinguished company. No less a figure than

Jean-Paul Sartre can be called to your support. For him, emotion is not simply a feeling in the breast or the head: 'it is not a pure, ineffable quality like . . . the pure feeling of pain' (Sartre, 1962: 56). Like many before and since, he depicts emotion as a manner of apprehending the world. However, for him this manner is not innocent; it is the basis for a conscious strategy on the part of the feeling subject – a strategy to change situations and events. There may be a tendency to think of Tom's anger at Dick as the object of his state of being angry with him, as if to be angry is to be aware of a feeling of anger (just as to be hurt is to be aware of a feeling of pain). On the contrary, Sartre would argue, to direct anger at Dick is fundamentally a way of taking Dick as an intentional object (McCulloch, 1994). Sartre's thesis is that a subject *chooses* an emotion. So instead of suffering an emotion, Sartre argues we actively choose and adopt one as a means to alter a state of affairs in the world. We are prone to do so especially in situations of failure or embarrassment or insecurity. Thus perceiving himself to be cornered, Tom chooses irritation and aims to change the situation. Even if he fails in this, he can at least change himself. For Sartre, emotions frequently serve purposes of self-deception. Emotions, Sartre asserts, are always functional; Tom's emotion is his answer to a situation that he perceives as getting out of hand.

Sartre's representative on earth is Robert Solomon, whose early work on what he termed the passions draws heavily upon the master. He argues that emotions are judgements and 'can be rational in the same sense in which judgements can be rational.' He asserts that emotions are purposive, they serve the ends of the subject; they are rational responses to unusual situations. Strongly echoing his mentor, he goes on to argue that emotions are actions, that they are 'our projects' concerned not only with 'the way that the world is but with the way the world *ought* to be'. He believes that we are thoroughly active with respect to our emotions. Instead of having them, we make ourselves have them: 'we make ourselves angry, make ourselves depressed, make ourselves fall in love'. An emotion for Solomon is 'a judgement (or set of judgements) . . . something we do.' Echoing Aristotle, he asserts that

> I cannot be angry if I do not believe that someone has wrongly offended me. Accordingly, we might say that anger involves moral judgement . . . an appeal to moral standards and not merely personal evaluations. My anger is that set of judgements. . . . An emotion is an evaluative (or a 'normative') judgement, a judgement about my situation and about myself and/or all other people. (Solomon, 1976: 67–74).

Harré and Gillett consider that Sartre 'is too extreme' (1994: 46). However, they appear to share his cognitive approach to emotions and are heavily committed to the idea that emotion feelings and displays are functional. They also share his view that emotions are judgements and that they constitute social acts. Their particular contribution is to stress the place of display in emotion. They quote with approval Ekman and Oster (1979), who use the expression 'display rules' for the cultural conventions that determine how an emotion should be expressed. They are also keen on the work of Theodore Sarbin (1987), who argues that in performing any social act we do so within particular dramatistic conventions. In particular cultures at particular times there are certain characteristic feelings and displays that express certain judgements and perform certain social acts. Each vocabulary of feelings and displays expresses a local taxonomy and theory of emotions. Harré and Gillett assert that 'We must see emotion displays and feelings as discursive acts, based upon natural and inculcated patterns of bodily reactions but with meanings defined by their role in the discursive interactions of members of particular cultures' (1994: 52).

Something of a mouthful, but the straightforward argument is that emotions are *embodied* and conveyed in discursive acts. These acts or displays allow one to understand and appreciate the emotional attitudes that the other is projecting, and, conversely, to project one's own emotions when they become so pronounced that they need to be expressed to others in striking and unmistakably clear ways. R.S. Perinbanayagam argues that in many interactions – such as the one involving Tom, Dick and Harry – there occur moments in which quick, decisive and unambiguous assertions have to be made in 'order to protect the self, affirm a value, and/or define a situation and a relationship by [say] expressing anger'. In such circumstances one doesn't have time to think of the really smart put-down. One simply reacts in order to 'elicit the desired response from the other'. Such a frame assumes that one can know someone's purpose or intent because 'members of a society, using the word in both a broad and narrow sense, are expected to make use of a common idiom when displaying intentions' (Perinbanayagam, 1991: 34). Harré and Gillett make a similar point in a characteristically more long-winded fashion when they argue that emotions are 'situated contributions to a discourse' which depend for their effectiveness 'not only on the use of shared language but on a certain common background of knowledge and belief' (1994: 53).

In the present case such an analysis would assume that Tom could read Dick's intent. It would argue that Tom probably takes it that Dick intends to belittle him, make him look silly in front of his boss. In the circles he moves in, questioning someone's business knowledge may be the accepted idiom for such an intention. In response he will seek to convey his irritation and anger (if that is what he feels). If so, the issue for Tom is how does one 'do irritation' in this setting? As we have seen, according to Harré (1986) and those of a similar persuasion, the expression of a social act, the signalling, for example, of 'I am feeling pretty upset by your comments', is subject to local standards of correctness. In some organizations one's expression may be more forceful than here; in others less. Seeking to belittle a fellow member of the Mafia, for example, may lead to a more demonstrative display of anger than attempting something similar to a fellow member of the local co-op. The cognitive perspective on emotions holds that Tom, Dick and Harry will have developed a vocabulary of emotions appropriate to their circumstances. Such a vocabulary is not just a list, but is a system of words and expressions that indicate differences of kind and degree among the emotions.

Discursively articulated emotions such as the irritation which may be on display here are not only acts in themselves, but often they may initiate further acts in the form of verbal or physical signs. Even mild displays appear to signal that if one does not take note of this now there may be trouble ahead. As indeed there could well be in this instance.

Scene Two: Later the same meeting after a series of exchanges between the two managers

Tom: Cut it out Dick!

Dick: It's true. You know it's true. You can strut about as much as you like back at Tadcaster, but it cuts no ice anywhere else

Harry: Come on. Come on. Let's get on with it. The figures do not seem to add up to me.

Dick: Poncing about: 'look what we've done.' Climbing on the back of other people's hard work that's all you've done.

Tom: If *you're* looking for a smack *you're* going in the right direction.

Dick: Oh ho ho. Whatever next.

There is a perceptible pause in the proceedings. Harry appears preoccupied with the figures. Dick and Harry do not attempt to make eye contact with each other.

Tom: Right. Well. Let's get on with it shall we.

Here we may be in different territory. Importantly it is not Tom's subjective experience of irritation or anger that matters here. What matters is what Dick *takes* to be Tom's feelings because this is what elicits Dick's response. The signalling in the second scene appears to be more overt. So much so that it is safe to assume that there can be no question of Dick attempting to laugh Tom's comment off in the same way he laughed off his earlier gesture. Were he to do so he could well run the risk of a further escalation and perhaps even physical assault. The actors here may well have gone beyond the expression of standard emotions and may be edging towards that which Perinbanayagam (1991) terms *hyperemotion*. He argues that social actors are socialized into an understanding of the degrees of emotionality appropriate to particular situations. Emotion, in his succinct phrasing, is a semiotic achievement. Thus one could argue that Tom has moved from a display of mild irritation through to a demonstration of moderate anger and may well be heading for a bout of extreme rage. If this point is reached, events may well get 'out of control'. Being in the grip of hyperemotion suggests that an interaction is about to break down. In such circumstances there is little or no chance of an orderly pattern of exchange. Emotions may be seen as waves that may become more or less pronounced and may, on occasion, completely overwhelm the participants. Those of a cognitive persuasion hold that most exchanges do not break down because most are undertaken according to the scripts that we have mastered for their performance. Indeed, it can be held that the very existence of hyperemotions serves to emphasize that in *most* situations we have learned to submit our feelings to the control and direction of signs and rules, scripts and scenarios.

The somewhat rudimentary and very partial summary of views I have attempted here appears to confirm the value of the cognitive perspective. I can readily agree that emotions are in many cases ways of accomplishing certain 'social acts'. I can appreciate why Harré and Gillett devote a great deal of space to talk of rules and conventions before they conclude that 'emotion displays and emotion feelings have a cognitive role as bodily expressions of judgements about stimulus situations' (1994: 26). For them feelings are to be taken as emotional when and only when they are expressions of judgements. For example they argue that, when one feels or displays envy, this is an expression of the judgement that someone has something that one would like to have oneself. Extending this line, we can see that Tom's displays initially of irritation (if such it is) and then of anger (if such it is) express judgements on the moral quality of Dick's actions. Aristotle himself would recognize this kind of analysis. In his *Rhetoric* he writes, 'Anger may be defined as a desire accompanied by pain, for a conspicuous revenge for a conspicuous slight at the hands of men who have no call to slight oneself or one's friends' (Aristotle, 1984: 58). Dick's performance, if carried off successfully, may also be seen as an act of protest, ostensibly aimed at Tom but actually directed towards Harry, the person giving offence. From such a perspective an emotional feeling and its related display may indeed be understood as a discursive phenomenon, an expression of a judgement and the performance of a social act.

Stripped down to its essence, the cognitive position depicts emotional interaction as a series of more or less aware moves. Played out in slow motion, Tom reads Dick's behaviour, considers its implications for himself, constructs what he takes to be an appropriate response and presents it. Dick reads Tom's response (which is now a stimulus to him), considers its implications, constructs what he takes to be an appropriate response and presents it. And so on. The negotiation of order within this exchange takes place within local rules as to how to do irritation and anger. Stated like this, it all appears terribly cerebral. Most writers of the cognitive or discursive school, whilst not denying the role of feelings in emotions, tend to major on the cognitive aspects.

Hearts and Minds

R.S. Perinbanayagam (1991) is an exception since he reminds us that students of emotions have always been confounded by the mind–body problem. Despite the brave attempts of a number of writers, we have yet to arrive at the proper language with which to describe and explain emotionality. As can be seen from my analysis, we have a very fundamental problem. The language I have used in these analyses is a linear language of cause and effect: these physiological disturbances give rise to these cognitions, these cognitions give rise to these acts, and so on. Thus I am forced to put one before the other. Perinbanayagam, however, argues that emotions are *simultaneously* cognitive and physiological events, interpretative and felt, and that it is what he terms our entrapment in a Newtonian ontology that makes us seek to find primary or causal significance in one part or another of the pairs. He considers that emotionality and the physiology of the self are complementary phenomena. He takes issue with the argument that emotions are individual and separate, to be captured in neat categories. He goes on to assert that social acts are not calculated efforts simply based on rational and purposive considerations. In another rather nice phrase he claims that such acts are 'limned with emotion'. Indeed, he holds that 'emotions limn all social acts, both circumscribing and delineating them' (Perinbanayagam, 1991: 45).

An interesting word 'limn'. The kind of word I trust that stopped you in your tracks. The *Oxford English Dictionary* offers the following definition: 'To illuminate (letters, manuscripts, etc.) Also **2** To embellish with gold or bright colour; to depict in (gold etc.).' I like the metaphor; it offers me a way forward, but it does not take me quite as far as I want to go. Perinbanayagam appears to be saying that emotions are important because they serve to embellish and illuminate social conduct. I want to accord something more to emotion than that. First, however, I want to give priority to feelings. I want to look at the circumstance where social actors show no awareness that another person's 'weal or woe' is at stake (Blum, 1980). Then I want to pick up on his view that emotions are simultaneously cognitive and physiological, interpretative and felt.

Let me return to how you, the reader, may have responded to the scenes I presented earlier. You may have considered the emotions that they stimulated in Tom and Dick as explicable by one or other of the theories that I have put forward *or* you may have been completely puzzled by the exercise. You may not have seen that there was anything to be explained. For you the scenes had no emotional or moral import. Not only do you feel nothing about these exchanges; you cannot see why Tom or Dick should feel anything either. It could be that you were quite incapable of being transported, becoming full of, being pervaded by, being attuned to, abandoning yourself in, becoming caught up in, being immersed in, sharing, participating in, responding to, merging with, forgetting yourself in, being absorbed by the interaction that occurs between these actors. On the other and more likely hand, it could be that the reporting of the interaction is too thin to enable you to make any connections. Only fiction can approach the richness, opacity, indefiniteness and obliquity of real life (Nussbaum, 1990). For the sake of this exposition, let us assume that it is the former. Down to you rather than to me. In this respect, therefore, your perspective may be similar to Harry's. He appears to be indifferent to the emotional life of his colleagues. It could be that you and Harry have failed to develop empathy. If so, then you will be unable to appreciate that Harry's initial decision to split the business between these two managers may have been something that he

undertook without any awareness of the possible interpersonal consequences. Being an affectless person, neither you nor he is in a position to
appreciate the importance of affect to others. It could be that neither you nor
Harry has any appreciation of the hurt that may have been done to Dick. If
so, it is probable that neither of you will have any appreciation of the
consequential damage that the latter is seeking to inflict on Tom in these
scenes. I trust that you can see this line of argument leads to the conclusion
that emotions are important for making good evaluations (Crisp, 1996).

From this perspective, the exercise of judgement is made possible by our
possessing the ability to have certain emotions. If I am right about Harry, his
judgement is likely to be impaired since he appears not to have the ability to
have access to the feelings that would enable him to *apprehend* that there is
an issue between Tom and Dick and between Dick and himself. It could be,
of course, that his ability to apprehend what is going on is not entirely
absent, but is simply inhibited or suppressed. It is entirely possible that the
organization that he directs has a culture that systematically plays down the
importance of feelings, emotion and morality. This would not be unusual. It
is also possible that in becoming the managing director of the enterprise,
Harry has learned to adopt an 'objective attitude' to other human beings,
precluding, as Strawson puts it, 'the range of reactive feelings and attitudes
which belong to involvement or participation with others in inter-personal
human relationships' (1974: 78).

This is a matter of no little consequence. Strawson argues in *Freedom and
Resentment* (1994) that emotions are constitutive of human life; that having
and being the subject of feelings is central to being a person, and that having
shared feelings is central to being a member of a community. Stocker (1996)
agrees with him in his concept of 'emotional engagement'. He suggests that
we can appreciate what the term means by imagining cases where the affect
and the emotional engagement are missing. He gives as examples the
circumstance where an affectless parent and an emotionally engaged child
are playing or a friend is talking with you about amusing matters, 'but
affectlessly, not engaging emotionally with you' (1996: 69). My example is
drawn from the theatre. Consider this review by Charles Spencer of a
production of *Uncle Vanya*:

Not a tear in the house for an all-star Chekhov

It is, I suppose, absurd to judge a Chekhov production by the wetness of your
handkerchief at the end. Nevertheless, though Bill Bryden's starrily cast new
staging of *Uncle Vanya* is full of good things, I found myself with dry eyes
throughout.

   This is strange, because I've seen greatly inferior productions of the same play
which have moved me more, and Bryden is the most generous and emotionally
committed of directors. Here, though, he and his cast often seem to be observing
their characters, capturing them with sharp psychological detail but rarely
revealing that sympathy, that sudden flood of feeling, which goes straight to the

heart. I suspect Bryden's aim was to get away from the wistful melancholia which once dominated Chekhov productions.

The acting is precise, and there is a real sense of ensemble. You get a vivid impression of an ill-assorted group living in rural isolation. Resentments lurk, and at any moment you know exactly what the characters are thinking about each other. . . . What is missing is the aching sense of waste, of love unreturned and lives left to wither on the vine. As Vanya, Sir Derek Jacobi . . . expertly captures the character's self-mocking cynicism and festering indignation, but I never felt the full force of his hopeless passion for Yelena, or the unbearable sense of failure that torments him at the end. As his niece Sonya, Frances Barber . . . too fails to penetrate to the heart of the character. Her silent Munch-like screams seem artful, and in the great last speech she misses the desperation that should accompany Sonya's longing for rest in the afterlife. . . .

This is a fascinating, intelligent production, and I just wish Bryden and company had combined their almost surgical dissection of a family with a greater depth of compassion. (*Daily Telegraph*, 11 July 1996 © Telegraph Group Limited, London, 1996)

I saw this production and would agree with every word of Spencer's review. It was an intelligent, skilfully played performance expertly depicting some sharp psychological detail. The cast appeared to be markedly aware of their characters and their interactions. They failed, however, to engage each other as characters emotionally and they failed to engage the audience. In this particular circumstance, as a member of the audience I wanted engagement – emotional engagement. For me one of the most important reasons for going to the theatre is to be emotionally engaged with the characters on the stage. Here is Spencer again, this time on a performance that succeeded in engaging the audience.

Ibsen's dream team

John Gabriel Borkman was Ibsen's penultimate play, written in 1896 when he was 68. But it shows no diminution in the grim Norwegian's theatrical energy. The drama moves from naturalism to extraordinary poetic intensity, from icy hatred and resentment to a sense of transcendent reconciliation.

In this outstanding production Richard Eyre has assembled a dream cast, with the three leading roles taken by Paul Scofield, Vanessa Redgrave and Eileen Atkins, as well as a lovely supporting cameo from Michael Byrant. On opening night there were signs of nerves at first as if these marvellous actors were uneasily aware of how much was expected of them. But the production grows impressively in strength and by the end there is no doubt that you are in the presence of greatness . . .

Occasional hesitancies aside, the performances are magnificent. Eileen Atkins superbly captures Gunhild's consuming bitterness, as well as her obsessive maternal love for her son Erhart. Her snide put-downs of the sister who also wants to possess Erhart are often devastatingly funny, but it is her silent scream when she is left alone and tormented with doubt that sends shivers down the spine.

. . . Redgrave . . . is like an improvising musician, and bum notes give way to inspirational flights of astonishing spontaneity. The scene in which she accuses Borkman of killing her own capacity for love has a rawness and an aching tenderness that are almost unbearable to watch.

. . . Scofield brilliantly portrays a man who fatally sacrificed love for power. In the great last act, set in a splendidly conjured snowstorm, he recaptures his lost vision in rapt, hauntingly poetic speeches. But the most moving moment follows his death, when Gunhild and Ella finally come together and clasp hands.

It is one of those rare moments when a whole theatre seems to be holding its breath and puts the final seal on a production of remarkable strength and depth. (*Daily Telegraph*, 15 July 1996 © Telegraph Group Limited, London, 1996)

I am aware of the dangers of taking the theatre as a guide to everyday interaction; nonetheless I feel the point can be generalized. In many circumstances I want engagement with others. I take it that Tom and Dick want engagement with each other. Less certainly I take it that they want *emotional* engagement with each other. Harry and a host of management gurus may prefer alienated, machine-like interaction, but many of us may wish our important activities and relations to be infused with emotions. They are central to the nature, meaning, and value of a great deal of human life. Stocker argues that 'if we are unable to see, understand, and appreciate the emotions of others, we will be unable to see, understand, and appreciate a great deal of what their relations, activities and lives are, and are like, for them' (1996: 89).

Emotional Disclosure

Vetlesen pushes similar ideas much harder. He argues that perception is a cognitive and emotional accomplishment. He argues that emotions are active in disclosing a situation to us. His position is that emotions 'partake in the prior and constitutive accomplishment of perceiving, or recognising, or apprehending, the given situation as being such and such a kind in the first place' (1994: 206). If I understand his argument correctly (and he takes a couple of hundred densely argued pages to arrive at this conclusion), Tom does not work out at a cognitive level that he is under attack from Dick, feel disturbed and then 'do anger'. Rather his very act of perceiving is informed by anger and thus constitutes the situation in which anger appears to be the appropriate response. From this perspective emotions are ways of seeing. They are a fundamental first cut at a situation where mine or someone else's 'weal and woe' may be at stake. Emotions are crucial in making us aware of 'the peculiarly *human* reality of a specific situation' (1994: 190). Vetlesen quotes Charles Taylor's argument that feelings incorporate an 'understanding of our predicament, and of the import it bears'. Feeling a certain way, we simultaneously know something to be of a certain nature. In Taylor's words: 'We can feel entitled to say on the strength of certain feelings, or inferences from what we see through certain feelings, that we know X is right, or good, or worthy, or valuable' (Taylor, 1985: 30).

If Taylor is correct, a feeling incorporates a particular definition of our situation, and if this is so, feelings may be subjected to further definition. Such further definition enables us to consider our first, intuitive apprehension of the situation. It enables us, that is, to define it more carefully, and this further articulation may transform the feelings. On reflection, Dick may decide that the circumstance is one in which mild amusement or even studied indifference is a more appropriate response. As Stuart Hampshire (1971) has argued, emotions are not immediate data of consciousness, uncorrupted by reflection and description. The emotion is partly constituted by the act of description. This leads Hampshire (and Vetlesen who quotes him) to conclude that 'If my belief or assumption about the cause of the feeling is displaced by an argument that shows me that the belief or assumption about the cause is unfounded, my sentiment will change also' (Hampshire, 1971: 189). The important contribution here is the idea that feelings incorporate and call for definition, and then for further definition. Articulations of what we feel are never definitive, never complete. As we reflect and redefine, the feelings themselves alter simply because we are reflecting and redefining.

I need to outline one more step in Vetlesen's argument before I draw the threads of this argument together. Again following Taylor, he proposes that we do not merely define and redefine our emotions, we also evaluate them. We subject them to scrutiny to see whether or not they fit with our goals and desires. We also submit our goals and desires to scrutiny and re-evaluation. For example, were Dick so minded he could look at his anger and evaluate whether or not it was important, vital, good, bad or a matter of no consequence in his constant attempts to belittle Tom. He could also subject his goal to re-evaluation. Is it appropriate that I try to work off my anger with Harry by attacking Dick? Vetlesen asserts that this capacity for engaging in 'strong evaluation' is peculiarly human, but not all make use of this activity. Some – and managers instantly spring to mind – actively shun it. We judge or evaluate other people by their willingness to engage in such self-reflection and evaluation. A 'deep' person is one who is ready to question his or her own judgements, one who is prepared to question the worth of his or her goals and intentions and willing to change judgements, goals and intentions that do not stand up to radical self-reflection. Vetlesen takes irrationality to mean the 'unwillingness to engage in any self-evaluating process'. A rigidity or inflexibility with regard to one's own emotions, goals and intentions marks irrationality. In this domain, he concludes, rationality signifies the 'preparedness to question oneself and, significantly, to let others do so as well' (Vetlesen, 1994: 196).

Summary and Conclusion

I have attempted to show that changing notions about the nature of emotion still leave us with a difficulty. Earlier attempts at definition gave priority to the body or the soul and were found wanting. The more recent attempts at definition, whilst not denying the role of the body, tend to have stressed the cognitive and strategic aspects of the deployment of emotion in interaction. Contemporary accounts such as those provided by Michael Stocker (1996) and Arne Johan Vetlesen (1994) attempt to bring feelings and cognitions together whilst stressing the important role that emotions play in our lives.

It is difficult to summarize a piece which itself has been a summary of views. I am, however, broadly persuaded by Vetlesen's formulation. He conceives of an emotion as a feeling, 'a being moved and affected by something, a first, intuitive grasp of a situation, one awaiting further articulation' (1994: 22). The sequence is clear. We are moved by emotion, we obtain our first 'take' which is simultaneously physiological and cognitive on a situation, and we elaborate, question, modify, deepen, this 'gut' reaction by further use of our cognitive powers. In this way, Vetlesen argues, 'emotional and cognitive capacities join company and assist each other in a joint preoccupation with the situation we have tuned in to' (1994: 254). This process seems to me very similar to the process used by some actors and some directors in rehearsing a play. One can take the Bryden route and carefully examine the motivations and psychological relations of the characters, or one can take the Eyre route and simply run the piece. In effect, one invites the performers to disclose their relationships through engaging with each other. Subsequently one can look at the run and debate whether such and such an emotion appears to be appropriate. One can at the extreme – and Redgrave appears to be an example of extreme spontaneity – invite the actors to maintain this exploration even during the performances themselves.

Actors, of course, are subject to reviews. Their emotional performance is scrutinized in a way that few other performances are. The willingness of actors to respond to such reviews is, of course, variable, but the best of them in rehearsal and in performance are prepared to question who their characters are and what are their intents, and how they relate to other characters and their intents. I do not wish to labour the analogy. My point, I trust, is clear. Tom, Dick and Harry and many, many managers inhabit organizations in which emotions are considered irrational. They create and maintain settings in which displays of emotions are suppressed to the point where – at best – they constitute nothing more than weak signals. These circumstances are compounded by a system of management recruitment which selects people with little or no capacity for empathetic perception and develops its future leaders by systematically extirpating any capacity that remains. Harry is well on his way to the top.

In some circumstances displays of emotion may well be early warnings of issues that need to be tackled. Tom, Dick and Harry are involved in a battle over the structure of the organization. They may or may not be aware that the emotions they generate in this battle will impair the performance of the entire company. If Harry were capable of having an emotion it ought to disclose to him that there is an issue in need of urgent attention. Reflection on his own feelings and exploration and reflection on the feelings of Tom and Dick with them might just offer a more rewarding way forward. Practical wisdom is likely to be deeply informed by emotion.

4 Talk and Action: Conversations and Narrative in Interorganizational Collaboration

Cynthia Hardy, Thomas B. Lawrence and Nelson Phillips

Insights from postmodern work have drawn our attention to the discursive, textual and social nature of organizing. For some, 'to tell a story is to act upon the world' (Cobb, 1993: 230). But these approaches raise an important question: if our world is purely social, can we simply think up – or talk up – a new one? It would appear not: the link between talk and action is more problematic than some voluntaristic explanations of social action might suggest (see Palmer and Dunford, 1995). This chapter attempts to explore the link between talk and action by integrating discourse theory (Fairclough, 1992; Parker, 1992; Mumby, 1998) and narrative theory (Cobb, 1993) with the insights of micro-sociological approaches (Collins, 1981; Knorr-Cetina and Cicourel, 1981; Swidler, 1986), and applying them to an empirical example of collaborative talk and action. By integrating cultural and discursive approaches to organizing, we hope to explain how we move from thought to action, and to identify how to facilitate collaborative action.

A discursive approach to action is thus central to this paper. As Laclau and Mouffe (1987) argue, not everything is discursive but most of what we know is through discursive means. For example, while many of the effects of natural disasters fall clearly outside of the realm of discourse, most of us do not experience them directly, but discursively, through television or newspapers. Similarly, our experience of an organization's strategies and mandates is as much through written and oral 'stories' as by directly observing decisions and actions. At the same time, however, we do not believe that meeting and talking are the only potential effects of organization; buildings are built, products are manufactured, services are rendered beyond (and because of) all this organizational talk. Thus, discourse and talk are central to organization and organizing (Alvesson, 1994; Watson, 1995), but so is non-discursive action.

To assume that all discourse – all talk – translates into action underestimates the impact of existing practices (Fairclough, 1992): existing patterns of talk and action constitute social structures (Berger and Luck-mann, 1966) in the form of rules (Giddens, 1984) and nodal points (Laclau and Mouffe, 1987) which both enable and constrain courses of action. By defining obligatory passage points through which discourse is forced to pass (Callon and Latour, 1981), dominant groups can achieve some closure on meaning and institutionalize it in organizational practices that reduce the scope of possible action (Phillips and Hardy, 1997). At the same time, closure is never fully achieved, as rules and nodal points are always subject to resistance, contest and reinterpretation (Clegg, 1989; Laclau and Mouffe, 1987). While discourses embody power, they also embody resources on which 'social actors draw on in different ways at different times to achieve their particular purposes' (Watson, 1995: 816–17). In other words, not all talk may translate into action, but within talk lies considerable scope for action.

The context within which we consider the relationship of talk and action is that of interorganizational collaboration. These non-competitive relation-ships between organizations have been suggested as a solution to a wide range of managerial and organizational problems – from entering new markets to dealing with environmental crises. Although management aca-demics have examined interorganizational collaboration in a wide range of forms and from a variety of perspectives, its discursive aspects remain relatively unexplored. This situation is ironic considering that a central issue for many participants in collaborative initiatives is the ability of the collaboration to move from simply providing occasions for talk to generat-ing sustained collaborative action.

In the remainder of this chapter, we present our argument in three steps. We first develop a theoretical model of the relationship between discursive and non-discursive practice – between talk and action. We begin by elaborating our perspective concerning the role of conversations in generat-ing action, drawing on both micro-sociological approaches and narrative theory. We then examine in more detail how conversations discursively produce identity, skills and emotion. In the second section, we discuss a collaborative initiative that brought together government organizations, universities, community groups, employment counsellors and training organizations to address the problems of the unemployed in Canada. Here, we show how conversations around this collaboration generated action by producing skills, identity and emotion in this particular context. Finally, we draw some conclusions concerning research and practice.

From Talk to Action

Talk About Conversation

In this chapter, we draw extensively on Collins's (1981) work on conversa-tional activity, supplementing it with narrative analysis (Cobb and Rifkin, 1991) to show how, through the production of meaning, collective action is generated. Micro-sociologists such as Collins (1981; also Garfinkel, 1967; Goffman, 1967; Knorr-Cetina and Cicourel, 1981) contend that the only truly empirical grounding for social processes lies in micro-events. From this perspective, concepts such as 'culture', 'state', 'economy' or 'collaboration' are only real to the extent that they are enacted in the micro-contexts of individuals interacting. Thus the social world exists neither as an objective entity nor as a set of meanings that people carry in their heads, but in repeated actions of communicating usually around limited, routine matters in a 'few physical places and with the particular people usually encountered there' (Collins, 1981: 995).

Collins (1981) conceives of these communicating actions, or conversations, as rituals that create beliefs in common realities, or myths, which, in turn, become symbols of group solidarity (Douglas, 1973; Durkheim, 1995; Goffman, 1967). Individual chains of conversational experiences over time re-create people's cognitive beliefs about social structure and, in turn, promote collective action based on these tacit understandings and meanings. If, however, no such myth or shared meaning arises, the conversations will not be sustained and collective action will not ensue. Thus conversations generate collective action through both non-verbal modes and verbal content – through the *activity* of talking and the chain of conversations in which the individual takes part (or from which he or she is excluded) – as well as its *content*.

According to Collins, social order is inevitably physical and local. Social structure is simply 'people's repeated behaviour in particular places, using particular physical objects, and communicating by using many of the same symbolic expressions repeatedly with certain other people' (1981: 995). It is the activity of conversational interactions, which includes an irreducible physical component in the form of space, time and numbers, that shapes the micro-behaviours of individuals. Coupled with the *where* and *when* of conversations is the question of *who* is participating in the conversation. Both Collins (1981) and Westley (1990) have drawn attention to the empowering effects of not only being included in conversations, but also being able to contribute to them; both represent a source of power. Similarly, narrative theory (O'Connor, 1995) asks: who is the narrator, who is the narratee, and what are their motives? In other words, part of what we know to be social structure, or think of as 'reality', is the result of who takes part in conversations, and when and where they do so.

In Collins' model of social interaction, the importance of conversational content is largely ignored: social structure lies in 'the repeated *actions* of communicating, not in the contents of what is said; those contents are frequently ambiguous or erroneous, not always mutually understood or fully explicated' (Collins, 1981: 995). Certainly, part of what we 'know' about 'an organization' is what we experience directly in the form of interactions with particular people in particular settings. However, we also 'know' things about organizations outside our immediate physical experience. We 'know' things from the *narratives* that emerge from conversations, which tell us stories about an organization or parts of an organization that we may never directly experience; and we may hold many, different, contradictory stories in our heads (Boje, 1995), suggesting that the cognitive limits are not so great as Collins (1981) implies.

Such stories may constrain action by 'defining characters, sequencing plots, and scripting actions' (Boje, 1995: 1000). But stories can also *enable* action: as the story-teller and story listener co-construct the story, multiple, contradictory and ambiguous meanings emerge which are, according to Boje (1995), empowering in the space that they create for resistance and trans-formation. For example, Brown and Duguid (1991) provide an example of how story-telling about a broken machine enabled the individuals concerned to repair it. They constructed a coherent account of the malfunction in a long story-telling procedure which was, effectively, a diagnosis that resulted in a communal understanding of the machine: collaboration in narration provided a shared understanding of the problem that helped individuals to act. The key element in Brown and Duguid's analysis is that the production of understanding – of meaning – was achieved through a narrative process which allowed the various facts of the situation to be integrated through their verbal consideration using a primary criterion of coherence (also see Orr, 1990: 178–9). In other words, the mere activity of conversing would not have been enough to repair the machine – people might simply have stood around conversing about the fact that they did not know how to repair it. Rather, the solution – the action of repairing the machine – lay in the co-constructed content, or narrative, of the conversation.

Although Collins (1981) downplays the importance of the content of symbolic communication, his theorizing does leave a space for narrative. For example, he argues that a conversation is a ritual which invokes a common reality or myth, which may or may not be true; this is what stories and narratives do. Moreover, he argues that some conversational resources, such as individuals' reputations, *transcend* individual conversations. The only way for this to happen is when the contents of conversations (that is, stories about an individual) circulate and aggregate to create a reputation. He also talks of how these reputations change as a result of dramatic events. But many such events are not personally experienced – our knowledge of them is derived only from stories and narratives. Finally, he notes the existence of abstracted 'generalized conversational resources' concerning various solidarity groupings that exist in society, such as religious, educational and political affiliations. Understanding these groups must inevitably involve stories and narratives that describe them. So, it would appear that the content, story or narrative of a conversation is as important to the social construction of reality as are the numbers of individuals acting in relation to physical objects over time and space.

To summarize, collective action is generated by conversational activity *and* content that produce shared meaning. Some conversations, because they occur between certain people, at certain places, at certain times, mean something and lead to something. In contrast, conversations that occur between the 'wrong' people, in the 'wrong' places, at the 'wrong' time, mean 'nothing' and will lead nowhere. To start the process of understanding the link between talk and action, then, we might ask *who* is talking, *where* and *how*, and *what* they are talking about.

Generating Action

But the question remains as to exactly *how* do shared understandings, created by conversational narrative and interaction, lead to action? In this section, we examine how conversations, by discursively producing identities, skills and emotion, help to generate collective action.

Conversation creates *identities* for individuals through their physical presence or absence, through being dominant or passive in the conversation (Collins, 1981; Westley, 1990), and through the characters, myths and stories that emerge from narratives (Brown and Duguid, 1991; Dutton and Dukerich, 1991; O'Connor, 1995). Conversations also produce *skills*. They are the medium through which skills are acquired, since learning involves conversation (Weick and Westley, 1996), and they are the arenas in which particular skills are invested with (or stripped of) meaning and value. Finally, conversations also effect *emotion* (Collins, 1981; Westley, 1990), both positive and negative. It is through the interaction of identities, skills and emotions that conversations are able to generate collective action.

Identity Conversations generate identities for the people included in and excluded from them. Collins (1981: 999) emphasizes how membership ties are created through conversations every time an individual negotiates participation in a conversation. Similarly, Cobb and Rifkin (1991) show how narratives produce identities. In other words, individual identities are created as people talk particularistically about an individual, constituting her or his reputation. Thus, one acquires an identity through inclusion, by being 'on' the collaboration team; for being 'a member' of the management committee, for being 'important', perhaps by sending out the memos, for deciding where the meetings are held. Similarly, one might also acquire an identity through exclusion. Czarniawska-Joerges (1996; also Alvesson, 1994) reminds us that identity is a result of discursive processes. There is no 'true' self or even selves. Instead, 'it is useful to treat identity as a narrative, or more properly speaking, a continuous process of narration where both the narrator and audience formulate, edit, applaud and refuse various elements of the constantly-produced narrative' (Czarniawska-Joerges, 1996: 160).

Not only are individual identities created, so, too, are collective identities. Collins refers to 'generalized' membership ties – the more abstract content of the conversation:

> Some conversational topics are *generalized*: They refer to events and entities on some level of abstraction from the immediate and local situation. Talk about techniques, politics, religion, and entertainment is of this sort. The social effect, I would suggest, is to reproduce a sense of what may be called status-group

membership: common participation in a horizontally organized cultural community, which shares these outlooks and a belief in their importance. . . . Successful conversation on such topics brings about a generalized sense of common membership, although it invokes no specific or personal ties to particular organizations, authority or property. (Collins, 1981: 1000)

In other words, a generalized sense of common membership, a *collective* identity, emerges. With generalized membership ties, the identity extends beyond the individual and his or her immediate experience. Collins argues that a collective identity may be more stable than individual identity. In the former, generalized memories of the past create the perception of stability which prove resistant to specific changes to personnel and practices. Individual identities are bound up with specific ties to particular conversations – exclusion of a particular individual from a particular set of conversations may immediately and radically change his or her identity.

Identity is both constraining and enabling. Cobb and Rifkin (1991) show how, as stories are elaborated, persons are co-opted into identities they do not author and cannot transform. Often, in stories, individuals attempt to construct themselves in relation to others in a way that 'good guys' (usually self) and 'bad guys' (usually other) emerge, which affects how they behave and how others behave in response to them. So, people have identities constructed for them, and people assigned negative positions try to reposition themselves as legitimate and appropriate participants in the discourse (see Phillips and Hardy, 1997). In this way, stories are political because they establish positions from which persons must speak and from which material consequences flow (Fairclough, 1992; Parker, 1992). Identity matters not only because it affects others' valuations, but because it affects action: identity has been found to be a key factor in influencing whether issues are noticed, considered legitimate and important and, hence, acted on by different organizational members (Dutton and Ashford, 1993; Dutton and Dukerich, 1991; Dutton and Penner, 1993; also see Weick, 1995). Czarniawska-Joerges argues that the strategic employment of identity is limited by the manner in which it is co-constructed with others: 'identity must be accepted by other actors involved, both those who are operating on an established stage with a clear identity . . . and also by others who find themselves in a similar situation' (1996: 169). There is never one, single 'autobiography' but, rather, many autobiographical acts, formal, informal, that contradict, dominate, and subvert. It is in the space created by this struggle that the possibility for action and change resides.

Skills   A common view is that culture plays an important role in shaping action by providing the fundamental goals and values which individuals try to attain (see Swidler, 1986). According to micro-sociologists like Swidler (1986), however, culture does not shape action by supplying these ultimate ends or values; instead, culture provides a *tool kit* of symbols, stories, rituals and world views that people can use in varying configurations to solve different kinds of problems. Individuals act as they do because they have the tools or skills that make certain actions possible. Hence:

> A culture is not a unified system that pushes action in a consistent direction. Rather it is more like a 'tool kit' or repertoire . . . from which actors select differing pieces for constructing lines of action. Both individuals and groups know how to do different kinds of things in different circumstances. (Swidler, 1986: 277)

So, values do not determine actions; instead actions occur which capitalize on competencies and for which particular culturally shaped skills and habits (see Bourdieu, 1977, on 'habitus') are useful. Both actions and values 'are organized to take advantage of cultural competencies' (Swidler, 1986: 275).

This is a discursive view of skills. As Dougherty has pointed out, competencies 'do not exist apart from the people' who develop them, 'nor from the social processes of interpretation and construction through which people make their experiences meaningful' (1995: 115). Skills are discursively produced in conversation in a number of ways. First, conversations are the medium through which skills are acquired, since learning rests on conversations between individuals (Weick and Westley, 1996). Second, conversations are the means whereby the repository of accumulated wisdom – and particularly tacit knowledge – necessary for particular actions is disseminated (Brown and Duguid, 1991). Third, conversations are arenas in which particular skills are invested with (or stripped of) meaning. Finally, conversations do not just help individuals acquire 'technical' skills, but also provide arenas in which rhetorical and persuasive skills (Watson, 1995), which may be important in convincing other to act (Dutton and Ashford, 1993), are acquired and practised. In other words, the social production of culturally valued skills predisposes individuals to act in particular ways because they know they can.

Emotion In a field dominated by views of rationality, emotion has only recently been considered as an important organizational topic in its own right. Fineman (1996a) defines emotions as personal displays of affected, or 'moved' and 'agitated' states – such as joy, love, fear, anger, sadness, shame, embarrassment – and points out that they are socially constructed phenomena. Extending the performative aspect of this approach, Mangham (in this volume) describes emotions as semiotic achievements that are learned, constructed and improvised through performances. Such performances inevitably involve conversations. Collins (1981) has argued that engaging (or not) in conversational activity affects emotion in either a positive (energizing) or negative (de-energizing) way. Westley (1990) has taken this work a step further by emphasizing the importance of whether the individual is allowed to frame or co-frame the conversation. The positive experience of being able to contribute to the conversation generates emotional energy (Westley, 1990). Conversely, if the participant is subordinated, energy is likely to decline rapidly:

> [E]motional energies . . . can change in either direction. If one encounters a series of situations in which one is highly accepted or even dominating, or in which the emotions are very intense, one's emotional energy can build up very rapidly. . . . On the other hand, if one goes through a series of ritual rejections or subordinations, one's energies can drop fairly rapidly. (Collins, 1981: 1003)

Similarly, the conversational content also impacts upon emotion: stories shape human conduct because they embody motives, feelings, aspirations, intentions and goals (Rosaldo, 1993).

The consideration of positive emotion in the organizational context is important because it drives action. As Fineman (1994) points out, emotion is integral to the construction of social order. Individual action is based not so much on the result of rational calculation as on the emotional energies that are generated as individuals move from situation to situation. Greening strategies, for example, have been found to be linked to the emotions that managers attribute to the environment (Fineman, 1996b). Despite the importance of positive emotions, however, the study of emotion in organizations has largely focused on its negative aspects. Many writers who have addressed emotion have used a critical lens, focusing on 'emotional labour' which emphasizes the exploitation and commodification of employee emotion by management (Hochschild, 1983; Wharton, 1993). Hochschild's (1983) study of airline flight attendants, for example, focuses on the manner in which organizational systems of training and discipline work to ensure that flight attendants provide a pleasantly sexualized emotional atmosphere, regardless of how obnoxious or demanding passengers might act. Flight attendants are, then, trained not only to express the appropriate emotions, but to 'feel' them as well. Other writers have studied how negative emotions like shame, embarrassment and guilt are important to the self-regulation that allows social enterprises to function and the status quo to be maintained (Fineman, 1996a).

Although the role of positive emotions in organizations has been less closely examined, it is equally important. The connection between positive emotions and work helps to explain why people toil away, take risks, come up with new ideas, and challenge the status quo (see Mumby and Putnam, 1992, and Martin et al., 1996, on bounded emotionality). So, while it is commonplace to accept that work in aesthetic occupations, such as dancing, designing, decorating, painting and pottery, is intrinsically pleasurable (Sandelands and Buckner, 1989), it is also seems true that apparently more prosaic occupations afford considerable positive emotion too. Moreover, the influence of postmodern approaches on the study of organizations (Alvesson and Deetz, 1996; Alvesson and Willmott, 1992) suggests that we cannot dismiss such emotions as the simple product of management ploys but should give credence to individuals' exclaimed experiences.

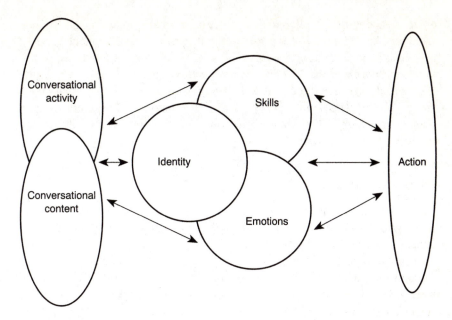

FIGURE 4.1   *The links between talk and action*

A Model of Talk and Action

We are now in a position to present a model of the links between talk and action (see Figure 4.1.). We argue that the activity and content of conversations discursively produces identities, skills and emotions which, in turn, produce action. So, for example, certain individual and collective identities react to particular information and events; frame issues in distinctive ways; and are predisposed to certain kinds of actions which reinforce identities that are experienced as positive or transform identities that are experienced as negative. Skills accord us both the right and the ability to take particular actions. Emotions generate the energy to act or not to act. These are not neatly self-contained categories. For example, identity carries with it certain emotions (Knights and Willmott, 1989); certain skills are associated with identities; skills – and the ability to act successfully – generate emotion. The interplay of these factors leads to actions and, while complex, it is possible to conceptualize the conversational foundations of action in this way. In turn, action feeds back into skills, identities and emotions which then influence the conversations which discursively produce them.

A Case Study of Talk and Action

We believe that the model of talk and action developed here has practical, as well as theoretical, significance. In this section, we describe the application of this model to a collaborative process in which one of the authors facilitated a collaboration workshop for a group of employment services agencies. Data collection for this case study included pre-workshop interviews with each of the 13 participants, extensive note-taking by a research assistant during the three and a half-day workshop, and an open-ended survey at the workshop's close.[1] This case provides an example of the manner in which talk is transformed into collaborative action through the production of identity, skills and emotion.

The Community Partners

The Community Partners[2] are a group of 13 organizations that provide employment services to the unemployed, including counselling, training and support, in a mid-sized Canadian city. The group includes publicly funded post-secondary educational institutions, private-sector organizations and not-for-profit organizations that range in size from fewer than 20 employees to over 3,000. The centrality of employment services ranges widely in these organizations: from a specific organization-wide focus (for example, private and not-for-profit counselling and training agencies) to a relatively minor part of the organizational agenda (for example, the post-secondary institutions).

The services provided by these organizations are funded by either provincial or federal governments. The Community Partners was formed when the manager of one of the primary funding agencies, referred to here as the Employment Office, called together all of the organizations with which it had contracts to provide employment services. He wanted these agencies to work together to serve his agency's clients – individuals collecting employment insurance living in a particular geographic area – more effectively. He also hoped that the group would serve as an information conduit between the Employment Office and the wider employment services community.

At the manager's request, the Community Partners met monthly for two-hour meetings for approximately 18 months prior to the collaboration workshop. At the first meeting, the manager of the Employment Office told the participants that cuts in government funding demanded the elimination of any duplication of services and other inefficiencies; there was to be no 'fighting over clients' among the employment service organizations. He also made it clear that the membership of the Community Partnership was within the purview of the Employment Office; it would include only those organizations that had long-term contracts with the Employment Office. Consequently, the membership could be expected to change over time with new players added and others being dropped. Finally, he simply told them that they 'would work together' and then left the room, leaving the Community Partners alone to work out how that would happen.

The Collaboration Workshop

The collaboration workshop was instigated at the initiative of the Employment manager and one of the partners, partly due to the lack of progress of the meetings over the previous 18-month period. It involved the Community Partners meeting for three and a half days spread over six weeks. Preparation for the workshop began with the facilitator and/or a research assistant interviewing the representatives of the participating organizations in order to identify the critical issues facing each of them. A diversity of opinions surfaced regarding the importance and potential benefits of the partnership: some participants viewed the collaboration and the workshop with scepticism, wondering what benefits could possibly justify three and a half days away from their regular organizational duties; others saw tremendous potential for the group as a social and political force; still others looked forward to forging closer personal and professional links with the other participants.

Although it is too soon to know all of the outcomes of the collaboration workshop, it is clear that the members moved much further in generating collaborative action than had previously been achieved. While the 18 months of meeting prior to the workshop were important in allowing the members to know each other better and to establish a degree of trust, its results had been limited. The focus of the partnership remained on information sharing, and the single attempt at concerted action, in the form of a joint funding proposal, had been unsuccessful. In contrast, by the end of the workshop, the group had founded a new organization, developed its mission and vision, articulated, prioritized and set dates for major goals, and assigned teams to each goal. We demonstrate below how this progress was linked to the discursive production of identity, skills and emotions.

Identity

> [Before the workshop] it was a loosely knit group of people who did not know each other very well. At the end, I think we had a stronger commitment to the group.

> For the first time with the group I felt we were trying to define who we are in a creative and visionary not a dull and bureaucratic way.

> I feel we emerged as a new group representing several bodies.

> I think previously many of us wondered about our own membership (certainly I did) in a group brought together by an outside agent. I think the significant outcome was that we were able to formulate our own reasons for existing as an independent organization.

> (Comments from post-workshop surveys)

If identity is understood as a narrative (Alvesson, 1994; Czarniawska-Joerges, 1996), then the identity of the Community Partners prior to the workshop was a simple, ineffectual story, having little impact on the behaviour of the partners. Thrown together by an external body on which they are dependent for funding, members felt less connected to each other than to the Employment Office. Two issues, in particular, exacerbated the lack of collective identity. First, the group's mandate, procedures and name were imposed on them by the Employment Office. As one of the partners recalled, '[The manager] pulled the partners together and said: "I have seen some examples of fighting for the pie, and I'm not going to tolerate it. You *will* work together. There *won't* be duplication of service. It will be based on need".' Second, the composition of the group – its membership – was also outside of the partners' control: the manager of the Employment Office decided who were Community Partners on the basis of which organizations had long-term funding contracts. This control was made explicit at the Community Partners' first meeting, when the manager announced that: 'Some of you my not be here for the next meeting. Some of you will.'

During the course of the workshop, however, the members developed a much stronger collective identity, both formally and informally. Much of the first two days of the workshop was devoted to developing a mission statement for the group. Through a series of brainstorming, prioritizing and decision-making sessions, the group worked to develop a statement that would capture their enduring reason for existence as a partnership and their collective vision of the future. Never having discussed who they were as a group or what their purpose was, other than to secure funding from the Employment Office, these discussions elicited strong arguments and serious disagreements.

An identity crisis occurred on the morning of the third day. In reviewing the mission statement, participants began to pick out elements which described the group as they wanted it to exist, but which were inconsistent with the responsibilities laid down by the Employment Office. Their new mission statement defined the group more broadly than the original mandate in terms of its geographic area, the types of unemployed persons served, and the scope of their political action. Suddenly the group was at an impasse: accepting their previous mandate meant radically changing the mission statement which they had spent two days developing; accepting the new mission statement took them well beyond their mandated responsibilities. Several participants suggested that they change the name of the group to reflect the new mission statement, effectively creating a new collaborative organization. This suggestion resulted in serious conflict over the legitimacy of such a move. A compromise was reached when the group agreed to 'try on' a new name for the remainder of the day – City Works.

The second major issue concerning the group's identity – the question of membership – proved to be even more contentious. Having identified themselves as City Works in the morning of the third day, the group decided to establish membership criteria for this 'new' partnership as opposed to the original Community Partners membership, set by the Employment Office. A variety of alternatives were suggested, ranging from restricting membership to the 12 founding organizations to accepting any organization that wished to join. Rationales for membership policy included restricting competition,

ensuring administrative efficiency, broadening political influence and increasing the operational efficiency of the region's employment services. At
the end of the day, a great deal of frustration and some anger had been
generated, but no membership policy had been agreed upon.

The final day of the workshop began again with a heated discussion of
membership. After some debate, a suggestion was made that the policy
regarding membership remain open; that any new members be ratified by a
two-thirds majority vote; and that the initial membership simply be limited
to the founding partners. It was at this point that the meaning of such a
membership policy was articulated in the discourse of the group. In calling
for a vote to ratify the new membership policy, one member suggested that:
'I guess it's a question of do we really want City Works to exist? Right now,
it's kind of pretend. A membership policy means we are real.' The vote
carried unanimously and there was considerable self-congratulations all
around. So, by the end of the workshop, a new collective identity for the
collaboration had been enacted by the participants.

Skills

> Because we came together to learn, it 'levelled the playing field'
> somewhat.
>
> The collaborative decision-making roles were particularly effective in
> maintaining the focus and clarifying issues within tight time frames.
>
> I feel [the skill development sessions] helped steer the group through
> creative thinking to useful decisions – quickly. I believe they provided the
> group with a skill that will prove useful for future meetings. I think it
> helped bring the group together and learn from each other how to
> communicate.

> (Comments from post-workshop survey)

The understanding of skills presented here focuses on their role as cultural
resources that shape behaviour and which are constituted in conversation.
Skills provide the basis for action, not simply by enabling individuals, but by
situating their abilities in a cultural context. In other words, skills represent
abilities that are culturally meaningful. The development of individual and
collective skills was an explicit part of the collaboration workshop, and was
seen by the participants as a crucial element in the process. Each of the first
three days included a one and a half- to two-hour skill development session:
Collaborative Decision-Making; Building a Strategic Mission and Vision;
and Conflict Management in Collaboration. These sessions provided participants with the opportunity to develop a collective approach to problem-
solving and strategic decision-making. The models utilized in the workshop
were intended to provide a semi-structured, non-hierarchical approach to
collaboration. The decision-making model involves the rotating assignment
of a variety of roles (chair, facilitator, task manager, time keeper, scribe)
and specific procedures (brainstorming, 'bundling' of ideas, prioritizing).
Although many different decision-making models could easily have been

substituted, the use of this approach and the reactions to it from participants highlight three issues of particular importance.

First, the process of skill development illustrates the discursive nature of their construction. Many of the participants had had significant previous training in facilitation and group decision-making, but their expertise in these areas had not been utilized in the context of this group. From the perspective we develop here, the members' knowledge of group dynamics had not been enacted as a cultural resource through conversation and, as a result, these skills had not been legitimated. Consequently, despite well-developed individual abilities prior to the workshop, the group lacked the necessary skills *until* they were collectively articulated and legitimated in the conversations that comprised the workshop.

Second, collaboration involves interorganizational relationships that are not governed by either hierarchical or market mechanisms (Lawrence et al., 1988). Consequently, control in a collaboration is achieved through social means, rather than through authority or exchange. Accordingly, collaborative decision-making must reflect the relative autonomy of those involved and extend participation to all members of the group – coercive or authoritarian decision-making undermines the collaborative initiative. Consequently, the skills developed in the workshop became an important aspect of the formation of a collective identity. Prior to the workshop, a few outspoken members had tended to dominate discussion and decision-making, while the approach taken in the workshop allowed more voices to enter into conversation and a stronger sense of collective identity to emerge.

The third critical aspect of the skill development sessions was that these skills were learned collectively rather than individually. The skill development sessions were completed in either one large group or a few small groups – never on an individual basis. They primarily revolved around group discussions and exercises that applied the principles to the issues at hand. As the participant quoted above indicated, the collective learning approach served to level the playing field, particularly in the minds of those who lacked business expertise and who had previously felt somewhat incompetent in discussions of 'visions', 'missions' and 'strategies'.

In summary, the collective development of skills ensured that these skills were legitimated through conversation and negotiation rather than by fiat. This became clear as the workshop progressed and participants' initial discomfort with the roles and procedures transformed into an open desire to protect the process when others did not fulfil their assigned roles or ignored decision-making rules. Participants' conceptualization of the decision-making skills changed from 'the facilitator's rules' to 'the way *we* operate'.

Emotions

Total frustration from a lack of understanding on behalf of many of the community partners.

Satisfaction and a sense of pride at the end that we had all had the tenacity to stick with the process and accomplished a great deal.

This was a challenging but energizing thing to do and it gave everyone a chance to relax their more reserved, professional manner and have some fun for a serious purpose.

I felt tension in the group during our initial attempts at learning a new process – that is, having a facilitator, etc. – and during the discussion on membership. In both cases, I felt we were able to take risks and the outcomes were positive.

(Comments from post-workshop survey)

The collaboration workshop was at times a highly emotional experience for the participants, illustrating both the potential positive impact of allowing participants to co-frame conversations as well as the frustrating, negative consequences of a failed conversation. Positive emotions grew out of the fact that the services provided by the partners, both individually and collectively, were targeted at unemployed persons in the local community. This 'cause' provided a moral basis for the workshop that was invoked regularly by participants to supersede the interests of the individual members, their organizations and the partnership in general. Although this occasionally prompted clashes within the group in terms of how the interests of unemployed persons might best be addressed, it generally served as a catalyst for positive emotional energy and the formation of collective identity. Strong feelings of membership are often associated with a sense of moral superiority on the part of group members (Douglas, 1973). These strong, positive emotions were often drawn upon to move the group beyond conflict around sectional interests – someone would 'remind' the group of 'why they were really there'.

Although the emotional tone of the workshop was generally positive, negative emotions also surfaced, particularly during discussions of membership. As discussed above, the issue of membership was highly contentious partly because it signalled a transition in the collective identity, from a group of agencies under an externally imposed mandate to a self-determining, collaborative organization. Before the group arrived at this point, however, there were strong disagreements about the nature of the group and why it might want to control its membership. The most heated concerned the rationale for membership: several members wanted a restrictive membership policy to protect their competitive advantage in terms of access to funding; others felt that such a policy was 'unethical' for a group that served the unemployed through political advocacy and inter-agency cooperation.

The discussion of membership occurred in two stages. During the first stage, the facilitator deliberately did not intervene when the argument became heated and, as a result, participants were left openly frustrated and angry. The second stage occurred later in the workshop when the skills and identity of the group were more solidly in place. This time, the participants invoked processual and identity discourses when the discussion heated up. Although many of the same concerns regarding competition and ethics were voiced and the conversation remained contested, the additional cultural resources – the new identity as City Works and decision-making skills – led to a far more productive resolution to the conversation.

Outcomes of the Workshop

We can conceptualize the history of the Community Partners as two sets of conversations: those that took place during the original 18-month period and those that took place during the workshop. In both cases, the activity of talking was much the same – the participants were one and the same – but the narratives changed. Specifically, the narratives that emerged during the second series of conversations helped to discursively produce identity, skills and emotion. Consequently, we believe that much of the progress made by the workshop is due to the transformation in identity (collectively from the Community Partners to City Works, and individually in terms of their commitment to the partnership); the collective learning of skills for collaborative decision-making; and the positive emotions which stemmed both from the underlying rationale for their partnership (serving the unemployed) and from the perceptions of success associated with their achievements in the workshop.

Conclusions

We have argued that the interaction of conversational content and process produces action through the generation of identity, skills and emotion. The relationship between these processes is not merely additive, where a surplus of emotion can overcome a skill deficit. Rather, the components are inextricably tied to one another: for an ability to be enacted as a culturally valuable skill, it must be consistent with the participant's identity and be motivated by appropriate emotions. This model of talk and action has significant implications for both research and practice.

Implications for Research

For researchers interested in the dynamics of organized action, and particularly collaborative action, the relationship between discursive and non-discursive practice is critical. The theoretical model and empirical case presented here demonstrate the importance of recognizing the discursive foundations of non-discursive practice. Both the model and the case highlight the discursive nature of identity, skills and emotion. The formation of a collective identity is explicitly a product of discourse. The Community Partners openly struggled with who they were and what that meant for their ability to act in particular ways. Research into collaboration cannot treat the identity of that collective initiative as external to the process, or simply as a result of the particular organizations that are represented in the collaboration – a collective identity includes not only which organizations participate, but their relationship to one another, and their relationship to other stakeholders.

Similarly, the discursive foundation of skill development in collaboration has largely been overlooked. The tendency in management research has been to treat skills as synonymous with individual intellectual or physiological abilities. This approach ignores the social context of skills: an individual's skills are social constructs, made valuable by the social context and enacted in discourse. This has implications for how we conceptualize and 'measure' organizational skills. If skills are understood to be products of a social context, they are not properties of an individual, but ongoing discursive constructions that are only evidenced in social interaction. Consequently, we might ask how skills are discursively constructed and what are its effects, rather than who has how much of what skill.

Finally, while we welcome the increased attention to the role of emotions in organizations, an overly narrow focus on the exploitative and manipulative side of emotion, ironically, leads to a similar conclusion as that of the rational view of organizations: both conclude that emotions are (or should be) the private domain of individuals and should not be considered as organizational phenomena. We believe that a more balanced view of emotions is warranted, which critically examines both the positive and negative relationships between organization and emotion. We certainly feel passionate about our own work and would like to think we can do so without necessarily feeling exploited by our universities or our disciplines. At the same time, we realize that the exploitation of emotional labour does occur. The theoretical model developed here places emotion in a context in which it can be rendered more understandable at an organizational level.

Implications for Practice

For practitioners interested in the generation of collaborative action, either as managers involved in a collaboration or as facilitators responsible for leading the process, an integration of discursive, narrative and conversational approaches also has important implications. Two points in particular are highlighted by the theory and case presented here: the role of the convenor and the relative importance of process and participants. In the case of the Community Partners, the convenor played a paradoxical role. Without the manager of the Employment Office, there would have been no partnership: he was the one who 'forced' the organizations to cooperate and provided the organizational framework in which it could happen. At the same time, however, the Community Partners needed to move beyond the convenor's mandate to pursue their own vision. In this case, the Employment Office and its mandate for the partnership provided a necessary nodal point for initial interorganizational cooperation. As with all social structures, however, it was simultaneously enabling and constraining.

The convenor is particularly important from a discursive perspective as he or she potentially has a very large impact on the group's identity. If the group is formed under the auspices of a powerful, central convenor, its identity will evolve in relation to that individual or organization, as was the case with the Community Partners. If the group wishes to engage in actions that take it beyond that relationship, tension is likely between this identity and the skills and emotions it attempts to generate. This highlights once again the interrelated nature of these three components; as practitioners work to generate collaborative action, they need to pay special attention to the discontinuities that participants experience between the identities, skills and emotions that are produced during the process.

The second issue for practitioners stems from the organizational nature of interorganizational collaboration, where participants are engaged as representatives of organizations rather than as individuals. In this situation, the generation of a collective identity must account for a potentially changing composition. Thus the basis for identity must transcend personal motivations and, particularly, personal emotions. In the collaboration workshop, there were two consistent themes running through the discourse concerning why the participants would want to stay together as a group independent of funding from the Employment Office. The first concerned their personal attachments to each other and the emotional support they received from the group – working at the intersection of government bureaucracies and unemployed persons can be very stressful since both groups make high demands while offering little in terms of resources. This theme, however, was necessarily secondary to the more abstract notion that the participants represented organizations who, together, could serve the needs of the unemployed more effectively. So, while the personal rewards from the partnership were considered important, they were left out of the formalization of the group's identity. Thus the collective identity represented the interorganizational level of cooperation more closely than the inter-personal level.

In closing, the manner in which conversations are situated within social structures and simultaneously constitute those structures is one of the foundational ideas of the so-called 'linguistic turn' in the social sciences. In this chapter, we have attempted to bridge two streams of research in this broad tradition. The first focuses on the micro-sociology of conversations (Collins, 1981; Knorr-Cetina and Cicourel, 1981; Swidler, 1986) and highlights the importance of processual aspects, such as face-to-face presence and ritual. The second stream focuses on the role of discourse and narrative (Fairclough, 1992; Mumby, forthcoming; Parker, 1992) and narrative theory (Cobb, 1993) and highlights the importance of the content of conversation – the text of the stories, myths or arguments. We believe that an understanding of collaboration as conversation requires attention to both process and content: understanding one without the other would be to hear the story without knowing the participants or the context; or to see the participants conversing without hearing what is being said.

Notes

1 All quotes used in the discussion of the case are taken from the interviews and surveys with partners.

2 All personal and organizational names have been disguised.

Part II

STORIES AND SENSE-MAKING

5 Same Old Story or Changing Stories? Folkloric, Modern and Postmodern Mutations

Yiannis Gabriel

'Once upon a time, a cat drank a bottle of green ink. At once, the cat turned green. . . .' Thus is a story announced. Thus does it command attention, no less firmly than the opening bars of a Beethoven piano sonata or the first sight of a new mountain peak. Thus does each story hold a promise, a promise which, as every story-teller knows, will be tested. An audience which has gone along with the possibility of cats turning green does not easily forgive a poor story.

'Story' shares a common etymology with 'history' – they both derive from a Greek group of words which include *histos*, meaning 'web', *histanai*, meaning 'to stand', and *eidenai* meaning 'to know well'. Story-telling is an art of weaving, of constructing, the product of intimate knowledge. It is a delicate process, a process which can easily break down, failing to live up to its promise, disintegrating into mere text. This is why good story-tellers and raconteurs have commanded power and esteem. Good stories are valuable; they can hardly be mass-produced. Teachers, orators and demagogues have long recognized their value – good stories entertain, explain, inspire, educate and convince. Bad stories do not merely disappoint; they insult the intelligence of the audience, they undermine communication and can challenge the very possibility of sensical discourse. The interest of organizational studies in stories is as belated as it is enthusiastic. Although this interest is undoubtedly connected with the more general interest in narrative processes in organizations, it cannot be reduced to that.

Organizational stories are currently studied in different ways, including as elements of organizational symbolism and culture (Allaire and Firsirotu, 1984; Hansen and Kahnweiler, 1993; Mahler, 1988; Meek, 1988), as expressions of unconscious wishes and fantasies (Bowles, 1989, 1990; Gabriel, 1991a, 1991c; Stein, 1994), as vehicles for organizational communication and learning (Barnett, 1988; Boje, 1991, 1994; Elmes and Kasouf, 1995; Martin, 1982), as expressions of political domination and opposition (Collinson, 1988, 1994; Gabriel, 1995; Martin and Powers, 1983; Meek, 1988; Rosen, 1984, 1985a, 1985b; Trice and Beyer, 1984; Wilkins, 1983), as dramatic performances (Boje, 1991; Boyce, 1995, 1996; Case, 1995; Mangham, 1986, 1995; Mangham and Overington, 1987), as occasions for emotional discharge (Downing, 1997; Fineman and Gabriel, 1996; Gabriel, 1991a, 1991b) or as narrative structures (Mahler, 1988; Martin, 1990; Martin and Meyerson,1988; Martin et al., 1983).

The mileage that as scholars on organizations we are currently getting from the concept of stories (and other currently fashionable concepts) ought to alert us to certain risks. Are we being seduced by the idea of 'stories' just as that famous sultan who found himself addicted to the yarns spun by Scheherazade? And if stories are proving such a serviceable concept, could it be that they offer a smoke-screen against awkward questions that we prefer to avoid? Postmodernism has invited us to mistrust many of the revered categories of the human sciences, including 'self', 'body', 'society', 'family', 'organization' and 'choice', revealing them to be linguistic mirages or constructs of convenience, indeed 'stories'. Is it not time that we sought to deconstruct the concept of 'story' itself?

Why is the Concept of Stories So Useful?

It is now widely agreed that stories create, sustain, fashion and test meanings in and out of organizations. They are part of a sense-making process which can be researched *in situ*, without that burdensome requirement of social science research – the need to establish the validity of claims, the facts behind allegations, the truth behind the tales. For as it has been widely argued, the truth of a story does not lie in *the facts*, but in the meaning. If people believe a story, if the story has a grip over them, whether events that it describes actually happened or not is irrelevant. It is for the pedant or the unreconstructed positivist to question poetic licence, seeking to convert story-telling into testimony.[1]

Any analysis of the concept of story must return not only to its implicit juxtaposition to fact, but, more importantly, to the current tendency of *privileging* of narrative over fact. Most conventional positivist research privileged facts over narratives, steering stories in the direction of facts, denying their standing as stories and using them as raw materials for establishing facts. By contrast, much research under postmodernism is happy to go about as though facts do not exist, or as if they do not matter, even if they do exist. What matters are narratives. Even when 'facts' do crop up in the text ('I saw him with my own eyes . . .'), they are sometimes seen as narrative constructions, amplifying or elaborating a story. Once narratives were freed from their enslavement to facts, an immense new landscape for organizational research opened – a landscape dominated by linguistic structures and tropes. What is strange is that once this freeing had taken place, a wide variety of entities which had been previously thought of as solid facts, like 'organization', 'culture', 'commodities', 'the body', meekly surrendered to being treated as texts.

This chapter is the result of a long-standing love for and fascination with stories. It is also the result of serious misgivings about the current conceptualization of stories in organizational studies, a conceptualization which at times stretches to encompass virtually everything that is not a fact, and since facts do not exist, simply everything. In particular, the following will be argued:

1   Stories are not the only things that generate and sustain meaning.
2   Not all stories generate and sustain meaning – some stories may actually undermine and destroy it.
3   Not all narratives are stories; in particular, factual or descriptive accounts of events which aspire to objectivity rather than emotional effect must not be treated as stories.
4   Stories are relatively special narrative phenomena in organizations, where discourse is dominated by other forms.
5   Stories should not be seen as automatically dissolving 'facts'. Instead, narratives and experience must be treated as having a material basis, even if this material basis is opaque or inaccessible.
6   Not all stories are good stories, nor are all individuals effective story-tellers.
7   Organizational stories rarely achieve the depth and complexity of myths and should not be treated as part of a mythology. Instead, they may be profitably treated as folkloric elements.
8   The importance, quantity, quality and character of folklore differs across organizations.

It will be noted that several of these points may be seen as matters of definition. Why should we not treat every text as a story? Why indeed not treat every object, including a gleaming motor-car, a tattoo or a building, as a story? I shall argue that by obliterating distinctions between stories and other types of texts and narratives, stories lose precisely the power which they are meant to possess, namely the power to generate and sustain meanings. They then disintegrate into chic clichés into which meaning disappears. Restricting the concept of stories to those narrative phenomena which can rightly claim to be stories is not an act of semantic policing but an attempt to preserve that which makes stories unique both as social phenomena and as instruments of social research.

It will be argued that the concept of stories has undergone a radical transformation as it moved across three discourses: folkloric, modern and postmodern. It concludes by seeking to rehabilitate certain qualities of stories from folkloric discourses (stories as entertainment) and certain qualities from modern discourses (stories as opposed to information being subject to interpretation), and fitting them within a discourse broadly commensurable with postmodernist ideas regarding stories as narratives sustaining fragile meaning structures.

Stories and Folklorism: Stories as Entertainment

Story-telling has always been an art of the people, of 'ordinary folk'. In the early nineteenth century, a folkloric revival was signalled by the publication of the Grimm brothers' stories (in 1812 and 1835), collected by the two brothers with the assiduous zeal of archaeologists. As with other archaeological finds, the admiration and interest which the stories aroused at the time coincided with their transformation into museum pieces. For all the Grimm brothers' good intentions of recording the stories intact and preserving the dialect and nuance of their delivery, their work marked an ossification of story-telling from a folk art into written texts. To be sure, this ossification did not kill the stories' symbolic resonances but it drastically altered their meanings. It also obscured what folklorists insist is the most important function of stories, namely *entertainment*, which can only be grasped when stories are experienced *in situ*, as performances (Dorson, 1969; Georges, 1969, 1980, 1981; Newall, 1980). Of course, stories have carried other functions, besides entertainment. They stimulated the imagination and offered reassurance (Bettelheim, 1976), provided moral education (MacIntyre, 1981) and justified and explained (Lévi-Strauss, 1976, 1978). But folklorists are adamant that, when seen in the practice of story-telling, stories were above all else recreational. As no less an authority than Joseph Campbell has argued:

> The folk tale, in contrast to the myth, is a form of entertainment. The story teller fails or succeeds in proportion to the amusement he affords. His motifs may be plucked from the tree of the mythological order. His productions have to be judged, at last, not as science, sociology, psychology, or metaphysics, but as art. (1975: 862)

Entertainment distinguishes stories from other narratives. In moral tales or fables, for example, the didactic function eclipses the recreational. Legends, on the other hand, are often said to have a historical grounding, though this is enhanced by supernatural accretions from myths or fairytales. Myths, for their part, carry grand sacral meanings which are alien to stories; they seek to explain, justify and console. They may exist in many variants, but they are not liable to the embellishments and elaborations which are part of the story-teller's craft. The folklorists' insistence on the entertainment value of stories accords with the story-teller's willingness to do virtually anything that will please his/her audience, unencumbered by considerations of morality, factual accuracy or even decorum. Aristotle was keenly aware that story-telling involves *poetic licence*, the sacrifice of everything for effect:

The fantastic quality is a source of pleasure, as appears from the fact that we all tend to embellish a story, in the belief that we are pleasing our listener. Homer more than anyone else has taught us how to tell lies in the right way. . . . [In stories] a likely impossibility is preferable to an unconvincing possibility. (*Poetics* 1460a)

And this relates to the second much noticed quality of folk stories, their plasticity. Vladimir Propp, the pioneering Russian folklorist known for his morphological analysis of wonder tales, has argued:

[Folk] performers do not repeat their texts word for word but introduce changes into them. Even if these changes are insignificant (but they can be very great), even if the changes that take place in folklore texts are sometimes as slow as geological processes, what is important is the fact of *changeability of folklore compared with stability of literature*. (1984: 8; original emphasis)

Folklorists have noted that the plasticity of stories is compounded by the nature of their dissemination. Unlike film or theatrical audiences, the audiences of stories are potential story-tellers or disseminators of the story. Thus do stories travel from mouth to ear and from ear to mouth, undergoing embellishments and elaborations along the way, mutating, disappearing for long periods of time and then resurfacing in new variants. Indeed the quality of the story lies in its delivery as much as in its plot. The story-teller is understood by the audience to be inventing rather than merely recounting. Mark Twain has expressed this admirably by saying that: 'If you wish to lower yourself in a person's favor, one good way is to tell his story over again, the way you heard it' (in Flesch, 1959: 124).

The fact that story-telling aims to entertain does not preclude unpleasant, sad or terrifying twists in the plot. Such twists can be quite important in establishing a happy end, following a crisis or a cathartic conclusion. They also accentuate the oppositions between good and evil, young and old, success and failure, which lie at the heart of stories.

The plots of folk tales are relatively uniform, in spite of an enormous invention in matters of detail and embellishment. They can delight by coming up with new variants on old themes, and new twists to old plots, in short, through a creative blend of the totally familiar and the totally unexpected. Their characters are also quite one-dimensional. They may go through tremendous adventures, face moments of crisis or decision and display great virtues and vices, but their behaviour is essentially non-psychological, they experience little inner conflict. They are driven by the plot, instead of driving the plot. A villain behaves in villain-like ways, just as a princess behaves in princess-like ways. Consider the following story retold by MacIntyre:

In the saga account of the battle of Clontarf in 1014, where Brian Boru defeated a Viking army, one of the norsemen, Thorstein, did not flee when the rest of his army broke and ran, but remained where he was, tying his shoestring. An Irish leader, Kerthialfad, asked him why he was not running. 'I couldn't get home tonight,' said Thorstein. 'I live in Iceland.' Because of the joke, Kerthialfad spared his life. (1981: 123)

In this story, a classic plot is presented, that of a person extricating him/herself from an awkward situation through wit. The effect is compounded by the hero's apparent absence of fear (courage) and the dry qualities attributed to Nordic people to this day. In this way, characters in stories manage to find new and strange ways of behaving true to form.

Characters of stories grow and mature, they experience powerful emotions, they learn or fail to learn from their adventures and mistakes. Yet, the changes they undergo are themselves specific to the plots and to the characters themselves (immature characters will mature, arrogant characters will be humbled, cunning characters will disentangle themselves against the odds) rather than psychological changes. One may ponder at length on the motivation of a Hamlet or a Raskolnikov, though not of an Iron Hans or a Snow White (see Benjamin, 1968: 91; Propp, 1984: 27). Unlike the heroes of novels or plays, the characters of tales do not pose many psychological puzzles. The puzzle which they pose is whether they can find unpredictable ways of behaving predictably, a puzzle which mirrors the *challenge* facing the story-teller, that of telling an old story in a novel way, so as to entertain his/her audience. The story-teller buys his/her audience's suspension of disbelief at the cost of delivering a good story. The story is a dare, which he/she must pull off. The more outrageous or unusual the beginning of the story, the greater the narrative feats that must be performed to redeem it. Failed stories may actually feed a good story, that of a pretentious person failing to deliver his promise. Alternatively, however, aborted stories and stories that are not understood also may lead to a collapse of meaning, just like a text or a joke in a foreign language which leaves us suspecting that there is meant to be meaning somewhere though the meaning eludes us.

To summarize then, within the folkloric universe (as opposed to the universe of modernism) story-telling is a process whose primary aim is to entertain audiences. This is achieved through a creative blend of the unfamiliar with the familiar, the natural and the supernatural, the reassuring oppositions between primary forces and the story-teller's performing craft. Stories travel easily, mutating along the way, resurfacing in unexpected places in unexpected shapes. Good stories represent a successfully met challenge, whereas poor stories may either be seen as personal failures on the part of the story-tellers or as instances where meaning is drained out of discourse.

Modernism and Stories: Stories as Non-Facts, Stories as Symptoms

It is hard to imagine reading the folkloric discourse without the prism of modernist discourses – even committed folklorists doubt that it is possible to capture the story-teller's craft as applied on audiences unacquainted with electric light, mass entertainment and scientific theories (see Colum, 1975). The very word 'folklore', coined by W.J. Thoms in 1846, is itself an invention of the age of reason, denoting, at least initially, the customs, superstitions and stories of the folk, a euphemism for the rural poor, the 'uncultured or backward classes in civilized nations'. Over the nineteenth century, the cultured classes of Europe appropriated elements of folklorism in their civilized discourse (as did Gustav Mahler in his song collection *Des Knaben Wunderhorn*), though folklore retained its connotation of rustic unsophistication.

Stories, as part of their folkloric discourse, were redefined by modernism, primarily through their *opposition to fact*, losing much of their connection with entertainment or communication. As such, stories and story-telling occupied a very secondary position in the modernist narrative pantheon – far inferior to scientific theories, vast novels and painstakingly detailed historical texts. In their ongoing opposition to fact, stories have remained firmly subordinate, being part of the realm of fantasy and uncontrol rather than the world of science and control. While casting occasional nostalgic glances at this realm, modernism moved forwards confidently with its large visions and projects.[2]

In this way, modernism invented what the great American folklorist Alan Dundes has called 'folklore without folk'. Folklore scholarship, for its part, has come to be characterized by progressive de-humanization, a collection, comparison and analysis of texts without regard for the fact that they were once used to entertain people or that they may have acted as media of communication in a universe without mass media. Modernist scholarship, especially as embodied in Propp's morphological studies, Lévi-Strauss's structuralism, as well as the more conventional historical and comparative approaches, is summed up by Dundes as the 'folkless study of folklore' (1980: 33).

By the 1930s it was not rare to regard story-telling as virtually moribund, folk tales themselves being a part of the folkloric past and to be studied as such. Writing an entry on folklore for the *Encyclopaedia of the Social Sciences* in 1931, cultural anthropologist Ruth Benedict wrote that 'folklore has not survived as a living trait in modern civilization' and 'thus in a strict sense folklore is a dead trait in the modern world' (1931: 288). Writing about the work of the Russian novelist Nicolai Lescov in 1936, Walter Benjamin laments the passing of the story-teller's art:

> Familiar though his name may be to us, the story-teller in his living immediacy is by no means a present force. He has already become something remote from us and something that is getting even more distant. . . . The art of story-telling is coming to an end. Less and less frequently do we encounter people with the ability to tell a tale properly. More and more often there is embarrassment all around when the wish to hear a story is expressed. It is as if something that

seemed inalienable to us, the securest among our possessions, were taken from us: the ability to exchange experiences. (1968: 83)

In Benjamin's argument two factors have conspired to bring about the demise of story-telling. The first factor, widely recognized by diverse scholars, relates to technical and social changes which have caused the audiences of story-tellers to disappear or turn elsewhere for entertainment. Thus, electricity has eliminated the long periods of winter darkness, opening up huge opportunities of mass entertainment; urban living with its cultural abundance and privatized living has marginalized story-telling; and the mass media have delivered the finishing blow. The second factor is one that Benjamin terms intriguingly the 'decline of the value of experience' in modern times. The point he makes here is not that traditional know-how and lore accumulated through experience is supplanted by scientific knowledge. Instead, he remarks that

with the [First] World War a process began to become apparent which has not halted since then. Was it not noticeable at the end of the war that men returned from the battlefield grown silent – not richer, but poorer in communicable experience? (1968: 84)

In Benjamin's imagery, the unanswerable brutality of modernity makes people silent – their experience eclipsed by information. Story-telling has been silenced by facts, hard facts in every sense. In sharp contrast to the glib expression 'stories for the trenches', Benjamin argues with some justification that the trenches spawned few stories among those who experienced them first-hand. (They did, of course, generate a new genre of poetry far removed from the heroic poetry of earlier wars.) In one way, Benjamin furthers the argument that modernity marginalizes stories as non-facts. Interestingly, however, he shifts the meaning of stories away from *narratives about characters* towards *narratives about the self*. This is why he views the travelling artisan as the story-teller *par excellence*, the person who collects stories in his/her travels, but whose travels are stories in themselves. If the folklorist views the story as the product of invention and elaboration on traditional materials, Benjamin views the story as the product of personal experience – it is this personal experience which modernity devalues, debases and ultimately obliterates.

Benjamin's argument contains in embryo the modernist treatment of stories: that stories grow out of subjective experience; that the social and technical conditions of modernity undermine the art of the story-teller; and that modernity devalues subjective experience in favour of information. (This argument is further developed by Lévi-Strauss, 1978: 6, who casts science in the crucial part of supplanting experience.) In short, modernity does away with the art and craft of story-telling just as it deskills and destroys other old crafts. This is what I shall call *narrative deskilling*. Mass entertainment is then to story-telling what mass production is to artisan craft. Narrative silence is the equivalent of the lost skills of traditional artisans.

Interpretativism

Yet, modernism spawned another discursive line on stories. This line, like Benjamin's, views them as products of experience riven by conflict, domination and resistance, control and uncontrol. Instead of lamenting the passing of stories, however, this line has seen them as marginalized but present in various nooks and crannies of modernity, from the psychoanalyst's couch to the impersonal spaces of organizations, from the private spaces of parents reading to their children at bedtime to the public areas of shopping malls. This approach is broadly interpretativist, seeking to unmask the hidden symbolism of stories, reading them as depositories of meaning and expressions of deeper psychic, interpersonal and social realities. Exponents of this approach include Geertz, Douglas and Devereux among cultural anthropologists; Dundes among folklorists; Bettelheim, Ferenczi and Freud among psychoanalysts; and Studs Terkel among urban ethnographers. This approach draws from Marxism and phenomenology, literary criticism, ethnography and psychoanalysis, but its ideological root lies undoubtedly in romanticism. It seeks to restore a kind of modern folk, a set of ways which people discover for behaving outside the large modernist structures and institutions, evading controls, laughing at the absurdities of impersonal systems and rediscovering their humanity in their ability to mould reality to their wishes and fantasies through story-telling.

In contrast to the rationalist tradition within modernism, interpretativist approaches have tended to emphasize emotion and desire as well as their repression. Freud's *The Interpretation of Dreams* stands as an almost paradigmatic work in this tradition – dreams, far from being anomalies, are seen as compromise formations resulting from conflicting mental forces, whose interpretation opens up the royal road to the unconscious. The approach pioneered by this work, which treats texts as distorted expressions of unconscious wishes and desires, has found a bewildering array of applications in neurotic symptoms, works of art and literature, slips of the tongue or the pen, political ideas, material artefacts, jokes and, of course, stories and folkloric creations. Dream interpretations come closest to interpretations of folkloric materials in respect of symbolism:

> This symbolism is not peculiar to dreams, but is characteristic of unconscious ideation, in particular among the people, and it is to be found in folklore, and in popular myths, legends, linguistic idioms, proverbial wisdom and current jokes, to a more complete extent than in dreams. (Freud, 1991: 468)

Interpretativism found an awkward place in modernism, generating much hostility, and – erroneously – often being defended by its advocates as scientific. Yet, in truth, what interpretativism achieved was to offer a model of explanation different from that of positive causality, which – at least in the human sciences – enjoyed a modicum of respectability. When applied to stories, interpretativism, unlike the rationalist tradition, did not much concern itself with their opposition to facts but rather with their attachment to meanings. Unlike rationalism, interpretativism located stories at the symbolic margin of reality, one that gives clues *about* social and psychological reality, but not a pre-eminent component of reality. If folklorists (with some notable exceptions, like Dundes) have generally shied away from interpreting the symbolism of stories, believing that interpretation usually kills a story, interpretativists have been keen to unlock the symbolic riddles of stories, seeking to uncover different meanings. In his work *The Uses of Enchantment: The Meaning and Importance of Fairy Tales*, Bruno Bettelheim (1976) argued that stories are vital in children's development. They help children make sense of a threatening and seemingly cruel reality, reassuring them, stimulating them and entertaining them. This work did to fairytales what Freud's *Interpretation* did to dreams – it opened up their symbolism, while honouring the multiple meanings that fairytales have for different audiences.[3]

Postmodernism and Stories: Sense as Stories

Interpretativism, while offering a different type of explanation from rationalism, remains firmly within the modernist tradition. It preserves distinctions between fact and story, story and other narratives, plot and embellishment, story and interpretation, strong and weak interpretations. Postmodernism has tended to blur such distinctions, along with many others. If modernism questioned the survival of stories, postmodernism sees stories everywhere.[4] Postmodernism has reinvented stories beyond the dreams of the most ardent folklorists. If narratives are favoured objects of postmodern discourses, stories are favoured among narratives. Virtually any piece of text, any sign, any object that has drawn a gaze unto itself, tells a story; indeed the failure to tell a story is a story in its own right. Advertisements, material objects (including all commodities, branded and unbranded), images of all sorts, human bodies (especially as pierced, tattooed and surgically modified), consultants' reports and performance appraisals, official documents and works of art, legal arguments and scientific 'theories', do not merely furnish the material for stories, but, in as much as they make sense, *are* stories.

Organization and management studies, no less than consumer studies, cultural studies, media and communication studies, oral history, as well as substantial segments of legal studies, accounting and studies of the professions and science, have enthusiastically adopted the idea that in creating a meaningful universe, people resort to stories. The proliferation of information in late capitalism does not lead to a 'decline of the value of experience', as Benjamin and the modernists imagined, but rather to a massive process of turning information into experience, of signifiers into signifieds, through the medium of stories. The more 'people are buried in a mind-numbing avalanche of information' (Boje and Dennehy, 1993: 155), the greater the importance of stories: 'stories make experience meaningful; stories connect us with one another; stories make the characters come alive; stories provide an opportunity for a renewed sense of organizational community' (Boje and Dennehy, 1993: 156).[5]

Stories and experience are linked in postmodern discourses like Siamese twins – not only do stories transform into experience, but experience turns into stories. 'If we listen carefully to the talk around, it is not difficult to think that story-telling goes on almost non-stop. People transform their lives and their experiences into stories with practised ease' (Mangham and Overington, 1987: 193). If organizations are, *par excellence*, jungles of information, stories come to the rescue of meaning. 'In organizations, story-telling is the preferred sense-making currency of human relationships among internal and external stakeholders', claims Boje (1991: 106) with character-istic aplomb, a point which can be found in endless variants. Stories appear to sweep all other sense-making, explanatory or indeed narrative devices aside. This is difficult to demonstrate here, though a few examples will illustrate the extent to which sense-making in different contexts has become dominated by stories:

> *Members of organizations*: Telling and listening to stories . . . is fundamental to human processes of making sense of the world. But story-telling, which might take the form in the broader management context of biographies of famous managers like Lee Iacocca, Michael Edwardes or John Harvey Jones, or be manifested in the corporate tales and legends retold by Peters and Waterman, does not just give us moral anchors and pragmatic guidelines to help us through life. The stories we engage with also provide the languages or 'discourses' which . . . influence the very way we talk about the world and hence, the way we interpret and act towards it. (Watson, 1994: 113)
>
> *Management consultants*: [Management] consultants successfully satisfy and retain their customers by telling stories. (Clark and Salaman, 1996b: 167)
>
> *Material objects*: Ours is a world in which it is our products that tell our stories for us. (Davidson, 1992: 15)
>
> *Social workers*: The theoretical vacuum existing in the 'social' professions has been largely filled by a model of explanation we term 'narrative'. (Harris and Timms, 1993: 53)

To generalize, postmodernist discourses have privileged stories and story-telling as sense-making devices; in so doing, many have lost sight of the qualities of story-telling as entertainment and challenge, and have blurred the boundaries between stories and other types of narratives, including interpretations, theories, and arguments. From a postmodern angle, this current text is itself a form of story-telling, a story about stories, at once reflexive and self-referential.

Organizational Story-Telling: Terse Narrations or Narrative Deskilling?

This story-telling perspective now permeates a large part of organizational studies, generating quite a formidable bibliography (see Boyce, 1996, who has diligently assembled five pages of references). Yet, one searches in vain for massive volumes of organizational stories to match the painstaking labours of folklorists. A few collections of organizational stories have been published, mostly for their pedagogic rather than their research value (Boje and Dennehy, 1993; Fineman and Gabriel, 1996; Sims et al., 1993). A few research texts report several stories (Kunda, 1992; Watson, 1994), many include the odd 'story' or two, though several papers explicitly devoted to organizational story-telling fail to quote a single story.

A few research pieces have studied organizational story-telling *in situ* (for example, Boyce, 1995). This is the great virtue of a justly acclaimed piece of research by David Boje, who collected or rather extricated stories from some 100 hours of taped material in an office supply firm. Boje views organizational story-telling as the 'institutional memory system of the organization' (1991: 106). It is reflexive, in the sense of continuously re-creating the past according to the present, interpretations becoming stories in their own right. It is interactive in the sense that most stories are multi-authored, with organizational members alternating in the roles of teller and listener, adding 'factual' cues or interpretative twists as a story unravels. Thus, stories hardly ever feature as integrated pieces of narrative with a full plot and a complete cast of characters; instead, they exist in a state of continuous flux, fragments, allusions, as people contribute bits, often talking together. Boje's key finding is that 'people told their stories in bits and pieces, with excessive interruptions of story parts, with people talking over each other to share story fragments, and many aborted story-telling attempts' (1991: 112–13).

Boje describes the stories he collected as 'terse' and acknowledges that in all his transcripts hardly a single story bears repetition outside its home territory as a 'good story'. He offers only one story with a plot:

> Doug [the recently appointed CEO], in almost his first meeting with the executives, uprooted a 'reserved for the CEO' (one was also reserved for each of the VPs) parking sign and threw it on the executive meeting table, demanding to know 'who put up this sign? This is not the kind of leadership I will have around here.' The offending executive, for this and other good reasons, was fired by the week's end. (1991: 119)

Boje collected this in several variants, apparently without substantive differences; in his view 'a year from now this might be tersely referred to as the parking-sign story' (1991: 119). Thus organizational stories have the tendency to shrink into coded signifiers devoid of narrative. Observers who are not familiar with such taken-for-granted information may miss the point or the catch or may not be aware that a story is actually being alluded to or performed at all. Boje asks the logical question of 'just how abbreviated can a story be and still be classified as a story?' (1991: 115) and gives the extreme answer that the mere exclamation 'You know the story!' constitutes a story. A single word may thus be seen as encompassing an entire story. One suspects that Boje is driven to this conclusion because his commitment to viewing organizations as story-telling systems does not square with the anaemic quality of the stories he collected. Yet, in taking this extreme position (and the strength of Boje's argument lies in its extremism), Boje loses the very qualities which he cherishes in stories: performativity, memorableness, ingenuity and symbolism. His terse stories amount to little more than delicate fragments of sense, communicating metonymically, as if they were product brands. Why do such stories shrivel over time? One suspects precisely that meaning drains out of them, so that the effort is hardly worth making to narrate them. Again, this is a quality shared with product brands, which, in spite of advertisers' attempts to turn them into signifiers of difference, are lost in a meaningless cacophony of freely floating signifiers (Baudrillard, 1983a, 1983b; Gabriel and Lang, 1995). Doug's parking sign heroic may end up reduced to something barely meaningful: yet another CEO pulling off another tantrum in order to appear different from his predecessor. In a similar way, many 'official' organizational stories reported by researchers may amount to little else than slogans, virtually drained of meaning and unable to generate emotion. This view would lead to the conclusion that organizational story-telling is victim of the narrative de-skilling noted by the modernists, which itself results from the increasingly fragile nature of experience when choked by information. Members of organizations, overwhelmed by data, are neither story-tellers nor story listeners, but information handlers. All that remains are relics of stories, coded left-overs from impoverished narratives, uncrafted and unappreciated. Story-telling would then be silenced (as *per* Benjamin) by the semiotic cacophony of flying signifiers (as *per* Baudrillard).

It is, however, possible to retain the concept of a story for proper narratives, with beginnings and ends, held together by action, entertaining for audiences and challenging for tellers, while acknowledging that other narrative devices are used to sustain or negotiate meaning. These include three devices noted by Czarniawska-Joerges and Joerges (1990), namely clichés, platitudes (including traditional proverbs) and labels (and Boje's terse stories can aptly be described as labels of stories rather than stories). They also included many other sense-seeking and sense-saving devices, often used in combination, though not amounting to stories – arguments and explanations, slogans and soundbites, lists (especially acronymic ones or featuring in overhead transparencies) and numbers (occasionally acting as labels, for example, the '£67 million fiasco'), logos and images, opinions and stereotypes, metaphors and metonymies (especially in the form of slogans, like 'quality', 'service', and so on), symbols and signs of all types, fragments of information, puns and *jeux de mots*, fantasies and day-dreams, displays of emotion.

However, story-telling, in the narrow sense of the telling of stories with plots and characters, involving narrative skill, entailing risk and aiming to entertain, is not dead in most organizations. Organizations do possess a living folklore, though this is not equally dense or equally vibrant in all organizations. This folklore, its vitality, breadth and character, can give us valuable insights on the nature of organizations, the power relations within them and the experiences of their members. My argument is based on a piece of fieldwork on organizational story-telling in five organizations – a hospital, a public utility, a large manufacturing company, a consumer organization and a consultancy firm. Unlike Boje, I actually elicited the stories from 126 interviewees by explaining to them the rationale for studying organizational stories: 'Stories often express organizational realities and people's feelings more accurately than responses to direct questions.' In this way, I represented an audience interested in hearing good stories. This contrasts with other researchers on stories, whose 'fly-on-the-wall' approaches undermine the story-teller's challenge and pleasure. Tape-recorded interviews lasting between 45 and 75 minutes generated 375 organizational narratives.[6]

It was clear to me that the majority of respondents quickly saw the point of the research and that they related directly to the idea of stories. A few individuals instantly responded with some story, others suggested I talked to a specific individual known for their story-telling ability, some held back answering until they had a clearer sense of what was meant by 'story', and some indicated that they knew what I meant but commented that 'Nothing interesting ever happens here' or 'People only ever talk about work in this place'. This is in itself a significant finding – respondents made sense of the category 'story' and clearly differentiated it from other types of talk. Some of them regarded their organizations as story-free spaces. Their willingness and ability to relate stories varied widely. Twenty-two failed to relate a single story, while 18 related seven or more. Some individuals were able to convert the flimsiest material into interesting narratives, whereas others seemed unable to convert into meaningful stories what seemed like rich symbolic, emotional and narrative raw material. Like Boje, I found few stories which would be highly rated by folklorists. Only 12 stories exceeded 300 words when transcribed and only 30 had more than three distinct characters or groups of characters. Yet, there were some stories which were good enough to bear repetition. Here is one as narrated by a clerk of a utility:

> There was a chap driving a lorry and he hit a cat so he got out of the lorry and saw this cat on the side of the road and thought I'd better finish it off . . . smashed it over the head, got back in and drove off. A lady or a chap phoned the police and said I've just seen a Board lorry driver get out and kill my cat. So they chased after the van and found it and asked the driver whether he had killed the cat so he said he had ran over it and couldn't leave it like that . . . it's cruel so I finished it off. So they said can we examine your van and he said yes by all means so they

examined the van and found a dead cat under the wheel arch. So it was the wrong cat [he had killed] sleeping at the side of the road. (Narrative 432)

A narrative like this meets most folkloric criteria of story-telling: it is entertaining, it is well timed, its plot is a road-story involving a central hero and other characters, its story-line contains typical elements like accident, coincidence, mistaken identity (of the cat) and misdirected motives. It certainly invites repetition and further embellishment. It does *not* invite factual verification. (Did he *really* kill the cat? Did the police record the incident? And so on.) Looking at this narrative as a myth would be wrong. A myth about the deaths of two cats does not bear comparison with the great myths of humanity; it would lead to the conclusion that organizational mythology is trite. Looking at it as folklore, on the other hand, highlights its vitality and invention. Slang, jokes and idiosyncrasies, which are so alien to myth, all lie at the very heart of folklore (Dundes 1965, 1980). It is perfectly possible and meaningful to talk of Xerox or Internet lore or the folklore of computers or, indeed, the folklore of lorry-drivers and network-surfers without debasing the concept of folklore. The story of the driver who killed two cats is a fine example of lorry-driver folklore, capable of yielding telling and fruitful interpretations. It illustrates that, contrary to modernist ideas, story-telling is still alive and story-tellers can be found in organizations. It also illustrates that, contrary to postmodernist tendencies, some organizational narratives *are* proper stories.

Here is a piece of car-park folklore, resulting from the visit of one of the company's own engineers to fix a problem at regional headquarters. It is a 'proper' story and is reported exactly as told by a senior clerk:

Lakeside is [our regional] head office; our engineer went out there, he thought it was an emergency call. The area is murder to park, he couldn't park anywhere and as far as he knew it's an emergency job he's got to get there; he goes round the back of the building and there is the company's own car park, so he sees a vacant place and puts his van there. Goes into the main building, it wasn't an emergency job, just that they wanted priority treatment if you like, run of the mill job, he comes back out again and one of the senior managers had blocked him in with his car. And he wouldn't let him out . . . and that was one of the top cats in personnel department and he said to the car park attendant and he told him his name and he virtually refused to come down and shift his car. That's senior management and he just lost his rag because it is costing him money . . . and he threatened to smash his car with a hammer or get the police to tow it away for causing an obstruction, the engineer this was, he was raving and that's what they think of senior management. But by the same token that's what they think of them. . . . You, you peasant you dare park there and blocks him in. There was a lot of sympathy for him here. (Narrative 674)

This story, like the previous one, can rightly be seen as a piece of workplace folklore, whose analysis can yield substantial insights on the nature of the organization, its power relations and its culture. Like the previous story, it describes events second-hand, the narrator being neither a character in the story, nor a direct eye-witness. His narration is replete with passionate commitment, anger interfering with the narrative's grammar, yet amplifying its poetic effect. Most of the good stories I collected refer to events in which the teller is the central hero or which were witnessed first-hand. The following one, told by a computer analyst, combines a self-deprecatory sense of humour with a sense of sexual dare:

> I had an office next to the girls in the legal department, and they were talking about the sexiest man in the building and came up with all these men I'd never heard of before, so I said, 'Sorry about this ladies, I thought that I was the real myo-star, the hulk' and they cracked up laughing and said, 'We had a vote and you were voted the most boring old fart in here.' (Narrative 132)

Narratives of this quality were not common among the 375 collected. As a typical listener, I rated the quality of each story on a scale of 1 to 10, a highly subjective measure of how interesting, memorable, repeatable, mean-ingful and telling each story seemed to me. Only 11 stories, including the three above, got the top rating. It was also the case that most of the good stories were told by a few individuals, with five individuals accounting for half of the 30 stories rated 9 or 10.

Opinions, Descriptions and Proto-stories

I have described elsewhere different ways of classifying, interpreting and analysing stories (Gabriel 1991a, 1991b, 1992, 1995, 1997b). What I wish to do here is to introduce three particular types of narratives which I encoun-tered which should be distinguished from proper stories, even if they are not unrelated to them. The first are *opinions*, often strongly held, often contain-ing some factual or symbolic material, but lacking plot, characters and action. In the following example the opinion expressed by a clerk is that repetitive work causes mistakes:

> Certain tasks are repetitive and tedious, we've got a particular task on the computer screen, it is called work reading. . . . It is very repetitive, the screen is not pleasant to look at . . . it is not an easy thing to do and you need a lot of knowledge to do that . . . some people do it for 8 hours a day and that is a boring job, being stuck in front of the computer for that time. Mistakes happen not because they don't know what they are doing but because of the tedium of it. (Narrative/Opinion 262)

Opinions, like this, seem to announce a story, which never materializes. They receive support from generalized assertions, without singling out a particular incident around which to construct a story. The listener may then encourage a story by prompting 'Can you think of any such cases?' though, in my experience, such prompting rarely generated high-quality stories. Opinions may not be stories (and were not included in my database of 375 stories), though they are part of an organization's sense-making apparatus.

Unlike opinions, the second type of narrative I wish to distinguish from stories does have a plot and characters. Yet, its attitude towards them is stubbornly 'factual', refusing to read any meaning in the events described. A fire, a sacking, an accident, are described just as facts devoid of symbolism or emotion. I have compared elsewhere three embellished accounts of a fire at a research and publishing organization (Gabriel, 1995) and contrasted them with the following purely descriptive account offered by a manager:

> The most memorable thing I can think of was when the emergency fire control system in the computer room blew up. The pressurized system blew a cap off and punched a hole through the glass separating the computer room and went through just over our head; it nearly took our head off. A couple of months ago. (How much damage did it cause?) It looked worse than it was; but it was pretty spectacular. The safety officer had just moved the compressed whatever it was, so the cap on the compressed system was facing across rather than up and when it blew off, a fairly substantial piece of brass came off like a bullet and went through the glass, so there was glass everywhere. Of course, the computer went down, the place was then flooded. It was out of operation for a couple of days. It didn't affect the working of my department very much other than the e-mail going down. (Narrative 46)

Such factual accounts were common in the research organization where members prized the factual accuracy of their work and appeared generally reluctant to deviate from 'facts'. I decided therefore to classify such narratives as *descriptions*, presenting facts-as-information rather than facts-as-experience. Alternatively, they can be seen as historical accounts in which accuracy is valued above effect, maintaining the Aristotelian distinction between history as analytico-descriptive and of poetry as emotional-symbolic.[7] Descriptions may lack the compelling narrative power of stories but are not outside the sense-making apparatus of organizations. In fact, I suspect that in most organizations they are more prevalent than stories. A narrator like the one above acts as a historian or a forensic scientist, inviting a causative rather than a symbolic explanation of the event, concerned about damage and cost limitations and preventative measures rather than about keeping his/her listener entertained.

The third type of narrative I wish to distinguish from stories are *proto-stories*. These are fragments of stories, similar to Boje's terse stories, sometimes highly charged emotionally and symbolically. Yet, their plot is very rudimentary. Under certain conditions of repetition, embellishment and cross-fertilization, such narratives may yield fully fledged stories. Here are two examples, the former from a chemical company, the latter from a hospital:

> There is the gentleman across the corridor; I notice him because he's always working, he's such a nice gentleman, such a nice character, and I always say, 'I just met him on the first floor, I think he's madly in love with me,' silly things like that. We just laugh about them. (Narrative 92)

We have got a chap that lives on the streets, it is quite sad, he was a prisoner of war and he hates to be confined, and he comes in lots, he sort of lives in the centre. Occasionally he suffers from hypothermia and someone will call an ambulance and he will come in; he is quite a character and can be quite aggressive sometimes. (Narrative 857)

Both of these narratives focus on a potentially interesting character who acts as a spur for fantasy, but their plot is rudimentary; they have a beginning, but, unlike true stories, they lack a proper end. A total of 119 of the 375 narratives in the database were classed as proto-stories. Clearly distinctions between stories and descriptions or proto-stories are not as clear-cut as those between opinions and stories. A narrative may have different symbolic resonances with different listeners: one listener may hear a story where another hears merely a proto-story, just as one listener may hear a weak story where another hears a strong one.

Facts and Stories

The distinction between description and story seems especially problematic. Many would deny that it is possible to give purely factual accounts of any event. The choice of facts to report, the choice of words used, the omissions made, the framing of the narrative suggest that all narratives involve the narrator's active engagement with his/her subject. Yet, I believe that it is vital to distinguish between description which deals with facts-as-information and stories which represent facts-as-experience for both tellers and listeners. The former is the craft of the journalist, the recorder, the chronicler; the latter is the task of the raconteur, the entertainer, the yarn-spinner. Now, as Habermas, following Danto, has argued, the chronicler who simply describes events is an ideal fiction:

> Completely to describe an event is to locate it in all the right stories, and this we cannot do. We cannot because we are temporarily provincial with regard to the future. . . . The imposition of a narrative involves us with an inexpungeable subjective factor. (1977: 349)

Yet, this ideal fiction is indispensable in distinguishing between two types of discourses, one whose loyalty ultimately rests with the facts and another whose loyalty rests with the story. The chronicler is committed to accuracy, the story-teller is committed to effect.[8] The former treats his/her material with the respect of an archaeologist, wishing to discover, preserve and display valuable objects, his/her own pride lying in his/her claim not to have tampered with the material. The latter treats his/her material in a far more cavalier manner; his/her skill lies precisely in turning plain material into something valuable and meaningful. Of course, many archaeologists end up framing their findings, they (including celebrities like Schliemann and Evans) tamper with their findings for effect, they manage their discoveries as shows in front of television cameras. They, like many chroniclers and their contemporary counterparts, journalists, can end up as story-tellers. In a similar way, experimental scientists may falsify the results of their experiment in order to use them in support of a theory. Such distortions differ fundamentally from the story-teller's distortions. No-one would accuse a story-teller of distortion, although a story-teller may be accused of spoiling a good story. In fact, the narrative test for a story is relatively straightforward: would a listener respond by challenging the factual accuracy of the text? By contrast, journalistic, experimental and archaeological practices are factually challengeable and distortions constitute serious offences. It is essential, therefore, to preserve the distinction between narratives which purport to represent facts (even if they fail to do so) and narratives which make no secret of their purpose to use facts as poetic material, moulding them, twisting them and embellishing them for effect.[9]

Only by treating stories as distinctive types of narrative, claiming special privileges and subject to special constraints, can we use them as windows into organizational life. Only then can we study the challenge that they represent for teller and listener alike, the meanings they carry or fail to carry, the pleasure or pain they afford, and the power they accord or deny. If we insist on treating every consultant's report, every cliché, every overhead transparency and every statistical table as 'telling a story', we inevitably assist in making story-telling, as a meaning-bestowing activity, in its very ubiquity, moribund. Even worse, we allow our fascination with discourse and narrative to act as a smoke-screen obscuring the political, psychological and social issues in organizations.

Notes

I would like to acknowledge the contribution of several individuals who supplied narrative material used in this paper. Several colleagues, including Steve Fineman, Annie Pye, Judi Marshall and Ian Colville, have given me valuable suggestions. David Sims and Andrew Sturdy have given me very extensive and valuable feedback on the original draft. Thanks to all of them.

1 The clear antecedent of this idea lies in Durkheim's approach to the study of religion as a 'social fact' irrespective of the validity of its claims.

2 Myths were more amenable to modernism than stories, whether as supports of massive projects of social transformation or as buffers against older pre-modernist myths.

3 In a similar way, Robert Bly's *Iron John* unlocks the multiplicity of meanings present in the Grimm story 'Iron Hans'.

4 I shall not enter the debate on defining postmodernism in its relation to modernism. I accept that many features of postmodernism are rooted in modernism. One obvious instance of this is the equation of story and interpretation, whose origin is to be found clearly in Lévi-Strauss's discussion of myth. According to Lévi-Strauss (1976) a myth consists of all versions *and all interpretations*; no single version is privileged as the right one.

5 Giddens has argued that the very idea of personal identity

is not to be found in behaviour, nor – important though it is – in the reactions of others, but in the capacity *to keep a particular narrative going.* The individual's biography, if she is to maintain regular interaction with others in the day-to-day world, cannot be wholly fictive. It must continually integrate events which occur in the external world, and sort them into the ongoing 'story' about the self. (1991: 54)

6 Details of the methodology and findings of this project, which was undertaken with the help of ESRC research grant No. R000232627, have been published elsewhere and specific stories have been discussed at length in different contexts (see Gabriel 1992, 1995, 1997a, 1997b)

7 Aristotle must be credited with the first clear statement of the difference between stories and other narratives. He viewed stories as emotional-symbolic texts and used the term 'poetics' to describe the type of work that is involved in transforming facts into stories. By contrast, he viewed history as analytico-descriptive. While poetry is a discourse of meanings, history is a discourse of facts, causes and effects. He is also credited with the first convincing statement of the distinction between comedy and tragedy, in terms of the emotions they generate. Both comedy and tragedy are poetic forms. (See Aristotle, *Poetics.*)

8 For a view of the chronicler similar to the one presented here, see Frye (1990); for a different view of the chronicler as story-teller, see Benjamin (1968).

9 A limiting case here is that of the memory recovery syndrome, where what a patient presents as factual discourse is interpreted by a therapist as a story–discourse.

6   As God Created the Earth . . . A Saga that Makes Sense?

Miriam Salzer-Mörling

– You know how it all began, don't you?
  I made an evasive gesture. I wanted to hear it again.
  – Well, in the beginning there was nothing, just stony land and poor soil.
  They showed me pictures of a barren landscape and continued the story.
  – But, there was this young boy, you know, who was thrifty and ambitious by nature. No challenges were too big to him, no problems were unsolvable. He dared to tread new ground. With small means he created remarkable results. Stones were piled upon stones. And that's the spirit that still reigns among us. That nothing is impossible.

As a newcomer in the community, I got to hear the story a number of times. The words vary, but the plot is the same. It is a story about a creation. It is a story that promises that nothing is impossible – that there is a future filled with opportunities.

I kind of like the story. It is an appealing legend, where there are good characters and evil ones. And we know that the 'good side' will win, finding its way across the world, attracting new followers all the time. It is a fascinating narrative about the young man who created a world of his own; a man who dared to question the conventional and to find new solutions to old problems.

It is also a story that confers meaning on the past and supplies direction for the future. There is a logic which explains how it all came into being and how it all evolved quite naturally over time. Events are linked to events, and a sense of meaning and purpose is given to an otherwise incomprehensible world.

The story gives you a feeling of how it all hangs together. That's nice. I mean, it's rather relieving to see that things are not just chaotic or devoid of meaning; that pieces can be put together into a coherent world where everything can be explained and understood. The telling of the saga is a never-ending story about accomplishments and achievements. 'It explains why certain things are done here – it gives you a basic understanding', a leader tells me.

What kind of story is this then? Is it a fairytale or a mythical fable? It is in fact a saga from our own time, a modern corporate saga filled with myths, heroes and glorious achievements. It is the saga of Ikea. How, then, do such sagas shape and form organizational life?

The Ikea Story

Far down in the south of Sweden, in the midst of an enchanted forest, there is a small village called Älmhult. Arriving by train at the village's small yellow station house, you will have travelled through a landscape of green fields with winding stone fences and thick forests where the sun does its best to grope its way through the dense foliage.

It is down here, in Älmhult, that the often told saga of Ikea begins. Let me retell you the story as I learned it during my stay within the 'Ikea World', while carrying out an ethnographic study of organizational identity. I got to know the saga both from members of the company and from various articles and booklets in which the saga has been documented. I would like to tell it to you as follows.

From Fish to Furniture

Once upon a time, as all sagas begin, there was a young boy growing up on a farm outside Älmhult, on the typically poor land of the county of Småland. From an early age this boy, named Ingvar Kamprad, was looking out for opportunities. When other young boys were reading Donald Duck, little Ingvar pored over mail-order catalogues, looking out for things to buy and sell. Soon, Ingvar was seen cycling around the county selling matches, pencils, ball-points and even fish.

The business went well and in 1943, at the age of 17, Ingvar registered his little venture as a commercial company. The name he gave to the company was Ikea, an acronym of his initials and the farm (Elmtaryd) and parish (Aggunaryd) where he grew up.

Within a few years Ingvar had abandoned his bicycle and expanded the company into a mail-order firm. He started to buy furniture from the local furniture-makers, and soon began sending out catalogues offering low-priced furniture. However, the big revolution was yet to come. . . . Furniture was bulky and expensive to package. Ingvar soon realized that if the customers were able and willing to assemble the furniture themselves, packaging and transport costs could be reduced and prices lowered. 'You do half of it, and we do half of it – together we'll save money!'

In the 1950s, Ingvar's company started to launch quick-assembly furniture in compact packaging and shortly afterwards the first Ikea furniture store was opened in Älmhult. The store became a new outing for people from all over Sweden coming to Älmhult to see and touch the furniture shown in the catalogue.

Fighting the Enemy

However, the road to success was not without bumps. There were threatening dark clouds in the sky. Evil enemies were lurking around. The little new company had to fight its Goliath. The traditional furniture dealers regarded the up-and-coming intruder on the furniture market with scepticism and hostility. Feeling threatened by Ikea's low prices, they urged their suppliers not to deliver to the company. Ikea was boycotted. The situation was delicate, but Kamprad was soon to find a new unconventional solution.

Since the company was boycotted by the Swedish furniture-makers, Ingvar started to develop his own in-house design department. The search for new manufacturers led Kamprad to Eastern Europe. Still today, a great deal of Ikea's products are manufactured in the former Eastern European countries.

The boycott of Ikea even resulted in Ingvar Kamprad himself not being allowed entry into the various furniture fairs held in Sweden. On one occasion, he smuggled himself into the fair by hiding in a rolled carpet in a van! It was in ways like this that Ikea found its own way – the Ikea Way – of dealing with problems.

Low prices together with unconventional business practices led to a questioning of Ikea's quality. Could low prices really be combined with high quality? The market was dubious. But in the mid-1960s Ikea had a breakthrough. In a big article in one of Sweden's most influential home decorating magazines, Ikea's low-priced furniture was favourably compared with other more expensive products. Gradually, the outsider was becoming accepted.

A Growing Family

The small Älmhult company grew. More and more people were gathered around Ingvar Kamprad. They worked closely together, always ready to pitch in wherever and whenever needed. These early members of the Ikea family were the ones who, following in Ingvar's footsteps, created the 'jeans-rolled-up-sleeves-snuff-look' as the relaxed 'uniform' for the unconventional company.

In time the question was raised: Could Ikea succeed outside Scandinavia? Could the novel Ikea concept appeal to home-makers in foreign markets? Once again Ikea took the unconventional route. Which market would be the most difficult and most conservative one in Europe? Switzerland, they agreed. So Kamprad and a co-worker went down to Switzerland with a fat wallet, bought some land, and opened the first Ikea store outside Scandinavia in 1973. This was just the first step in Ikea's successful conquest of the world. The following years saw rapid expansion, with new Ikea stores opening every other day.

The Ikea family grew larger and larger. Kamprad wanted his lifework to maintain what he called the 'Ikea-spirit'. Thus, the man who once started selling matches in the dark forests in Småland wrote his 'will' in 1976: 'The

Testament of a Furniture Dealer' with nine moral guidelines for all the family members.

'The Future is Filled with Opportunities'

Over the years Ikea has grown into an international home-furnishing group with more than 100 stores in some 20 countries. And some 20,000 co-workers have joined the family. Little by little, the Ikea concept has been developed: flat packages, large volumes, self-service, mechanical selling and gigantic furniture stores.

In homes all over the world you can find Ikea's bookcases, kitchens, beds, and so on. The Ikea catalogue is said to be the most widely circulated publication in the world, with some 70 million copies distributed annually. But the saga doesn't end here. Ikea will continue to grow and attract new followers. New problems will lead to new solutions. The future is filled with opportunities . . .

A Saga that Makes Sense?

Fascinating, isn't it? The saga is the classical 'from-rags-to-riches' story. There is the promising beginning with 'a man with two empty hands', who challenges the establishment. Then, there is the dramatic climax, where a hostile enemy has to be fought. But against all odds, the small outsider turns out to be the winner. The stiff old guard is outflanked by Ikea's unconventional 'common sense'. A romantic happy ending, where the challenger triumphs, the community rejoices, and so they lived happily ever after . . .

The Ikea story is a saga about how the company started and evolved over the years. It is a vivid and heroic story of the young man who created the 'Ikea World'. I personally find an association with a kind of 'genesis'. A story of the creation. As God created the Earth, Kamprad created the Ikea World . . .

The genesis explains how it all came into being. It creates a sense of meaning and purpose. It seems as if all events can be explained or understood in the light of this saga. The saga makes sense of the past and depicts a glorious future. The creator has even provided his community with moral guidelines – the nine theses that formed his 'testament'.

A Verbal Symbol

If we turn to the literature on organizational stories, the Ikea story could be described as a corporate saga. A corporate saga is often defined as an organization's epic or a vivid description of the 'living' and achievements of the organization (Alvesson and Berg, 1988; Bormann, 1983; Clark, 1972; Wilkins, 1983). As such, it consists of myths, heroes and legends in the organization's history, and expresses the view the organization has of itself and its world.

As a verbal symbol, the saga constitutes a dramatized history that expresses and legitimizes the company's philosophy and management. Bormann (1983) talks about corporate sagas as a shared fantasy that answers questions such as: What kind of organization are we and what kind of people are members in our organization? Sagas define who we are. Or perhaps sagas define what the management wishes us to be.

The saga makes sense. It puts pieces together. It is as much a myth of sacred qualities as it is a modern narrative of linear and unitary progress (Hassard, 1993). In an air of modern enlightenment, the saga tells us about the wonders of progress and achievements.

Writing the Autobiography

The Ikea story is often told, more or less as I have retold it here, at internal training seminars in the company, and it is also sometimes referred to in the ordinary working day. It is a story that is spread and maintained as a living oral tradition.

The saga has also been written down and spread in the form of a booklet. On one of my first days in the Ikea World I received a small booklet: *The Future is Filled with Opportunities* (Ikea, 1984). This is Ikea's 'autobiography', a book that is handed out to all co-workers in the Ikea World.

The book is easy to read. It embraces some 80 pages with a lot of illustrations. Here you find the glorious story told vividly and illustrated with authentic pictures from Ikea's past. There are pictures of one of the first Ikea catalogues, the old barn where the company's operations started, the inauguration of the Stockholm store, and so on – snapshots from the Ikea 'family album'.

The text is a chronological narrative of the company's evolution. Major events in Ikea's development are described in a light-hearted tone in short sentences and short paragraphs, as in this extract from the book where the opening of the Stockholm store is described:

> But on opening day new problems arose.
>   The prices were low. People bought. And the lines to the cashiers got longer and longer. The employees who were hired to fetch the goods from the warehouse simply couldn't cope. Irritation grew.
>   What to do?
>   Employ more people in the warehouse?
>   That would have been the conventional answer to the problem and therefore not the solution that Ikea chose.
>   Instead, Ikea took away all the people who fetched the goods for the customers and let the customers fetch their goods themselves. They moved the warehouse people to the cash registers and opened more lines so that customers could get through faster.
>   Once again Ikea met a problem. Ikea made friends with the problem and Ikea changed a bit. (Ikea, 1984: 54–5)

The language in the book is special. In many aspects it is similar to the language used in Ingvar Kamprad's testament, one of the first official written documents from Ikea. In the testament the language is very simple and rather abrupt. It is close to spoken language. The sentences are short, affirmative and not always complete. In the book on the corporate saga, the same writing style is exposed, giving the impression that it is 'his master's voice' that lies behind the text.

However, the author is not present in the booklet; the narrator of the glorious story remains unknown. Only the postscript is signed, written by Kamprad himself. This aroused my curiosity. Who had written the book? Who gave the saga its characteristic voice? I made some enquiries, but soon I understood that the authorship of the book is not a part of the official story-line. After a while I found out that the author was a copywriter, who wrote down the glamorous story on behalf of Ikea. The same copywriter also lies behind much of the copy in ads and brochures. In an anonymous way he has given the company its voice and special language – a hidden spokesman for the corporate 'self'.

Producing the Myth of the Self?

Glorified corporate sagas are a part of the discourse in organizations. Corporate sagas can be understood as a part of the company's official rhetoric – stories that are crafted and distributed for public consumption.

Perhaps the purpose of spreading and writing down the corporate saga is that of producing a 'corporate self'. The autobiography, as a sort of 'auto-communication' (Broms and Gahmberg, 1983), is a text written by and for the organization itself. It creates and then confirms corporate ideals, promoting the sacred qualities of the organization.

A *Corporate Ego*

The saga enhances and contributes to the corporate ego. As Ramanantsoa and Battaglia point out, the autobiography of the firm produces the myth of the self, where 'the ultimate effect is to broadcast an image of the company as autonomous, a central and ideal actor, all at once fully free and ever strategically alert by virtue of a strong and original personality' (1991: 8).

Ikea's saga depicts a company that is different. It is a company that has challenged the 'normal' and 'traditional' in the furniture business. The saga emphasizes that Ikea is not like the others. The 'self' is distinguished from the 'others'. Ikea's path from Älmhult to a successful conquest of the world is dressed in the expressive language of an organization which has had to fight the outside world all along the way.

The saga promotes the image of the company as a rebellious outsider that becomes a threat for the establishment. Borders are staged between 'us' and 'them', the 'Ikea World' and 'the others'. As a rather egocentric company, the 'self' is sustained against the outside world (Morgan, 1986). It produces a feeling of being unique, of sharing a distinguishing identity.

'That's What Makes Us Unique!'

The myth of the self seems to involve a notion of being unique. Ikea's saga gives the impression of a company with a unique self, characterized by, among other things, a special 'just-do-it' mentality, a certain 'family-spirit', 'unconventional solutions', and a 'special dress code'. 'That's what makes us unique!', Ikeans kept telling me. ('Ikeans' is what they sometimes call themselves, leading to associations of some kind of creatures from outer space. Martians . . . Ikeans . . .)

But the Ikea saga is probably not unique, neither in content nor in form. Iacocca's Chrysler story and Roddick's tale about Body Shop pop into my mind. The myths, legends and metaphors reappear. It is what Martin et al. (1983) refer to as the 'uniqueness paradox'. What is supposed to make the organization unique is thus far from unique.

The search for uniqueness in sagas and stories can be seen as a deliberate effort to create the illusion of the company as a distinct personality. Even though organizations probably are best understood as a number of individuals, the saga, and other such stories, makes us think about the organization as a thinking and acting persona – a supra-individual entity that incorporates all individual actions, desires, and thoughts into a single corporate 'self'.

A Managerial Monologue

Ikea's corporate saga promotes a coherent, unified, distinguished self. The managerial voice narrating the saga gives voice only to the corporate self, at the expense of the variety and multiplicity of voices in organizations. In this sense, corporate sagas are monologues – managerial monologues that spread the officially approved meanings and definitions.

In the production of the myth of the self lies an attempt to incorporate organizational members into the official world view as defined in the saga. The managerial monologue, I would argue, is a part of the managerial effort to control the organization. It is an effort to integrate multiple meanings and alternative realities into one coherent voice.

The managerial monologue is a singular and exclusive statement. No other views are allowed in a closed monologue. Monologic stories promote a sense of ultimate 'truth': a final statement. There is one voice, one logic and one moral.

His Master's Voice

'There are some strict rules about who is allowed to talk to the press and so on . . .', Per, a Swedish Ikea manager explained to me in a conversation at his office. '. . . and personal profiling is about the worst thing you can do, you know. Well, nobody should compete with . . . [he points upwards and giggles] . . . that is viewed with disapproval . . .'

The myth of the corporate self involves downplaying individual voices. A corporate self can only have one voice. One manager proudly told me that he got the job at Ikea thanks to the fact that he said 'we' all the time during the interview. 'Kamprad liked that.'

Within Ikea the only pronounced 'I' in the company seems to be Ingvar Kamprad. The founder of the company writes letters and official documents in the I-form. His 'self' is exposed in many writings. His 'self' becomes the corporate 'self', a symbol for the collective 'we'. He is the patriarchal father of the big family and the spokesman for the collective self.

Using the collective 'we' can be seen as a way of incorporating all the individual 'I's' into one voice. Multiple meanings and alternative realities are integrated into one coherent voice, thereby producing a corporate self: a unified entity, with one soul and one will, where the master's voice becomes the fabricator of and spokesman for the dominant world view (Boje, 1995). As a universal voice defines and sustains the corporate hegemony, the individual is replaced by the collective we. Fragmentation, individualism, differentiation or divergent views are downplayed or even neglected in the totalizing story.

A Man with Two Mouths

Recently, in one of my courses on Scandinavian management for foreign students, one of the students, a young man from China, taught me the sign for 'boss' in Chinese. It appeared that this sign, if I understood it right, was built up by the lines for man and two mouths. And he explained: 'A boss is a man with two mouths. He takes the mouth from the subordinate. The subordinate has no mouth, so the manager speaks for everyone!'

It is an interesting image of managers, people who 'steal' the mouth from others. And in this way the organizational stories are orchestrated by the managerial monologue. Giving the 'mouth' to managers can be seen as a part of how subordination and control are exercised in the process of organizing.

If we look at management as the management of meanings (Smircich and Morgan, 1982), leaders can be said to define the reality of others. This means that some people give up their definitions of reality in favour of someone else's definition. As Linstead puts it: 'power is the right to speak in the name of another' (1994: 63).

I think that is just what the Chinese sign is about, and this is how the managerial monologue is performed. It is an act of defining the reality of others.

Fabricators of Meaning

In the corporate world we find people whose sole purpose is to provide people in the company with definitions and officially approved world views.

Elsewhere I have called them 'fabricators of meanings' (Salzer, 1994). The division of labour in any society leads to a state where some people do not have to 'hunt and forge weapons' for their survival. Instead they can be totally dedicated to the 'fabrication of myths' (Berger and Luckmann, 1967). The fabricators of meanings, often located to the 'myth-factories' at the headquarters, construct and spread the myths of the self.

The spreading of corporate sagas, myths and stories can be understood as a wish to manage the 'hearts and minds' of the employees (see, for example, Kunda, 1992) in order to control and integrate people. The ideology of control appears to be an effort to offset differences and variations, to homogenize divergent meanings. The fabrication of meanings involves using stories and sagas as a means for controlling and defining the organizational world.

Labelling the World

  – What's that?
  – It's an organization.
  – I see, that's what an organization looks like!

By giving labels to things, we define what they are. We actually make the world as situations, events and things are given names or being labelled. If we look at world-making as an act of rhetoric, we could talk about management as the use of language to persuade (Watson, 1995).

For instance, when managers talk about their companies as 'a big family' they use a metaphor that fabricates a sense of community ('we all belong to each other'), as well as loyalty ('you stick to the family'). The individual and alternative world views are downplayed or even suppressed by the strong stories on 'togetherness'.

A corporate saga can be characterized as a linguistic symbol, filled with labels and metaphors that define the world. Labelling things and situations is a way of controlling how these things and situations are defined. Convincing labels are, as Czarniawska-Joerges (1993) argues, a means for defining the realities of others.

Creating a Discursive Community

As a more subtle form of control, labelling the world is the way managers construct the reality of others. Persuasion, or rhetoric (as the currently fashionable buzz-word goes), is then an endeavour for shaping organizational sense-making. Through persuasive sagas, managers try to spread an official world view.

When the saga is told and retold, a discursive community is created. Boyce (1995) says that story-telling is a part of the collective construction of shared meanings. In this sense, the saga should be a unifying symbol; something which integrates and holds people together.

Within the Ikea World, the saga is widely spread. The shortest version I heard of the Ikea saga was in a discussion with Janice, a young girl working in a Canadian Ikea store, who simply stated: 'You know, Ikea is so big today and it all started by him selling matches . . .'. As Boje writes, stories are often referenced 'with a nod of the head, or a brief "you know the full story", or with a code word or two: "His way!" ' (1995: 1000).

Sharing the saga, the common understanding, is being a part of the Ikea World. You don't have to fill in the full story, it's enough to hint at the saga by saying 'You know how it all began . . .'. And I know that you know that I know – a collective sharing of this symbol.

Towards Polyphony?

The corporate saga is a monologue; a universalizing story. It is a singular, exclusive statement, just as my story here tends to be. No alternative realities are allowed in an omnipotent saga. No other voices are heard. And yet we know that each person has his or her unique voice, and that sense-making is an interactive process.

Managerial monologues are often loud and dominant, but alternate stories are told everywhere, all the time. We are not merely listeners of ready-made stories; we are also co-authors. The organization can then be regarded (or rather heard) as being polyphonic. There are many stories and many voices that make up organizational life.

Often we do not hear the other voices. As Jeffcut (1993) argues, management-centric studies relate managerial voices, the official words that produce the myth of the self. Traditional organizational writings tend to synthesize the different voices from the field into one coherent story. But 'if we conceive of organizations as many dialogues occurring simultaneously and sequentially, as polyphony, we begin to hear differences and possibilities' (Hazen, 1993:16).

Fragmentation of Meanings

Hearing organizations as polyphonic makes us aware of the multitude of voices and stories in organizations. Traditionally, it seems as if organizations and organization studies have been concerned with the question of how to integrate people; that is, organizations have often been described in terms of coordination, integration, homogenization and shared meanings.

However, the idea of 'collective' sense-making and 'shared' meanings could be questioned. Organizations as shared meanings assumes that someone's meanings become universal: that the process of organizing is a process of unifying the individuals into a collective whole. The managerial monologue would thus become an all-embracing story.

But organizing can also be understood as a process through which meanings become differentiated or fragmented. The division of tasks, hierarchical structures and geographical dispersion can be understood as differentiating constructions through which people come to create local spheres and local sets of meaning.

This differentiation means that there are many meanings and many voices within the organization. Instead of describing organizations as coherent entities or unified systems, I prefer to think that organizations can be described as arbitrary boundaries around arrays of complex spheres of meaning. As much as organizations can be characterized by homogeneity, consensus and integration, they can also be characterized by heterogeneity, conflict and differentiation.

Organizational Tales

The multiple realities, local world views, and existence of marginalized voices put new demands on organizational texts (Clifford and Marcus, 1986; Jeffcut, 1993; Martin, 1992). Even though the text has grown out of a multitude of voices, texts and dialogues, the ready-made organization story is most often a totalizing tale. The search for a polyphonic text is the search for new forms of representation.

In the same way as managerial discourses in organizations often can be characterized as monologues, outvoicing all other stories, organizational writings tend to be authoritarian scientific monologues where 'data' from the field are presented by the 'detached observer' in an 'untouchable scientific language' (Salzer-Mörling, 1997). The author is often hidden behind neutral formulations and extensive writing in the passive tense; presenting *the* story as the ultimate order.

What would the polyphonic text look like? A text where multiple meanings permeate the story? Here, I am the one who is authoritarian in synthesizing the multiple voices into this monologue you are reading. It seems as if we cannot avoid what Geertz (1988) refers to as 'the burden of authorship'. So, with the authority of being the author, most of the time it is my own voice which is doing the telling in this text. And when others' voices are heard in the text, I of course have used my power to choose quotes, to edit the text, and so on.

Even though my construction of this story partly aims at creating a sense of the multiplicity of meanings in organizations, at the same time I am inevitably creating a sense of order. Where does the departure from the norm of order come in? Where is the way of writing that dismantles the structured and cherishes the kaleidoscopic?

Often organizational studies present a picture of organizations as being ordered and static realities. But how do we account for things that are not ordered? Do we as organizational researchers try to create order where there is none? The organizational realities that our writings are supposed to represent are often found to be characterized by conflict, heterogeneity, differentiation and ambiguity. How can we understand this mingling and mixture of meanings? Maybe there is a need for new metaphors and other types of stories for relating organizational tales.

Co-authoring Stories

Polyphony implies that there are many sounds; multifarious voices. Still, as I have argued above, the corporate saga can be seen as a managerial monologue; an attempt to overpower the other voices.

The corporate saga is often defined by managers located at the centre of the organization. As in much of the flows of meaning around the world, there is a sort of cultural imperialism in the complex company. The myths, stories and sagas are produced at the centre, whereas the local settings are receivers of the pre-fabricated definitions. To quote Hannerz, 'when the centre speaks, the periphery listens' (1989: 1). Some are exporters of meaning whereas others are importers.

But the 'periphery' is not merely a listener. We are all co-authoring organizational stories. Hence, pre-defined stories could be expected to be constructed, deconstructed, rejected or re-created in the ongoing process of sense-making in various local spheres within the complex organization.

Alternative Stories

At Ikea, the stories I heard which were not incorporated into the dominant saga were reactions to, or rejections of, the official story, rather than alternative stories. As for instance when in an internal training seminar in a French Ikea store we were discussing the company's history and the philosophy that is promoted in the saga. After all the presentations, Pierre, a young co-worker, concluded: 'It's not like that here – that's a utopia!'

At the Canadian headquarters an alternative saga seemed to flourish, which to me in many aspects stood out as a reinterpretation of the centrally fabricated (that is, 'made in Älmhult') corporate saga. The North American saga is about customer service (retold here in the words of André, a Canadian Ikea manager):

> I think that North America was the big awakening for Ikea. . . . Usually when Ikea opened in a new market, it was just to open the door, and boom . . . and here it didn't work, you know. So now we have to stop and reflect why. . . . Take customer service, for instance. When I first started at Ikea, take the return policy, I think we gave two weeks, and you had to turn in the goods with the packages, with your receipt, and we would take off 25%. It was very rigid. In North America you cannot do that. . . . I mean, we have to follow the route that American retailers have set. . . . So, we've changed our return policy, now it's very generous. . . .
>
> Ikea North America – we're the No-Nonsense Return Policy. That's what we stand for. . . . Customer service that is what Ikea is all about, I mean it's the way it works in retailing. And you know, we're a leading company now, thanks to that. . . . I heard about one of our stores where someone brought in a car tyre, and as you know, we don't even sell car tyres, but he wanted to return it, so we gave

him his money back. The customer is always right, and this service is what we are. . . .

As an alternative story, the Canadian saga can be seen as a competing definition of reality. Here Ikea is not just the Swedish 'mechanical selling machine', but a philosophy of customer service. Even though, during my stay, this saga was never as loud or dominant as the official saga, it constituted an alternative world view; another way of explaining 'what it's all about'.

Still, during my stay in the corporate setting of Ikea, few alternative stories came to my attention. Maybe I didn't listen carefully enough. Or maybe I was too trapped by the 'integrationist thinking'. Or maybe the official corporate saga was so dominant and loud that other voices were drowned.

Powerful Stories

The telling of stories is a way of making sense. By reconstructing events or actions into a sequential plot, that is, by the very act of telling a story, sense is made of organizational life (Weick, 1995). Corporate sagas can then be understood as managers' attempt to make sense and to define the world for others. 'Good' stories appear as powerful linguistic symbols in the shaping of organizational life.

Throughout this story I have tried to make sense of Ikea's corporate saga. This is a saga that is widely present in the company. In some aspects it seems to dominate sense-making. It frames, defines and explains an array of situations in the company. But at the same time, we can see how meanings are created and re-created in various local spheres.

Homogenization of Meanings

In organizations, the people who represent a dominant set of meanings, the cultural hegemony, often try to control the organization. In the fabrication of meanings lies a desire to offset heterogenization in meanings with homogenization, and thereby control and integrate people in the organization.

The fabricators, often managers, seem to become powerful as they succeed in promoting their definition of reality to others. Through the use of images, labels and metaphors, appealingly presented in a corporate saga, the fabricators of meaning underplay multiplicity in favour of unity and similarity. The saga is a powerful tool for shaping organizational meanings. Speaking in a louder voice, alternative meanings and local voices sometimes become marginalized or drowned in the managerial sense-making.

Defining organizational realities is thus not just an equal interactive process of sense-making, but a process which expresses a power relationship. Since power relationships are built on the social differentiation between leaders and led, they seem to deserve far more attention within the field of sense-making. Who has the power to speak in the name of another? Whose stories become dominant?

Dominant spheres of meaning define the reality of others, where the managerial monologue seems to orchestrate the polyphony into one coherent voice. It is a process of homogenization of meanings.

Heterogenization of Meanings

At the same time, organizing is a process of heterogenization. Spreading the corporate saga is not a mere transmission of meanings in the functionalist sense between senders and receivers. How strong the managerial definitions of the world ever might be, managers cannot control the meanings after they are 'sent out'.

Organizational members are not merely listeners to pre-defined stories. Rather, we all perform as co-authors in bringing reality into being. Organizations are polyphonic; there are many stories and many voices.

The corporate saga is sometimes rejected, and sometimes challenged by alternative sagas. Sense is made out of the world in various local spheres. The 'monologue' becomes interpreted, and meanings are conferred to pre-defined stories.

Complex organizations embody meanings that are not commonly shared by all. Different local spheres differentiate organizational members' views of the organization. Meanings are differentiated, fragmented and arbitrary. There is a process of heterogenization.

Not Either–Or, But Both

Are organizations thus polyphonic, where each individual has his or her own voice that expresses organizational meanings? Or are organizations 'monolithic', where managerial stories define the organizational world?

Even though sense-making can be regarded as an interactive process, where meanings are fragmented and local, such a polyphonic view tends to ignore the power aspects by which flows of meanings are shaped and homogenized. There is a certain asymmetry in the ongoing world-making, where certain individuals define the realities of others.

But on the other hand, regarding organizations as monolithic seems to imply a management-centric image of organizations, where the local spheres and the mutual parts of sense-making are neglected. 'Receivers' of managerial meanings are not merely listeners, but are also engaged in an active creation of meanings.

Thus, I would argue that there is a constant interaction, or perhaps struggle, between the homogenization process, in which meanings are fabricated from the centre, and the heterogenization process, in which local meanings are constructed. Pre-defined meanings from the top are interpreted, rejected or adopted in various local spheres. There are no mere givers and no mere takers.

Homogenization and heterogenization are simultaneous processes in organizational sense-making. Managerial meanings mix and mingle with local meanings. The dynamics of powerful stories lie in this interaction. Perhaps organizations are best understood as containing both monologues and polyphony.

'To Give Some Hope'

Finally, I would like to return to the Ikea saga. I started by saying that I liked it. I still do. How come some sagas, some stories, or some definitions of reality become more dominant than others? How come we tend to 'buy' some stories, while others are rejected? How is it that we sometimes give up our own voice to let someone else define reality for us?

As I have argued above, it can be interpreted as a question of rhetoric. It is not a matter of how 'real' or 'accurate' a story or definition is. Rather, it is a matter of how 'persuasive' or 'attractive' the meanings are. Attractive meanings will always find followers. Beautiful stories will always be told and retold. We need sense.

A while ago, a manager from a big Swedish company made a speech on 'leadership' where he concluded that: 'The only thing we can do as managers is to give some hope.'

And maybe that is what management and stories are all about. To give some hope. We give up our own voices to a voice that can give us a 'better' definition of reality. Is a saga which makes sense of the world, a saga that explains how things hang together, one that we readily take to our hearts, as long as it gives us some hope?

7   The Struggle With Sense

Anne Wallemacq and David Sims

This chapter explores the relationship between two perspectives on sense-making – the narrative and the phenomenological. Our aim is not to make a propositional comparison of the two approaches, but to observe them at work as heuristics; as devices which illustrate the process of making sense. At the core of our study is the way each approach can illuminate the process of sense-making by its opposite, which we call 'non-sense'. The uneasy relationship between sense and non-sense is what we mean by 'the struggle with sense'. The question of 'non-sense' requires more attention. This is for both empirical and theoretical reasons.

The empirical reason for studying the question of non-sense is that in everyday organizational life the question of 'non-sense' is not marginal. Initially, we set out to show how non-sense is simultaneously normal and problematic for organizations and their members. Using a narrative approach we demonstrate how we all have to deal with the question of 'non-sense' in the everyday life of organizations, and that this can be tense and time-consuming. The phenomenological approach is then applied in order to explore how managers may sometimes be confronted with what appears to be 'non-sense' when trying to understand and deal with their own organizations. This involves an investigation of the role of representations and sense-making in an organizational intervention. Subsequently, we assess both approaches and focus on the ways in which they problematize the question of sense and non-sense.

The second reason for paying more attention to the question of 'non-sense' is theoretical. The study of sense-making is in itself uneasy since we are *always* making sense. As Weick puts it: 'Sensemaking never starts. The reason it never starts is that pure duration never stops. People are always in the middle of things, which become things only when the same people focus on the past from some time beyond it' (1995: 43). Thus we cannot go outside the problem of sense-making in order to study it because of the inherent recursivity of the topic we study. We cannot avoid the fact that in studying sense-making we are part of the process we are studying since we are trying to make sense of sense-making. The analysis of situations where sense-making is obviously problematic can thus give us a counterpoint which can illuminate the process of sense-making. Thus, in our concluding section we discuss the contribution of 'non-sense' in understanding sense-making where non-sense is assessed from both the narrative and phenomenological perspectives.

Sense and Non-Sense in Organizational Life: A Narrative Approach

As a starting point, it is as well to remember that 'sense-making' is problematic (Garfinkel, 1967; Hewitt and Hall, 1973; Weick, 1995). People struggle with sense, while accepting some degree of confusion and the absence of sense. Such a struggle is highly apparent where, as social scientists, we consider the management of organizations. As frequent visitors to organizations, whether as researchers or consultants, we are struck by how frequently the members wish to tell us that their organization is more crazy and senseless than any other. One frequently seen poster in offices says, 'You don't have to be mad to work here, but it helps' (Sims et al., 1993). Newcomers to an organization are greeted with stories to illustrate just what a chaotic, senseless institution they have joined. Many of these stories will be tales of mammoth organizational stupidity – the ordering of expensive new equipment for the project that has just been closed down; the big promotion that involves giving away sunglasses in the winter; the security firm which keeps losing letters.

When we listen to the metaphors that are used when people tell stories about their organizations, they seem particularly drawn to words such as 'asylum' or 'madhouse'. Sometimes this is done with affection; the madness of the organization may be one of its more lovable characteristics. Often we detect a note of frustration that goes with the affection – the same kind of mixture of responses which enables adults to cope with puzzling behaviour from children.

We also note a touching faith that the craziness is an aberration which will not last too long. Television comedies about life in crazy organizations – such as *Yes, Minister* and *Fawlty Towers* – are popular; while university administrators laugh with each other about the chapter in Malcolm Bradbury's (1977) novel *The History Man* which gives an account of a long, futile, fierce, ridiculous but utterly lifelike departmental meeting in a university. One of the reasons why stories about crazy activity in organizations are so popular is that such stories go down well with listeners, who feel reassured to hear that life is just as crazy elsewhere, and that others too have trouble with sense-making. There are rewards and approval available for those who tell these stories.

This applies not only to people telling stories outside their organization, but also to internal stories, particularly those told between different organizational levels. Thus a head of department will often regale his or her subordinates with an account of the antics of the top team of their organization. They will laugh at the silliness of it all, and be relieved to know that their seniors are as confused, unsure and incompetent as they are themselves. At the same time the message being conveyed is that they should be grateful to their boss for protecting them from the worst consequences of this madness, for holding an umbrella of sanity over them. Similarly, stories are told by first-line supervisors and by junior managers about the craziness of much of what is said and done on the shop floor. Again the stories carry a range of meanings, including that others should feel grateful to those who absorb such madness on their behalf. This is the same sort of gratitude outsiders feel for the nurses in the secure psychiatric hospital, who keep all that madness under control. We like to be spared the encounter with non-sense, and are grateful to those who buffer us from it.

Everyday Sense-Making

Making sense is a spectacular achievement. Not everybody makes the same kind of sense in the same situation. Sense is crafted, put together with skill and care, not simply experienced as if prefabricated. We can see others, and occasionally ourselves, making sense in a way which does not seem to be conducive to productive action; it is not simply that sense is made or not made, but that there are consequences to the kind of sense that is made.

Everyday sense-making is not a matter of trying to make total sense of everything. There are levels of sense with which we feel comfortable. Too much sense – too clear an understanding of everything around us – may be boring. It may also be that we are able to make sense of parts of our lives, but not of how these fit together. Also, we may be able to make sense intellectually but not emotionally, as with the sudden death of a middle-aged friend from a heart attack.

For many of us, there is a sense of anomie knocking at the door of our consciousness; sense is always tenuous. The sense that we make is not usually conscious and deliberate. Sense-making is an integrated activity. We do not stop to make sense, in the same way as we do not stop to think (Weick, 1984). We make sense as we go along, and the only reason we know that we are doing it is that every now and then we fail to make sense. Sense is most visible in its absence.

Some people are denied the right to make sense, and if we look at their experience, we understand something more of how sense-making is done. The ultimate lack of sense is when you cannot produce a narrative to go with a situation. Funkenstein has argued that one of the Nazis' crimes against Jewish people was the destruction of their capacity to produce narrative accounts of the holocaust. Survivors are noticeably unable to give an account of the Jewish experience which makes any sense to others or apparently to themselves.

> The identity of an individual and the identity of a group consists of the construction of a narrative, internal and external. . . . The Nazis robbed [the Jews] of their identity, of their capacity to construct a narrative, of investing the events in their lives with meaning and purpose. They lost their individuality; and

survived or died, as Primo Levi describes, as if they were human atoms. (Funkenstein, 1993: 23–4)

We find in organizations some people who seem unable to give much of a narrative account of what is going on around them. At times we may attribute this to underdeveloped transcription skills on their part; they are presumed to be creating stories, but are not able to tell them well. Or they may not choose to tell us their stories; we are sometimes surprised to hear a lively narrative account being given to a friend by someone who would not give us any such account. But there do also seem to be many people who can tell a story about what they did at the weekend, or on holiday, or when they were young, but not about what is happening in their organization (see also Gabriel, this volume). This may be because they, too, have been robbed, if less dramatically, of the capacity to construct a narrative which endows the events in their lives with meaning and purpose.

It may be that there is something literal about sense-making. We are making something that we either take in through our senses or at least that we could imagine doing so. We find it hard to make sense of things that have no tangible reference or at least metaphor. So, virtual organizations may always be harder to make sense of than ones which have a physical plant. This is illustrated by Weick (1985) and Sims (1992) in examining the way in which information systems in organizations may make it more difficult for participants to make sense of what is going on. Jackson (1995) talks of the 'tactile' nature of organizations, and we would argue that this may be crucial to their members having any sense, literally and metaphorically, of what is going on in them.

Making Sense Through Stories

If we follow phenomenological principles and regard ourselves as embedded in sense, neither looking in on sense from the outside nor being lost in the mix of sense, we have to ask, 'How is sense-making achieved by people?' While we think our answer to this question is of wider application, we are looking at it within the terms of our own specialism – people in organizations. So how do people in organizations make sense?

We believe that the phenomenon which most fully realizes and illustrates this phenomenological stance is story-telling. Organizations are a great nexus of narrative story-telling, rumour and gossip (Dalton, 1993; Morin, 1971; Watzlawick, 1976). By narrative story-telling, we mean connecting the events of a story in some kind of sequence. Story-telling usually implies a piece of narrative in which events are connected causally with each other (O'Connor, 1995), although it is also possible to find stories that lack coherent narrative, which is why stories are sometimes dismissed as 'mere anecdote'. This is not always explicit; sometimes simply telling a story is intended to imply to the listener a connection between events, and filling in those implicit connections is left to the listener as his or her contribution to the story-telling. Some listeners may understand while others do not, and this can be intended by the story-teller. Stories can be multi-authored; Boje (1991) gives an eloquent account of how several authors can be involved in telling one story, particularly in an organizational setting. Stories do not always have to be told in full. In a group of people who share a history, shorthand versions of stories will often be enough. Sims and Doyle give an example where all someone has to say to recall a story to the minds of their colleagues is, 'It's the cow tied up in the wool again, Sally' (1995:194). Also, listeners are not passive; their contribution to understanding the story is more than simply providing an audience. They are also active as authors of the version of the story that they will remember, and highly skilled story-tellers will be aware of the activity that listeners will engage in (Barthes, 1974; Roe, 1994).

Widdershoven (1993) says that we remember entirely in stories; if we make any sense of anything in a non-narrative mode, we will only remember the sense we have made in story form. Linde (1993) argues that stories do not have to be mutually consistent, to the ears of a listener, for them to produce coherence for the teller. Indeed, it is important for the teller to have a repertoire of seemingly inconsistent stories to ensure that his or her coherence for himself or herself is robust.

Sims (1995a, 1995b), following Frye (1990), argues that people emplot themselves in stories. They give themselves characters, and may tell their stories as comedies, romances, tragedies or ironies. The form of emplotment they choose will have a clear effect on the type of sense that they make; we decide who to be in the stories that we tell.

One of the universal features of totalitarian life is the presence of a network of spies who report on other people telling stories, thereby making it dangerous for people to tell their own stories of what is happening. Why do totalitarian regimes (political or organizational) expend their effort on policing their members' story-telling? We suggest that it is because telling stories is the way in which people make their own sense of what is going on. This is how we express the paradox of our simultaneous embeddedness in our situation and awareness of ourselves within it. This is why, after a meeting or other major organizational event, people often get together in twos or threes to tell each other their story of the meeting – to try out their own version of the story on others whom they trust, and to hear their friends' story of the meeting to help them to make more sense of what happened.

Story-telling can be deliberately geared to strategic or tactical purposes, however. There are times when people make a quite deliberate choice of whether or not to tell a particular story to their boss. They may tell a story which brings some particular item to the agenda of their organization (Dutton and Ashford, 1993). Stories do not spill out; there is some choice about whether we tell a particular story or not.

Story-telling is not a universal privilege. A key indicator of power in organizations is who has the right to tell stories. There are some people in organizations who are treated as not being worth listening to, or whose stories are regarded as suspect. In one organization that we know, George was regarded by many of the powerful figures as 'a complete idiot', despite his relatively powerful-sounding post. In consequence, no-one was particularly interested in the stories by which he connected up events, and with no one to tell them to, it became increasingly difficult for him to take his own stories seriously. Conversely, some people's stories have to be listened to, however reluctantly, because of the power of their position.

There are circumstances in which stories are expected to be consistent. For example, lawyers and tax officials expect that their victims should be able to tell a consistent story about their activities. This seems to us to be highly unnatural: under most circumstances only those with something to hide are likely to restrict themselves to consistent stories (Linde, 1993).

Story-telling is also the means by which we pass sense on to others. We attempt to encourage people to make a particular kind of sense by telling them things which will act as raw material for them to go and tell others (and themselves) the kind of story we would like them to tell. In this way we pass the authoring on to the next person.

Sense-Making Through Intervention: A Phenomenological Approach

Phenomenology has been a spring of inspiration for several authors who deal with the question of sense. Our aim here is to adopt the premises of the phenomenological approach – and especially Merleau-Ponty's (1962) conception of perception – to analyse an intervention. The case we report is one we developed in a discussion group made up of three managers of small firms. Each firm had undergone important changes – a merger, a diversification and an internal crisis – and the managers were looking for tools to manage these transformations.

For each member of the group the definition of 'what went wrong' was not very clear. They met various problems with the reorganization of their firm, without being able to be precise about what the overall problem was, or if there was a problem. It appeared that they all held a vision of their firm – which they had taken for granted – which no longer seemed relevant. They were puzzled by their own organizations and very concerned since they had themselves been very active in the process of transformation.

This reinforced the idea that intervention should be first and foremost at the level of representation. Intervention, in other words, was explicitly conceived of as a process of sense-making. The aim was to shape with the participants an operating vision of their firm which would allow them to understand what was going on and to cope with the transformations. Our role was as a mirror, reflecting their ways of saying and trying to find out, through analysing language and the spatial organization of their firm, the basic images they relied on to think and act in their organizations.

This is a phenomenological approach to sense-making, and is very close to Merleau-Ponty's contribution. Merleau-Ponty (1962, 1964, 1989) is principally interested in perception: in particular, in the 'moment' things appear to us; that moment *before* intellectual constructions are elaborated to 'explain' what we have seen. This does not mean that perception has nothing to do with intelligibility, but that it cannot be reduced to intelligibility. The focus on perception stresses the importance of the moment things appear to us, and appear to us as 'given'.

Perception is seen in Merleau-Ponty's terms as the spring of sense, the apparition of a meaningful totality. But this 'meaningful totality' does not appear superimposed on a meaningless background. The phenomenal world is 'always already' impregnated with sense. There is always another pre-existent perception which we have to deal with in order to allow a new perception to appear. This pre-existent definition of things is – as Schutz (1967) put it – in the 'natural attitude', taken for granted and not questioned as such.

Intervention conceived as a sense-making process involves not only the construction of a new intelligibility but also a new perception that bears its own principles of intelligibility. But the word 'construction' hides the fact that it is not something that is simply put together. To be credible, this new vision has to impose itself with a 'necessity' that the word 'construction' does not evoke. We now analyse one of the cases from the discussion group in this light.

The Imperialism of the Spontaneous Perception

In order to bring about a new understanding of the firms, we offered different well-known concepts – such as legitimacy and organic/mechanistic structures – as a source for discussion. An important part of the work became the analysis of the participants' assumptive frame. It was the discovery of those frames and of the possibility of alternative views which were most enlightening for the participants.

It was particularly true for a woman of about 45 years old who, five years before, had founded a small firm providing intensive training in software. From a managerial point of view, the firm seemed to develop very well. Four new branches had been created in different parts of Europe. These new units were built on exactly the same model as the first one and did exactly the same job. The growing process did not involve differentiation of the units nor did it involve any enlargement of their products and abilities.

The way she described the growing process was extremely illuminating: 'The firm was becoming too big, there were too many of us, and so we decided to split; I asked my second in command if he would manage the new firm in Luxembourg; he accepted and so that is what we did.' The story continued in exactly the same way; other firms were created on the same pattern and for the same reasons.

Although the development of the firm was outstanding, she felt uncomfortable and marginalized. She realized that she no longer had any influence on those new firms, which were becoming progressively more independent of the original one. She could not stand losing her power over those firms that she had created and that she still owned.

As one of the participants noted, she was trying 'to reproduce her firm by photocopy'. Put together, all the points mentioned above could be seen as deriving from a basic implicit metaphor – the biological metaphor of cellular division (mitosis). The 'mother cell' develops – inside herself – a duplication of herself, and when she becomes too big, she splits into two different cells, built on exactly the same pattern as the original one, each being complete and self-sufficient. It appeared that her feelings related to the same metaphor for she could not accept the consequences of the image implicitly used – the self-sufficiency and the independence of the cell she had created and which did not need her help any more.

We had the opportunity to complete the analysis when we decided to visit the different companies. Hers was located in what, from the outside, looked like a private house. She took us into a small kitchen. After coffee she began speaking of her secretaries and the conflict which took place when she decided to tidy their office herself. We visited the different training rooms and she insisted on the importance of the family atmosphere which she tried to develop. When we commented that her entire staff were women, she replied that there was also a very young man, the youngest person of the company, whom she referred to as 'the Benjamin' (a phrase for the last child of a family).

With all these 'details' put together, it became clear that the role she embodied was the role of 'mother'. This time, we did not have to underline the clues. She spontaneously found the word, and this provoked a shock of greater intensity than the discovery of the mitosis metaphor.

The stories of the mitosis, on the one hand, and of the mother, on the other, are so close that we can wonder whether they proceed from the same analogy. But was it a simple analogy? We do not think so since an analogy is a concrete image you choose in order to better express things that are hard to define. Here the image is not chosen. On the contrary, it imposes itself as the natural frame in which phenomena take place. Everything is interpreted, even the woman's own feelings about duplication and separation. Thus, rather than the concept of 'frame', the image of a 'spring' gets closer to the way in which she was 'expressed' by this metaphor; she herself, her words and her feelings were 'shaped' by it. It was as if she was under the influence of the metaphor. She was closer to being 'used' by the metaphor than to using it.

Discovering or Constructing Sense?

Let us now look more closely at the result of uncovering the hidden metaphor. In both cases, it provoked a shock; the second far more intense than the first. That shock is the moment when the perception is strongly reshaped, when you see something different, a new image whose existence you had not even suspected. In this case, the sudden apparition of the metaphor strongly reshaped the vision she had of her firm and opened new ways of seeing its development.

Merleau-Ponty's (1962) description of 'the spring of sense' is very close to the discovery of the hidden metaphor. He describes it as like the discovery of a rabbit hidden in the leaves of a puzzle picture; a meaningful totality appears. We have to seek it but, at the same time, once 'discovered', it imposes a kind of 'necessity' as being obvious or evident.

That shock could be compared with the one we experience when we watch an artist who begins with details we cannot identify until the moment when the whole drawing, even though not finished, appears in its totality and becomes meaningful. To take another example, the process is like the revelation of the image when you print a photograph: you remain puzzled until the image, even though not totally formed, suddenly appears as a meaningful totality. Here the metaphor – though with hindsight it can be seen as having been foreshadowed by a whole set of clues – suddenly appeared formed at the same moment as being 'true'. As soon as it 'arrived', the metaphor was in a sense taken for granted when speaking of the relationship which linked that woman to her firm.

One important problem remains. Did we discover an embedded sense or did we create sense? The phenomenological view would lead us to neither of those interpretations, nor to both of them at the same time. Both are partly illuminating. The 'objectivist' one takes into account the fact that the mitosis was not just one of many interpretations we could give of what was happening. It imposed itself with a kind of necessity so that we could no longer avoid this image when we were depicting the firm. We had the impression of having discovered something rather than having created it – that the logic of the firm was following the mitosis process. The second type of interpretation, more 'subjectivist', emphasizes that, of course, mitosis is neither more nor less than a representation that we created together and which gave us a vocabulary to express the woman's way of looking at her firm. This recognizes that the 'mirror' that we embodied was, of course, not a passive one and that the discovery of the mitosis metaphor was not a magic event, but the result of several hours of discussions. But for all of us it was far more than one representation among other possible ones. It was the reflection of the real firm.

The 'spring' of the mitosis was neither a passive rereading of a pre-existent logic (the objectivist view), nor a simple construction of a repre-sentation (the subjectivist view); it was the very achievement of sense. The sense-making process is not a creation nor a discovery of a pre-existing logic; it is the birth, the achievement of this logic, the very accomplishment of it.[1]

The Status of Intervention

Intervention, conceived of as a sense-making process, has to take into account the importance of this deep reshaping of what we see. It is at that moment, and only at that moment, that a new understanding is possible. But this reshaping, to be valid and effective, has to appear to the participants. Intervention has therefore to be conceived as a process of making something appear in the eyes of the participant.

The image of the 'active mirror' we used to describe our role was related to this understanding of intervention. It echoes the process of 'making something appear' to the participant's eyes. The point is not to give a personal diagnosis or an image, but to let the participant look at him- or herself through you. But it gives another understanding of the shock that the manager experienced with the metaphor. It was similar to the one we experience when we look at ourselves in a mirror – a feeling of both strangeness and recognition. Strangeness, for the manager, because it was her own image that she was looking at. She was looking at herself as if she was an object or as if she was someone else. Recognition because she did not consider this image to be external to her. On the contrary, despite the fact that she could have considered the picture (in this case the metaphor) as being nothing more than a picture, she considered it as a representation of herself and therefore as far from being a matter of indifference.

This mirror effect is thus linked to the deep recursivity of the intervention situation: in order to make sense of what was happening in her organization, we reflected what we saw to her in a way which led her to change her way of shaping the situation. In other words, the frame she used (the implicit metaphor), instead of being 'transparent' and not perceived as such, as in normal life, was taken as the object of our investigation. Consequently there was a reshaping of the object/subject distinction. The woman was in fact both the subject and the object of her perception. She was 'perceiving herself perceiving', 'making sense of her own way of making sense within her firm'.

This is reminiscent of Merleau-Ponty's (1964) interest in self-portraits. In the self-portrait, the subject is no longer external to the painting but inside the painting. He is seeing himself seeing, perceiving himself perceiving. This is related to what is to our mind the most original contribution of phenomenology – the displacement of the viewpoint that it suggests. Put briefly, phenomenology is based on the assumption that we are inside the world we perceive. We cannot therefore go outside the perception. Analysing the perception process (as we were doing in the intervention) is therefore not from an external viewpoint but always from an internal one. We can no longer speak as if we could analyse perception 'from outside'. We are always perceiving. That gives this kind of situation an inherent recursivity. We were seeing the manager seeing, perceiving her perceiving, analysing her analysing.

Sense and Non-Sense: Making Phenomenological Sense With Narrative

Earlier we suggested that the question of 'non-sense' needs more attention since it is in no way marginal in organizational life. We now want to outline in a more analytical way how the narrative and phenomenological approaches we have presented construct the idea of 'non-sense'.

With the narrative approach, we have shown that non-sense is not at all exceptional. On the contrary, it is an everyday experience, and not necessarily a dramatic one. In the narrative approach, the phrase 'non-sense' is less an academic construction than a category used by individuals to make sense of their situation. Non-sense is a familiar idea that can be brought into different kinds of stories. Non-sense is not a failure of the sense-making process. It is a part of it; it is a categorization that permits sense to be made, even of 'non-sense'.

If non-sense is not the opposite of sense-making but a part of it, how in this narrative approach do we understand the process of sense-making? Sense-making is not a conscious activity. It is like the respiration of organizational life. We make sense all the time without the feeling of doing something important or indeed of doing anything at all. The sense-making process cannot be isolated without being destroyed.

The concept of story allows the researcher to grasp the process without destroying it. We tell stories the whole time, even to ourselves. Story-telling is part of us rather than a construction of our wills. With the concept of story, the process of sense-making becomes one of emplotment, the way we tell and retell the events. There is a simultaneous construction of the stories and the events since they are not events in themselves but only in relationship with a narrative frame which constitutes them as events.

One of the consequences of the concept of story is that the border between fiction and fact is explicitly not clear. The question of whether the story is true loses primacy. The narrative approach puts the stress on the functions of the stories rather than on their truth. Story-telling is the ongoing reassessment of organizational life, the ongoing elaboration of what is happening, and the permanent re-elaboration of our identities.

In the case of the 'mitosis', sense and non-sense are constructed at different levels of analysis. The manager did not define her situation as 'non-sense'. Nor would we define this situation as 'non-sense' since it would suggest the 'absence of sense'. 'Absence of sense' would be incompatible with the very premises of the phenomenological way of thinking. The world we live in is always meaningful. There is not an un-meaningful world, on the one hand, and a production of meaning, on the other. The world we experience is given to us as meaningful. The process of sense-making is therefore not one of assigning or giving a meaning to things. On the contrary, we are immersed in sense, we are 'condemned to meaning', as Merleau-Ponty (1962) puts it. The question of sense-making is not therefore how we make sense but how we deal with sense, how we manage it, how we 'swim' in that world of sense of which we are part, how we constitute ourselves in that world.

How, then, can we describe the situation in the case study? Rather than an absence of sense, the situation can be analysed as an absence of the 'necessity' which makes things appear as given, as objective, which makes the world appear as 'obviously' what it is. In the natural attitude, as the phenomenologists put it, we do not doubt reality; the definition of things is taken for granted. When she arrived in the discussion group, the firm's founder was still referring, quite strongly, to her natural vision of her firm. But at the same time, she felt uncomfortable. Her vision could no longer be imposed on the other members of the organization. The obviousness of her reading suddenly vanished. She was therefore in a crisis of interpretation, not being able to define what happened and whether something really was happening.

Here, sense-making consisted of the emergence of a pattern which was then taken for granted. It is not the 'truth' of the analysis but the fact that the woman suddenly saw the pattern that made the mitosis–mother interpretation convincing for her.

Conclusions

Both the narrative and phenomenological perspectives share at least three main features which are quite fundamental: we cannot go outside sense; accomplishment; and recursivity. These three features are deeply interwoven because the latter two rest on the first.

We Cannot Go Outside Sense

Even constructivists speak of a reality (even if we cannot reach it) on the basis of which the world is socially constructed. Referring to this underlying reality is not meant to imply that it exists but that we use it as a kind of counterpoint, allowing us to speak and to understand the process of sense-making. The concepts we use and our whole common language belong to our society where the 'fact' of a natural reality is taken for granted.

The phenomenological approach pushes this further, and takes it that the world that we experience is no longer conceived of as a (pale) reflection of the world in itself. The world of phenomena, the world we experience, is consistent by itself and has to be understood as such. Developing a way of thinking that tries to understand the phenomenal world as consistent in itself, and as not needing to be seen with reference to an 'objective' one, seems to us worthwhile. It is in this direction that phenomenology takes us. The consequence of adopting this approach is that – from the very beginning – the world we experience is seen as symbolically constructed. There is no meaningless, pre-symbolic situation.

Both of the approaches we have discussed above are based on these premises. The narrative approach does not isolate the sense-making process as a specific phenomenon. We make sense all the time without being aware of it. The narrative approach echoes the reflexivity of the process. We come back to our previous experience, to what happened yesterday, to what someone said or did. Even non-sense narratives are a way of making sense. It is a category, a type of story that is not different in nature from other types. In the case of the mitosis story, the 'moment' of making sense was isolated as special, due to the particularity of the situation reported – an intervention conceived as a sense-making process. The previous situation was not an absence of sense, but was a situation where a definite frame did not impose itself with 'necessity', so that many interpretations and perceptions could compete, none of them being totally convincing for the woman in situation. To put it another way, there were several different stories that could be told, none of which had hitherto imposed itself as being ultimately convincing.

Sense/World as an Accomplishment

The process we are discussing is the one described by Garfinkel's concept of accomplishment:

> [I]n in contrast to certain versions of Durkheim that teach that the objective reality of social facts is sociology's fundamental principle, the lesson is taken instead, and used as a study policy, that the objective reality of social facts as an ongoing accomplishment of the concerted activities of daily life, with the ordinary, artful ways of that accomplishment being by members known, used, and taken for granted, is, for members doing sociology a fundamental phenomenon. (1967: vii)

The discovery of the underlying metaphor was the very accomplishment of the fact that there was an underlying metaphor that was organizing the way the woman was acting, representing and feeling. Story-telling is the process by which the individuals or the group constitute their reality as real, as 'accountable', as 'member's methods for making those same activities visibly-rational-and-reportable-for-all-practical-purposes' (Garfinkel, 1967: vii).

Inspired by gestalt theory, Merleau-Ponty (1962) used the image of the 'discovery' of the rabbit in the leaves in a puzzle picture to describe the moment of perception as the apparition of a meaningful totality. The same image is used later by Garfinkel (1967) when describing the process by which scientists 'discovered' an optical pulsar, arguing that it is the method that they used to describe the object that created that object as visibly reportable and accountable, as 'objective and real'. Of course those expressions are quite paradoxical: how can we discover something that we create? But this paradox vanishes if we do not continue to contrast a world in itself with the world as it appears to us. If, on the contrary, we take it that the world of phenomena is embedded in meaning, the apparition of the optical pulsar, the apparition of the mitosis, and also the apparition of a new story is the very process of making something which unavoidably appears to us as objective, as independent of our creation, as 'already there'.

One more thing has to be pointed out. In the phenomenological view, it is assumed that in everyday life our interests are first and foremost practical. We do not wonder whether things are really what they appear to be; we simply use them. The consequence is that in everyday life the question of 'truth' is not dominant. As we mentioned before, one of the interests of the notion of story is that the border between fiction and reality is not sharp. The phenomenon of rumour (Morin, 1971) is a good illustration of how in everyday life we do not continuously verify what is assumed. In the mitosis case, rather than wondering whether the interpretation we produced was true or not, from the moment we saw the mitosis metaphor it appeared to us as obviously real and reportable. We do not mean here that some criterion of truth has nothing to do with the process of sense-making, but rather that it is the process by which things are seen as convincing stories which is at stake; one part of this is the question of verisimilitude.

Recursivity

We cannot avoid the issue of recursivity. The process of our analysis is related to the processes we are studying. If we adopt phenomenological premises, we are not outside the world we study and live in. We are part of it and the analysis we produce is similar to the general processes we study here. In writing this chapter we have not been interested only in the content of it. We have also been interested in the process of producing this chapter as a kind of sense-making itself. We could not stand outside sense to write about sense, any more than we could stop telling stories to write about stories.

The style of the section on the narrative approach is quite narrative. It attempts to avoid 'being boring'. And this intention was not an epiphenomenon; it was an aim to describe something – story-telling – without destroying the object itself. It was, in other words, an endeavour to find a style that suited the phenomenon that was described and from which the description could not be isolated. The case study of the intervention was quite paradigmatic. It was a process of phenomenological sense-making, and its presentation tried to make appear, in the reader's eyes, the powerful way in which 'mitosis' acted as the very phenomenon of the 'spring of sense'.

Thus in recursivity, accomplishment and the impossibility of going outside sense, we see that the conceptualization of the phenomenologists and the practice of story-tellers seem to bring us to the same place. In the struggle for sense, narrative and phenomenological approaches can operate as two sides of a coin: phenomenologists have emphasized our embeddedness, and stories never fail to illustrate it.

Notes

We are indebted to Yiannis Gabriel for his comments on this chapter.

1 Yiannis Gabriel has pointed out a parallel process with irony. Accounts are given along the lines, 'He won the pools on the very day that . . . [virtually anything goes here]'. This might be a narrative construction that can be imposed on almost any story, but the phenomenological contribution is to point out that when this construction has been so placed it imposes 'necessity', and becomes seen as 'Murphy's' or 'Sod's Law'.

Part III

DISCOURSE AND SOCIAL THEORY

8   Linearity, Control and Death

Gibson Burrell

On 1 August 1914, 11,000 troop trains were poised within Germany's boundaries to follow a very tight and punctilious schedule of movement to the frontiers. News came through that Britain would only become involved in the looming conflict if France itself was attacked.

'This calls for champagne', said the Kaiser. 'We must halt the march to the west.'

'It is impossible,' said General Moltke, mindful of the railway timetable. 'The whole army will be thrown into confusion.'

In 1915, the Allies made a series of offensives at Neuve Chapelle, Aubers, Ypres and Loos which made the essence of mechanized warfare plain to see. A German officer described a British advance thus:

> Ten columns of extended line could clearly be distinguished, each one estimated at more than a thousand men and offering such a target as had never been seen before or thought possible. Never had the machine gunners such straight-forward work to do nor done it so effectively. They traversed to and fro unceasingly. (Roberts, 1979: 32)

Robert Graves, the writer and poet, took part in the Flanders sector of fighting and describes the following events in *Goodbye to All That*.

> One of the (. . .) officers told me later what happened. It had been agreed to advance by platoon rushes with supporting fire. When his platoon had gone about twenty yards, he signalled them to lie down and open covering fire. The din was tremendous. He saw the platoon on his left flopping down too so he whistled the advance again. Nobody seemed to hear. He jumped up from his shell hole, waved and signalled 'Forward.' Nobody stirred. He shouted: 'You bloody cowards, are you leaving me to go on alone?' His platoon sergeant, groaning with a broken

shoulder, gasped 'Not cowards sir. Willing enough. But they are all fucking dead.' (Quoted in Roberts, 1979: 32)

Linearity kills.

Linearity, Control and Death

Linearity kills. Linearity kills? What could possibly be meant by such a trite assertion? This chapter is an exercise in extreme violence. Through this extreme violence it is possible to beat a path backwards and forwards across time in order to construct a highway of possibility with a number of historico-theoretical elements. The byways of other routings do not interest me here – at least to begin with. For the (rail)road I seek is to arrive at death via control having departed from linearity. Yet to arm oneself with linearity is to seek to kill the entrenched monster that we only hear and smell but do not see. That is the problem. Modernity, particularly this century, has embraced the hegemony of vision and its unbending linearity (Levin, 1993). It has slain the beasts of the other senses. The argument you are about to read is a typical one which is set up to conform to the pre-eminence of sight and to linearity. It concludes with a brief outline offering a more 'Cretan' view of the darkness of the textually labyrinthine. For, to quote Georges Bataille, perhaps 'it is time to abandon the world of the civilized and its light' (1985: 179). Perhaps we should seek the excitation of our full sensorium through the work of the likes of Deleuze and Guattari. For working in darkness, possibly among the rhizomes, we may discover lightning.

Use your eyes and behold Figure 8.1. It is a crude device through which to make an argument. It stands proudly as a cipher. Here is a railway line by which the North American Native Peoples were conquered, subdued and killed. I see here also the cause of the First World War as the railway lines of Europe hummed to the sound of mobilized troops hurtling towards No Man's Land between the front lines. I discern here the way in which McDonaldized cattle head for the abattoir. Here is the pattern of attack used by ex-West Point railway engineers trained in the disciplinary techniques of France. Here is the track which is so easy to be born on the wrong side of, bringing different life expectancy rates. Figure 8.1 is a bureaucracy of multiple levels, some within it waiting less than calmly to be de-layered. Here is a career ladder on which to trample your contemporaries. It is a hierarchy for rule by the sacred. Here is the greasy pole. It dictates the quest ahead. It is a thesis converging on the truth. It is a way out of the labyrinth of non-understanding and confusion. Figure 8.1 panders to the audience by adopting perspectivism and assuming the readers' point of view. Here is a list which can be presented as a set of *bullet* points. Here is a track driven through hostile country, killing as it goes.

FIGURE 8.1   *A cipher for linearity*

But does the assertion that Figure 8.1 is all to do with death imply that non-linear forms of life and of argumentation and of presentation are life-affirming? My answer would be 'a little perhaps'. Why don't we try it and see? Why don't we seek youthful adventure in escape from the doctoral thesis? There is an argument which suggests that the English word 'thesis' comes from the same root as the name Theseus. The story of Theseus relates the son of the Greek King, Aegeus, being offered up as a sacrifice to King Minos of Crete. Theseus and Minos' daughter Ariadne fall in love and she offers him a ball of thread with which, once he has killed the Minotaur, he might find his way out of the labyrinth of Knossos. Having safely disposed of the monster deep in the darkness of the labyrinth, he reaches the light of understanding by following the line of argument allowed to him in retracing the thread. Thus he straightens out the turns and twists of the benighted building in which he has been placed. Ariadne presented him with the means to find the light, but to do so he first had to murder a being which was at least *half*-human.

The Greeks' predilection for the straight line in their geometries of column and form reflects in part perhaps this concern for rendering visible that Other which prefers the darkness. Even Euripides (1973) has the Bacchae acting in daylight so that they may be closely surveyed by the shepherd. The classical Greeks had a desire to produce public spaces in Athens in which the speaker is not only heard but also seen and carefully observed. And as Nietzsche (1977: 216) shows us, the Golden Age of

Greece, both in sport and in debate, underlies much of the contemporary notion of 'civilization' which we promulgate in the West, yet it rests upon extreme violence of the body and of the tongue.

It is relatively simple to make a violently crude argument, thesis-like and driven as a straight highway through the past, which links Euclidean geometry to the typographic shift identified by McLuhan to the Cartesian perspectival scopic regime and thereby to full-blown perspectivalism and thence to positivism and finally to the effects of technocratic modernism with its baleful conclusion in 'the will to power' and murderous, anti-intellectual rationalism. And let us be clear here. Rationalism *can* be anti-intellectual in the sense that it seeks to degrade all talk of ethics, of aesthetics, of taste, of disputation and argument around qualitative matters. All is reduced to a quantitative calculus of ratiocination and the search for the right answer: the final solution. The Final Solution.

Linearity kills. Euclidean geometry imprisons the social sciences and makes sacrifices of us all. There is a photograph of a squash match set up just outside the pyramids at Cheops which sums up the delights of the appeal of the ideas of Euclid. Behind the Great Pyramid set red against the setting sun is the brightness of the transparent cube of the squash court in which two squash players hit the spherical ball, the movement of which will decide the victor. Whilst the ball cannot be seen in the picture, the players are caught in the act of playing with it. Social scientists are also caught in the act of playing with spheres and pyramids and cubes, but these are usually reduced in our theorizing to circles and squares and triangles. On paper we reduce three dimensions to virtually two.

Just as this page does.

In the eighteenth century the rival Dutch and British navies, having solved the problem of finding latitude, tried to overcome the problem of longitude through the enforcement of linear conceptions of space and time (Sobel 1996). Both astronomic and chronological methods were used until the 'mere' mechanic John Harrison developed timing devices which proved themselves to be superior in finding one's place on the planet. The dangerous activity of negotiating a ship through the trackless oceans called for surveying, for maps, for fixity, for stations, for grids of reference, for locating devices. These devices had to be portable. Indeed, this is why the 'Enlightenment' is such a precise term in English to describe this period, for it was the age of making less heavy these sorts of devices for ensuring 'action at a distance'. The British Navy perhaps contained the most advanced form of thinking about linearity in the period with its ships of the line, chains of command, log books (which measured distance travelled) and navigational position expressed as a grid reference. Social scientists today likewise encourage the mapping of fields and areas of study within disciplined imperial boundaries, the better to travel safely (Pfeffer, 1993). Thus, Euclidean geometry with its particular ethics of control brings us firmly into the Age of Empires. And the Age of Empires relied heavily upon the multiple crossings of linear coordinates. Take away these elegant but simple geometrical forms and how many theorizings in social science, diplomacy and warfare would be impossible to articulate? Non-Euclidean geometry was developed in the 1830s but its significance was not seen until the end of the century by natural scientists (Jay, 1994: 158). It still has to be recognized by social scientists. If we were to seriously embrace non-Euclidean geometries, we would recognize, perhaps, the multiplicity of perspectives possible upon the world. The perspectivism inherent in the concept of the reader might give way to the view from each of the 100,000 words in this book. Perhaps an exploration of the non-Euclidean world would allow us to be innovative or at least to escape the tyranny of the acetate and the video screen.

But, for the moment, we must proceed with the single-track voyage upon which I have embarked. The crew must be silent and keep no record of their own, otherwise they can only expect Sir Clowdsley Shovell's yardarm (Sobel, 1996). No room here for the non-linear. For we are reading, left to right and up and down. We do not hear. We are expected to read authors in all their author-ity. It is how *they* see the world that is important.

Perspectivism is closely associated with the Cartesian scopic regime in which the individual human being inhabits a uniform, infinite, isotropic space. The key sensory device is the eye, for visual perception allows the focus to be upon an object world. In perspectival painting there is a unidirectional subject–object relation which is de-carnalized. The I is made up of the eye. The body then is pitted against the eye and there is a fetishization of the power of sight. Other organs of sense are downgraded and the emphasis is upon the optocentric. The emphasis is upon the world of appearance. Consider but two brief examples. Hoskin and McLean (1997) have shown that 'the form' used by insurance companies to insure and assure their clients came about when the Prudential began to offer cover to the rising middle classes in the mid-1850s. They were inundated with over 10 million pieces of paper as putative clients talked to company agents before the process of actuarial assessment began. To reduce the complexity of two million individual lives to manageable proportions, the Prudential invented the form. Real individual lives were reduced to a two-dimensional representation on dead xylem. The depths of the soul, the frailties of the flesh, were thus made visible. Rendered illuminated by the form, we were made fit for serviceability in the interests of finance capital. We were (re-) invented as those who were calculable. The owner/controllers of the Prudential were and are those who hold the privilege of perspectival position. But in a real sense they are also managers of death. We may call it a 'life policy' but let us not fool ourselves with this euphemism. The 'man from the Pru' is a dealer in death, and from the company's perspective this certainty of mortality can be calculated with some statistical accuracy. That is why they deal comfortably in assurance. And it is also why we are assured in our dealings with them.

But it is not only those owners of capital who, as John Berger (1967) shows us in relation to the landscape paintings commissioned by the new landowners of the eighteenth century, embrace optocentric perspectivalism.

We do so ourselves with a startling eagerness. The dominance of the I and of the culture of narcissism help explain the egocentricism of the new virtual reality machines and their emphasis upon the world of the single viewer. New technologies do not free the viewer from perspectival biases. They pander to them, albeit in a version of a weak carnalized form. The eye is joined electronically to the hip and the thigh and the palm, but more important for the twenty-first century orgasmatrons is what is beheld rather than what is held. Thus the eye is carnalized – but by no means fully. And whilst we are on the theme of the carnalized form, Manguel (1996: 42–3) tells of Ambrose, a cleric in the fifth century, who was said by that paleo-organization theorist, St Augustine, to be an 'extraordinary reader'. In our terms what Ambrose did was to challenge the carnalized version of reading which was prevalent at the time. For as he scanned the page and sought out the meaning of the text his voice was silent and his tongue was still. He *never* read aloud. The reader today sits (which of course assumes the dressage of the chair, which was not common in western Europe before early Victorian times), with eyes scanning the page, tongue held still. Such forms of silent reading were not commonplace until the tenth century at the earliest. Prior to this, to sit in a library of the Middle East would have been to squat amidst a cacophonous din! Manguel gives other examples which predate Ambrose where extraordinary events reported on paper are read silently because of their impact; but it is not until the monasteries of the early middle ages begin to institute the regime of work and prayer and prayer and work (Noble, 1994) that silent reading becomes acceptable and as not rude and offensive. Before this, reading was an *oral* skill to be enjoyed by others as they listened, practising their aural skills. To read silently is to deprive others of both pleasure and access.

Of course it was McLuhan (1962) who produced a strong, oversimplified account of the importance of writing made possible through the printing press. McLuhan argued that the greater the number of senses involved, the greater the chance the recipient of a message would be able to reproduce the experience of the sender. For him, the spoken word was the best of the possibilities for reproducing our mental states in others. The spoken word in a face-to-face interaction involves the full range of the human sensorium. Hearing is hotter than sight but the written word has achieved the status of a 'momentary deity'. Now whilst this impoverishment began with handwriting and manual copying, it accelerates tremendously with the development of the printing press. Thereafter, the macadamized text allows the reader to rush along; for the surface has been tidied up and cleared of ambiguity. It is unobstructed by the personal potholes of the transcriber. Readers of this visual uniformity learn to inhabit a world of strict, logical, explicit and literal patterns. They come to live by timetables and are punctual, by tables of weights and measures and are productive, and by formal instruction and are expedient. The discovery of printing, more than writing, is the original sin which industrial civilization is now heir to. It has created a world of closely regimented text, of the notion of the author, of a fixed point of view, and of

the concept of proprietary rights over ideas. Typographic Man is Organization Man. And Typographic Woman is Organization Woman. McLuhan
(1962) goes on to argue that 'perhaps the most significant of the gifts of
typography to man is that of detachment and non-involvement'. Jay (1994:
67) suggests that the Greeks also possessed this 'gift', but that printing
multiplied the number of its beneficiaries, including, most notably of course,
René Descartes, whose campaign for a visually conceived cognitive project
led to 'the decay of dialogue' (Ong, 1958).

Jay (1994: 2) argues that modernism generated a frenzy for the visible.
There is a shift from the oral to the chirographic to the typographic. Visual
perception gives us the object world while the voice or the auditing of it by
the listener is associated with the personal world. The former produces
positivism, universal rationalism, the privileging of grids and flattened,
geometricalized, ordered industrial technological design. What the Cartesian
Revolution did, says Jay, was to decarnalize the eye and foreground the
perspectival scopic regime.

Descartes was always surrounded by death. He was present at the Battle
of the White Mountain outside Prague when the Magic Kingdom was
brought to an end in 1623. He attended the anatomy theatres of Paris and
undertook many a personal autopsy searching for the human soul, finding it
eventually in the pineal gland of a very recently deceased corpse. To his
contemporaries he was a secretive man, possibly a member of the 'Invisible
College' of Rosicrucians. Moreover, he was seen as wasteful of expensive
human cadavers since he went into the head first, leaving the bodies to
putrefy. He looked into animal hearts and human foetuses and published his
results based on research into optics. Through the anatomist's scalpel he
sought to reveal, to make visual, the interior of the human heart, body and
soul (Dale, 1997). This was to be done through perspectivism and the
revelation of deep interiority to human sight. Thus the body became
objectified and entirely divorced from a thinking, speaking being. A divorce
was made between an 'I' that thinks and an 'it' in which we reside, and it
quickly became, across the western world, a *decree absolute*. The mind and
the body in which it was housed became as separable as a horse from a rider.
And the human sciences had no interest in the riderless horse. They
concentrated on the rider.

What is absolutely clear is that to have a Cartesian understanding one has
to kill. Full-blown perspectivalism, indeed modern epistemology itself, is
often seen as originating with Descartes (Rorty, 1980: 45). He assumed a
natural geometry of the mind which he himself identified with that of Euclid
(Jay, 1994: 78–9), and sought to be a spectator and not an actor. The focus
thereafter was to be on the geometricalicized laws of optics and the
mechanical transmission of light. It assumed a unidirectional subject–object
relation which became the hallmark of perspectivalism. It assumed the
analysis of living objects by killing them and fixing them in space, the better
to allow their anatomization and the bringing of their body parts under the
microscope. It assumed the conditions for French positivism.

As Heilbron (1995) has recently demonstrated, the most popular of the French sciences in the eighteenth century was natural history, and the links between biology and the new sciences of society were very obvious. Moreover, the rise of sociology comes about at the feet of the guillotine as new notions gained currency in the ferment of the early nineteenth century. Under Napoleon there had been a strong emphasis on *linearity* for military purposes in terms of road building and army drilling and in the thought behind the Napoleonic Code. Both these came about as a result of the thanatocracy of the Revolution. They had been in train in the eighteenth century of course. Cuvier, for example, looks at the internal organization of humans and animals rather than their surface features to see why and how they should be classified. Indeed he brings the concept of organization into the contemporary world (Dale and Burrell, 1995). His classification system of life is functionalist and linear. And it is this vision which Saint-Simon and his aide, Auguste Comte, come to take as the basis for a scientific social theory we now know as positivism. Heilbron details the emphasis on linearity (as in the hierarchy of the sciences) and the text (as in the emphasis on writing) under positivism. He shows how Comte takes the Napoleonic Code as his own.

I wish here to focus upon military history to demonstrate the conjunction of linearity, control and death. The period in which we first find this conjunction is arguably the First World War. Linearity comes to us in the lines of battle which stretched across Flanders where the front line separated and yet connected the huge armies of the west and the east transported to the front from behind the lines by trains with their own particular and revolutionary form of linearity. As A.J.P. Taylor (1979) noted, the logic of the war in part comes about from the timetables for mobilization and the scheduling of the train networks of Europe. The timetable as text constrains military planners and speeds up the inexorable flow of death. The troop carriages are the cattle trucks which previously carried animals to the west European abattoirs. In 1916, French regiments came close to mutiny as they baaed their way to the front line in full knowledge of what awaited them. At Vimy Ridge, a dual carriageway was constructed in the chalk so that as one regiment left the front depleted, as it had to be, by 50 per cent, it would not be seen by the new troops coming up the line. Science and engineering meant that the coal miners of Europe were called to undermine and destroy the subterranean works of those others mining from the opposite lines. The tunnels and shafts in the hillside are again examples of the linearity in action of military thought. On the surface the generals planned to let the blood of a complete generation. The thinking was that the blood lines of their own forces were stronger than those of the enemy and if the opponent could be forced to lose more men over a long-drawn-out period then ultimate victory would be won. They would bleed their enemy white. It was a calculus of the crudest kind with which Mao was to frighten the West some 50 years later. The battles were fought with orders of the day. These were texts which drove the conflict onward. When British and German troops, amongst others, met and played football on Christmas Day 1915, the prospect of a united front against the generals by the troops was almost realized. The orders were for these footballing mutineers to be tried and in some cases executed for mutiny. The nature of the exchanges was seen as decidedly threatening by those in charge. The army had to move as one, over the top and into No Man's Land. Those who were to be found in this territory in-between were the dead and the dying. Life took place behind the lines.

Those First World War battlefields then give us straightforward connections between lines and death. The front line, the line of defence and attack, lines of command, lines of supply, and so on, are all obvious in the way in which linearity kills. At the Battle of Jutland at sea, ships of the line lined up against each other and began a mutual bombardment. The logic of the period was confrontation to the death across well-defined lines drawn by both parties in what was normally a two-dimensional space. Like the previous page. Of key importance here is the *map*, for it is the cartographers' representation of space that informs the action at a distance that the generals seek to engage in. They see a line and squares and symbols which stand for the real lives of men (and women) trapped in the mud flows and watery trenches of the battlefield.

As we move through the twentieth century we can see the forces first employed in 1914–18 become commonplace later. Technocratic anti-intellectualism, with its emphasis on instrumental rationality, which comes to fruition in 1915, does not disappear. Whilst the move to air-borne violence, to the rise of so-called 'wars of the flea' in the 1950s and the increased mobility of military forces after 1939 seem to indicate the decline in two-dimensional linear thinking, there is still the overwhelming dependence on the map and the technologies of visualization. The radar screen is a two-dimensional representation of space, the Viet-Cong's tunnelling under Saigon relied upon what were essentially inverted street guides, and the Panzers that reached the French coast in June 1940 were so far ahead of their expectations that they were using Michelin maps. Thus whilst the crude linearity of the First World War gave way, it did so only to a more sophisticated version of linearity, control and death.

Foucault pointed to the representation of the real lives of real human beings on pieces of paper. Hoskin and McLean's (1997) work on the form shows how the biographies of individuals become reduced to single pieces of paper. Our CVs are designed in exactly the same way to create the illusion of linearity in a three-dimensional life. Career is a linear concept of a hugely reductionist kind yet it fits in so well with these strategies for control. The form, the map, the CV, the share certificate, the passport, the love letter and the P45 all serve to control others by explicating the inexplicable simply and without room for doubt. They are uncertainty reducers, organizing the world for us. Without them we are unknown, we are lost, we have done nothing, we own nothing, we belong to nothing, we expect nothing, our future is nothing. Nihilism is kept at bay by the flurry of pieces of paper through which our identity is assured. Trees die to ensure my textual existence. My existential *Angst* is fought off by Scandinavian wood pulp.

'Fought off'? Military analogies are everywhere. It is worth pointing out that the importance of the military forms of organization are so under-estimated in contemporary organization theory. Yet if we look to techno-logical developments, the discourse of strategy, and so on, our language is replete with death and the means of dealing it out. Stories are legion about IBM's strategic thinking in the mid-1980s which had marketing executives from Big Blue engage in training sales staff training sessions dressed in combat jackets and talking of hit rates, bringing back orders in body bags and penetrating behind enemy lines. It's a war out there, soldier. A narrative becomes accepted in which it is legitimate to see business as the extension of warfare by another means. Colonel Urwick, Captain Harvey Jones and a whole range of ex-military personnel became influential thinkers in British management thought in the post-1945 period (Child, 1964). In the face of death, there is the encouragement to obey orders, follow routines and believe in the cult of the leader. At least that is what the leaders encourage in the followership. But of course you might say this word 'death' is merely a metaphor. It's not really dealing in death that is being spoken about. It is a symbol which is utilized when the going gets rough, nothing more. Death is not meant. It is a synonym for a serious situation.

Consider the managers of slaughter. The army officer, the funeral director, the safety officer, the doctor in casualty, the fire-fighter, the motorway police patrol and the assurance salesperson are clear examples of those who have to manage confrontation with death routinely. Death is their business. We are not talking here about metaphorical deaths. We are confronted in organiza-tional contexts with the death of human beings on a day-to-day, hour-to-hour basis. And the way these professionals handle this experience is through routine, through humour, through euphemism and through psychological distancing. These are precisely the ways in which the SS handled their tasks in the death camps.

But these are surely exceptions – aren't they? Human death is so medicalized and compartmentalized today that when I walk down Leaming-ton Spa's Parade I should see nothing of mortality. But there are restaurants that serve meat. Cars driven at speed. Shops that test products on animals. Gangs on the prowl. Dress shops with real furs in them. A passing hearse. Gift shops that utilize very cheap child labour in their goods for sale. Tobacconists. Shops selling aerosols and glues. Buses pumping out carbon monoxide fumes. Shops selling cheap cider and meths. Police wearing the newish extra-long truncheons on their belts. Defecating dogs on the pave-ment. Children standing on the back seats of people movers. Death stalks the streets in His absence and in His presence. Once one begins to tot up the calculus of death or threats to life and limb, then paranoia is but the next step.

Surely, you might say, even if this has some validity, death is not necessarily a negative. Rather it is a positive move to a higher stage which should be welcomed and certainly not feared. Most religions offer the hope of transcending the all too frail body and replacing it with a spiritual existence at a level of which we can only dream. Funerals often celebrate the passing on of the individual to this elevated state. So if the streets and organizations off them are about death, this is conceptualizable in a relatively positive light. It means they are about a better tomorrow. But this is sophistry. There are few religions which allow suicide and moving to this higher existence when the individual desires it. There are few religions which allow euthanasia. Much of contemporary religion justifies death *post facto* and certainly does not encourage its active embrace any earlier than appears essential. Cults which engage in collective suicide are seen as totally irrational. So let us not pretend that death is seen as unproblematic, as a step in a continuous process of improvement. For the vast majority of us it is a Giddensian destructuration which is unlikely to be matched in our lives. It is a discrete jump of frightening dimensions which few actively seek out.

A narrative develops of linearity, Euclidean geometry, printing, perspectivism, control, warfare and death which I happen to see negatively. Look in the streets and look in the organizations around and one sees a conjunction of forces which are about control using linear logic and are heavily implicated in death. The sense of this may come across from Figure 8.1. It is a cipher for what I mean. It looks like a *tree of knowledge* to which one must object. But in objecting to it what can one suggest? To construct an alternative to Figure 8.1 one might seek to appeal to the following: against the linear, the labyrinthine; against Athens, Crete; against Euclid, the non-Euclidean; against printing, the spoken word; against perspectivism, something cubist perhaps; against positivism, a stance drawn from cultural studies; and against death, a celebration of human life. In the place of One, we might elevate the Other. But what could we place against the tree of knowledge?

One alternative has been developed in the last 20 years in the work of Gilles Deleuze and Félix Guattari. They are both dead but their work has a vitality which is increasingly recognized. They offer an alternative to the linearity/control/death conjunction of forces outlined above and it may be worthwhile articulating what this Other is (see also Burrell and Dale, 1998).

One of Deleuze and Guattari's overarching theoretical endeavours is *nomadism*. Wandering is the key activity in which they seek to engage. There is no ultimate aim or direction. What is sought is a headlong flight from the centres of power. It is decidedly non-linear. In cartographic terms, they offer us a picture of the terrain where humans can *deterritoralize* and act in a nomadic way. 'We think too much in terms of history, whether personal or universal', said Deleuze. 'Becomings belong to geography' (Deleuze and Parnet, 1987: 2). Thus they speak of a *plane* of organization and a *plane* of consistency (Bogue, 1989: 152–3: Goodchild, 1996: 158). In discussing the first plane – the plane of *organization* – they often express the word plane as plan(e) to highlight the role of plans and this plane in forward-thinking human life. This first plane is a hidden principle which can only be induced or inferred from that to which it gives rise. It is the plane of organization *or* development. It is structural (or genetic) and gives rise to both structure and origin at the same time. It is 'the structural plan(e) of formed organizations with their developments, the genetic plan(e) of evolutionary developments with their organizations' (Deleuze and Guattari, 1988: 265). More important, however, is that this plan(e) always concerns the development of forms and the formation of subjects.

The second plane – the plane of consistency – contains no forms and no structures, no genesis and no development. There are only relations of rest and movement. These relations are between unformed elements which taken together nevertheless make 'collective assemblages'. This plane of movement knows only latitude and longitude and speeds. In a typical attempt at disruption of everyday meaning, Deleuze and Guattari say, 'we therefore call it the plane of Nature, although nature has nothing to do with it.' Notice here that no reference is made to plan(e). For in the plane of consistency there are no plans and no forms. The two planes are, or appear to be, in 'clear and absolute opposition' (1988: 265). In their view (1988: 268), the plan(e) of organization is upheld by Goethe and Hegel. It is a plan that is occupied by the 'abstract machine' which consists of immanent relationships in the form of a recipe. We are told that for these two luminaries, 'the plan(e) must indissolvably be a harmonious development of Form and a regulated formation of the Subject, personage, or character' (1988: 268). The plan(e) of organization covers the area that Deleuze and Guattari call stratification. It stands for hierarchy. I would argue that the plane of organization also signifies the conjunction of linearity, control and death. Opposed to it is the plane of consistency, where we might seek to explore. And who would be our guides? Nietzsche and Kleist, it is argued by Deleuze and Guattari, are concerned with the true soul of movement in the (decidedly unplanned) plane of consistency. They are associated with open, external fields. And at this most basic level, new planes of consistency can be constructed through more movement and nomadism by human beings. Indeed each of the 15 chapters of *A Thousand Plateaus* is presented as a plane of consistency which traverses many different disciplines. Each chapter is a *plateau* which is connected to each of the others, though not in some complete integrative way.

In reading *A Thousand Plateaus*, we do not have to be exceptionally perspicacious to see that Deleuze and Guattari privilege the plane of consistency over the plane of organization. Those who view themselves as theorists of the plane of organization would be seen by Deleuze and Guattari, one suspects, as dealing with an inferior, subordinate level of understanding. In my terms we would be seen as locked into the unhealthy and static conjunction of linearity, control and death. For we lack the nomadic spirit. In Deleuze and Guattari's metaphor of vegetation, the place of the structured tree of knowledge, with its brown narrow trunk leading to a mature lushly green growth and an open canopy of surface approaches, gives way, as they talk, to an exploratory *rhizome*. Rhizomes wander in a multiplicity of forms which are to hard to see and hard to predict in their location. For Deleuze and Guattari (1988: 3–25), unlike the arborescent tree, which is visible, hierarchical and predictably straight, the rhizome assumes very diverse forms as it ceaselessly establishes subterranean and grounded connections. Whilst the rhizome is made up of lines or lineaments, most importantly, the arboreal world is made up of lineages. Whilst the tree is a centred system with pre-established paths, hierarchical modes of communication and seeks to develop its selves further, the rhizome cares not for reproduction of self. It is acentred, non-hierarchical and anti-genealogy. It is an assemblage. And so too is *A Thousand Plateaus*. There is always the possibility of change, Deleuze and Guattari argue. They are unhappy with the notion, typically derived from a deep structuralism, that all is given and pre-ordained. Their orientation stands against the unchallengeable and the unquestioned. Fluidity is all. Determinism is out. No plans. No organization.

Nomadology, one plateau within *A Thousand Plateaus*, had such an impact that it was produced and published separately in 1986. Here, Deleuze and Guattari offer notions, concepts and provocations which have a clear relevance for organization theory. They argue in dichotomies. They say 'the war machine is exterior to the state apparatus. . . . It is the invention of the nomads. . . . The very conditions that make the state possible . . . trace creative lines of escape' (Deleuze and Guattari, 1986: 1; 1986: 49; 1986: 13). Typically the *war machine* does not necessarily have war as its object (Deleuze and Guattari, 1986: 110). Deleuze and Guattari's labels have to be read by us very circumspectly. Also annoyingly typical of their work is a reliance upon argument by analogy, and in this section their case is built upon the theory of games. That having been said, in this instance it is a very powerful analogy! Chess is a game of state. It is played by the Emperor and his courtiers. The pieces are coded, having intrinsic properties from which their situations, confrontations and movement are derived. They have qualities which are fixed and powers which are relative. Go, however, is played with pellets, disks, simple arithmetic units which are anonymous. These pieces have no intrinsic properties, only relational ones. Go pellets have a function of exteriority, located as they are within nebulae or constellations. They function to border, to shatter or to encircle. Chess pieces, on the other hand, have bi-unique relations with each other and thus their functioning is structural and internal. Their spaces are therefore different. Chess, the game of state, is a war but it is one with fronts. Go, the game of nomads, is a war without battle lines. Chess operates within a space that is striated. It is a space that is regulated, codified and quartered. The board governs all movement. In Go, space is *smooth* for it is open and it is possible to spring up at any point, without departure or arrival, without aim or destination. It is deterritorialized. Thus, the war machine is like the game of Go and the state apparatus is characterized by chess. I would argue that chess is a game of linearity, control and death. Go is a game of control and death only.

Deleuze and Guattari argue that it is a common confusion to see the war machine as identical to the state. 'The state has no war machine of its own' (1986: 6) for it is against war. They assert that 'the more discoveries archaeologists make, the more empires they discover' (1986: 14), implying that the state is as old as humanity. But so, too, is the exteriority of the war machine. Associated with the war machine is non-state science, which is characterized by the dominance of hydraulic metaphors not structural ones, with becoming and not being, with smooth space not striated space. This is what constitutes *nomad science* rather than royal science.

The state has always attempted, Deleuze and Guattari argue, to control nomad (or minor) science and subordinate it to royal science. The *compagnonnages*, or associations of journeymen, were roving groups of skilled labour. The state sought to sedentarize them and thus submit them to regularization and to governance by a hylomorphic model. The space inhabited by the nomad is a smooth space over which he [*sic*] slides and distributes himself. In a strange paradoxical way, however, the citizen of the city, which is a highly striated space, moves all the time across and between boundaries whilst the nomad '*does not move*' (Deleuze and Guattari, 1986: 51). He does not move because deterritorialization converts the earth for him into one homogeneous place – the steppes, the desert, the ice fields. For 'nomads have no history; they only have a geography' (Deleuze and Guattari, 1986: 73). The state seeks to capture all space and all movements within it. The nomadic thinker seeks to travel in a homogeneous space outside the imperial boundaries. Thus:

> On the side of the nomadic assemblages and war machines, it is a kind of rhizome, with its gaps, detours, subterranean passages, stems, openings, traits, holes, etc. On the other side, the sedentary assemblages and State apparatuses effect a capture of the phylum, put the traits of expression into a form or a code, make the holes resonate together, plug up the lines of flight, subordinate the technological operation to the work model, impose upon the connections a whole regime of arborescent conjunctions. (Deleuze and Guattari, 1986: 109)

This is another way of expressing the alternative possibility to the triadic linearity, control and death relationship.

One of Deleuze and Guattari's most difficult notions is that of a '*body without organs*'. For example, they describe metal as 'neither a thing nor an organism but a *body* without organs' (1988: 411). But what is, in terms of their own notation, a BwO? On 27 November 1947, they tell us, the writer Antonin Artaud declared war on organs. Why? Well, in a large number of cases of the psychologically 'disturbed' (for example, the hypochondriac, the paranoid, the drugged and the masochist), their desire is for their bodies to be sucked dry, sewn up and rendered empty. But bodies without organs are not fantasies of this kind where a longing for an emptiness of structures is what is being sought by the client on the psychoanalyst's couch. Since organs are a block to the flows which surround us, we must see the body without organs as assemblage of intensities through which the body is filled.

The crucial step is to move beyond the disturbed human's search for the organless and empty body to embrace a much more productive search for the organless yet *full* body. Structures in the form of organs are replaced by processes in the form of energy flows.

Deleuze and Guattari's ideas are of profound interest to those charged with understanding *the organ-ized*. For they are suggesting that the concern for organisms is a disturbed interest. The 'BwO is not the opposite of the organs. The organs are not its enemy. The enemy is the organism' (Deleuze and Guattari, 1988: 158). For the organism is stratified, subjected to science, stolen. One is labelled a deviant if one refuses to be an organism, refuses to be organized, refuses to open up one's body to surveyors. Deleuze and Guattari argue that the way forward is to dismantle the stratified organization of one's bodily organs. Hence, 'bodies without organs' are conceptualized as 'real inorganization', and real inorganization is much more interesting than the fixed, delimited and measured world of the plane of organization. Indeed, it is psychologically healing to 'disorganize'. They continue to play with this basic evaluative distinction and dichotomize between assemblages of war (weapons) and assemblages of work (tools) (Deleuze and Guattari, 1988: 399) which mobilize passions of different orders. The work regime is inseparable from organization and the development of Form. It relates to a passional regime of 'feeling'. But feelings are displaced and resisting. The regime of the war machine, however, is one of *affects* not feeling and is associated with the active discharge of emotion. Affects are active but feelings are passive. We, as organization theorists, do not rate a mention in this discussion of course, but we can hazard a guess that theorists who talked about organization, for them, would be concerned with assemblages of work and deal only with passive feelings. We would have no affect!

In the Preface to *Anti-Oedipus*, Michel Foucault says that Deleuze and Guattari are confronting three enemies of differing powers. These are 'bureaucrats of the revolution and civil servants of truth' (Deleuze and Guattari, 1984: xii); 'psychoanalysts and semiologists of every sign and symptom – who would subjugate the multiplicity of desire to the twofold law of structure and lack' (Deleuze and Guattari, 1984: xii–xiii); and 'the fascism that causes us to love power' (Deleuze and Guattari, 1984: xiii). This is a perspicacious commentary for, in the book, capitalism is the focus of attention. The Oedipus complex ensures that human desire is concentrated in the nuclear family where it can become individualized and thence commodified. Feelings are to be regulated in terms of their economic value. 'Schizophrenic' is the label we attach to those in whom Oedipalization has not taken and who have not found a way of acting on their desire. For Deleuze and Guattari, desire is a primary force that is produced. It is a process – not an absence nor a presence. They use the term '*desiring-production*', which neatly combines both a Marxian and a Freudian orientation. This combination works because of the development of a psychological model based on the experience of psychotics (Bogue, 1989: 90). We have already seen that the conceptualization of the body possessed by this grouping is often expressed in terms of ridding their body of all its organs. This is what Artaud himself desired. Deleuze and Guattari use the concepts of 'desire' and the 'body' to bring home their concerns about the importance of the physical and the personal to the psychological and the psycho-analytical. The body is quite, quite central to their work. When they talk of *desire* what they mean is something located on the plane of consistency connected to the body without organs. Every time desire is uprooted from this plane 'a priest is behind it' (Deleuze and Guattari, 1988: 154). The latest in a long line of priests is the psychoanalyst, they suggest. If they were interested, perhaps, one might suggest the theorist of organization, too, for nomination to this particular priesthood.

In summary, it has to be said that Deleuze and Guattari continually resort to the dichotomy as the defining way of analysis. It is my argument that they utilize dualisms to subordinate one perspective to another so that in their terms the 'line' where there is a 'lack' is downgraded in favour of the 'line' in which the fluid and the unusual exist. There is a *flight* from the centres of power to a nomadic existence within negative space. Negative space (which of course they value most positively) appears on the right of Table 8.1. On the left of the table appears the arboreal world in which theorists of organization may be thought to exist. It is the world which embodies linearity, control and death.

Most commentators on the writings of Deleuze and Guattari see them as adventurous, exciting and very different. So do I. The major problem I see in their work is the emphasis on dichotomous thinking. Despite clearly expressed objections to dialectical thinking and its emphasis on the lack (which is fully recognized), there is no doubt that in the depths of their writings they continue to privilege one side over the other. For example, there may not be a 'synthesis' in what they seek but there is a clear privileging of the plane of consistency and the rhizome over the plane of organization and the arborescent. Their language is difficult and deliberately

TABLE 8.1 *Some Deleuze and Guattarian Dichotomies*

The plane of organization	The plane of consistency
Organs (ization)	Bodies without organs
Work regime	War regime
State	War
Tools	Weapons
Form	Energy
Structure	Restlessness
Striated space	Smooth space
Abstract machines	Nomadic assemblages
Edifice	Orifice
Plugging of holes	Gaps, spaces, holes
Royal science	Nomad science
Reterritorialization	Deterritorialization
Arboreal	Rhizomatic

discomforting. They tend to adopt self-defined neologisms and their arguments shift throughout the course of a 'plateau' or chapter. Overall, however, they adopt what is discernible as, to use an old fashioned term, an anti-organization theory. This is where its power comes from and whence its attractiveness to colleagues derives. Its relevance to us arises from this very stance. One does not have to be a Situationist (Plant, 1992) to say, 'What we do is not nomadic. What we do is hierarchical. What we undertake is state science. Let us break free from it.' Deleuze and Guattari will certainly help us to articulate this, even if, unfortunately, not realize it.

Where, then, to find the nomadic? Where then to find approaches untouched by the arboreal? Consider the world of punk. In Fred Vermorel's discussion of the work of Vivienne Westwood, we see the influences upon the art college crowds of the period 1967–77. Dada, Situationism and even Stirnerism were all very popular, but as Vermorel says

> There are intriguing similarities between the relationships of the elite Situationist Internationale with their student and working class 'cannon fodder' and the Sex Pistols' management team's (Glitterbest) relationship with the youthful punks of 1976. (1997: 180)

These similarities were that of taking original material of some profundity and sloganizing it for maximum impact with an audience which was likely to be very hostile. The punks were given a voice but the book claims it was the voice of Malcolm McLaren, who was Vivienne Westwood's partner at the time. And it was in the interests of his career and income that the nomadic was advocated. The conduit for the nomadic may not have been internally generated from within punk at all.

Similarly, in academe the nomadic life is difficult to find, let alone sustain. For the organs of publication require a shared imperial language for commercial reasons. Their readership is often defined by the fact that it supposedly shares a common vocabulary. Their editors and publishers are worried about subscription rates and new business. Journals *are* a business! Those outside the state philosophy have smaller market opportunities and are less likely to be catered for. Should nomads subscribe to journals anyway? How might the nomad write? Should the nomad write?

Probably not. Yet I began this chapter with a crude assertion in writing that linearity kills. In suggesting a link between linearity, control and death, my argument, it may well be said, does violence to the issues and uses linearity as best it can in the development of the case. In place of linearity it is important to seek alternatives which are not simply elegant geometries. Deleuze and Guattari's notion of nomadic science gets us away from spirals and circles. It places random walks in our way. But would you read something that was as random as a nomadic trek?

A return to Figure 8.1 ends the chapter. As has been pointed out, the tree of knowledge is presented here. What might be needed is not so much a chopping down of the tree and the nurturing of the rhizome as a fundamental rethink as to what is knowledge itself. And in that very difficult recon-ceptualization can we begin to think without polarized dichotomies? And if we did think differently, how could we ever let anyone know? Indeed, could we ever become destructured bodies without organs and in so doing escape from linearity, control and death? Yes, but that way madness lies.

9 An Organization is a Conversation

Gerrit Broekstra

Playing God is a self-appointed role that many top managers tenaciously cling to. Despite a transforming world, they appear to be mesmerized by the illusion of being in control. Judging from their behaviour, these super-managers still fancy themselves sitting at the apex of a command-and-control hierarchy, in possession of ultimate authority, and in the secret belief of omniscience. Etymologically, hierarchy derives from the Greek words *hieros*, meaning 'holy', and *archein*, meaning 'to command'. Therefore hierarchy means 'holy management,' which is taken all too seriously by these managers and, in the comfortable warmth of their omnipotent aureole, by the devoted high priests of the corporate staff *curia*.

One day, these self-serving autocratic command-and-control pyramids will have become a tourist attraction. Many companies are already on their way to replacing such structures by more entrepreneurial democratic network organizations; systems of loosely coupled autonomous units held together by a common values-based vision (Broekstra, 1996b). Responding to an increasingly 'critical', intrinsically out-of-control (Kelly, 1994) business ecosystem, agile corporations are learning to run faster in order to hold the same place. The machine paradigm of control is thus being replaced by the ecological paradigm of autonomy and networking in which the maintenance of a robust identity and organizational resilience amidst intermittent avalanches of discontinuous change becomes an overriding concern (Bak, 1996). Not management, but how to *un*manage organizations has become the problem.

As cybernetician Francisco Varela (1979) put it, under the control perspective organizational interactions are characterized by *instructions*, where the unsatisfactory results are *errors*, to be dealt with through a carrot-and-stick system. Autonomy, however, means *self-law*, definition from the inside, assertion of one's own identity and self-organization. Control stands for external or *other-law*, definition from the outside and other-organization. By contrast, under the autonomy and network perspective, organizational interactions occur through *conversations*, and its unsatisfactory results are breaches of understanding (Varela, 1979: xv).

In this chapter I will build on these insights from cybernetics and its (post)modern offspring, the emerging science of dynamic complex systems. The outcome will be a new perspective – one of a triune architecture of organizing, and a complementary appreciative methodology for organizational change and renewal.

How To Do Change in Theory

Paradigms give rise to theories, whether explicitly formulated grand, general theories, perhaps in search of the ultimate reductionist ideal of a Theory of Everything, or small, privately held, mostly tacit theories, also called 'local knowing' (Okuyama, 1996). Everybody has theories about everything, particularly about one's self. This is how paradigms work. Through habituation and socialization, paradigms provide us with unquestioned assumptions and expectations of how to deal with one's self and the world. Theories thus become ways of acting.

Control-oriented managers hold a common background theory, perhaps even subconsciously, of how to change their companies based on control and instructionist intervention from the outside. This approach largely ignores the local knowing in and of the social system which is implicit in its autonomy – an autonomy resulting from self-organizing forces within the global system. Here, the experience of psychotherapy is relevant to organizational change. The Japanese child psychiatrist-cybernetician Makiko Okuyama (1996) noted that general background theories, though important for communication purposes in the community of therapists, are likely to have very little impact on the success of the therapy applied to a client system. By contrast, 'conversationalist managers' adhere to a different theory of change which tends to pay heed to the local knowing in and integrity of the social system as a self-organizing ecology of conversations, and the stories and metaphors associated therewith. They attempt to catalyse some form of self-control through dialogue and sharing. Obviously, both theories are not equally effective. So, let us examine the practice of theories a little closer.

Paradoxically, the problem with the practice of management is the dominance of theories. Whether they are home-made, of the motherhood/apple pie variety, or of an allegedly grander nature, and whether we refer to them by fancy names like mindsets, world views, philosophies, theories of action, paradigms, or just beliefs, rules of thumb, common sense or practical policies, most of them are, by any standards, largely untested. The question arises whether they primarily serve the purpose of communication among theorists and of anxiety reduction among managers, or whether they are intended to improve the change skills of so-called change agents.

Worse, we may observe a widespread lack of understanding of the epistemological role of theories in the practice of organizing, particularly where matters of radical change or transformation, rather than incremental change, are at issue. Indeed, with the prevailing Cartesian control-driven management culture in the West, it is about time we started to recognize that today's fervent peddlers of business fads, prime instances of theories in disguise, behave like the proverbial emperors of change who do not possess clothes.

Modern management culture abounds with untested and uncritically embraced theories of which we hardly know anything. Business techniques like re-engineering, total quality management, the learning organization and core competencies have claimed universal success as how-to-do-things differently. However, over the past decade, this unusual outburst of modern Taylorism provides excellent examples of how-to-fail differently (Broekstra, 1996b: 54). Change programmes are characterized by a typical Cartesian approach focusing on some part of the whole, whereas a transformation demands a focus on the whole, that is, on the organization as a total system. A holistic approach is required that pays heed to the integrity and self-asserting tendencies of the whole system of organization. Therefore, these transformational attempts are typical instances of what Michael Beer and colleagues (1990) have appropriately termed the 'fallacy of programmatic change'.

Yet, at a deeper level of understanding, change programmes are examples of the epistemological fallacy of confusing the domain of the system's experiential phenomenology with the domain of description. In such circumstances observers formulate theories about the system arising from their explanatory and communication needs. Thus, entangled in the circularities of their own observations and descriptions, theories inevitably may express more about the holders of the theory than about the system. Emphasizing the self-referential nature of observations, cybernetician Heinz von Foerster did not tire of emphasizing that 'anything said is said *by* an observer, *to* an observer', which could be oneself. This proposition implies the core of second-order cybernetics as an essentially constructivist epistemology, biologically, linguistically and socially conditioned. It gives rise to three fundamentally interrelated components: the *observer*, as the one who makes descriptions; what he or she thinks and says in *language*; and the *society* that observers constitute in talking to each other. More significantly from an epistemological point of view, 'you need all three in order to have all three' (von Foerster, 1979: 5–6; see also Glanville, 1996).

As a consequence of the intimate connections between observer, language and community, it is essential, according to Varela (1979), continually to perform a methodological bookkeeping of sorts by distinguishing what pertains to the system as constitutive of its phenomenology, from what pertains to the needs of the domain of cognitive description. Obviously, this position applies particularly to delicate human situations of integrity where improvement is needed through therapy or organizational change. This is why second-order cybernetics is sometimes alluded to as a theory of the observing system, that is, the observer. This is to be contrasted with first-order cybernetics, which is mainly a theory of the observed system. As such, it is worth noting that the inclusion of the observer in the domain of his or her observations has been recognized as a 'strong contribution to post-modernism in organizational theory' (Gergen, 1992: 216).

The Constructive Nature of Theory and Discourse

Theories belong to the domain of cognitive description and explanation which is also the consensual domain of language. Indeed, theories are often said to be ways of looking at the world. As the physicist David Bohm (1980), addressing the Cartesian problem of fragmentation of human consciousness, has argued, a theory is an insight, but not a description of the world as it really is. Derived from the Greek *theorein*, meaning 'to view' or 'to look at', a theory is, as it were, a self-constructed lens through which an observer views reality. The lens will determine what he or she will be able to see, and not see, and the view that unfolds is therefore not to be regarded as a representation of 'absolutely true knowledge of how things are' (Bohm, 1980: 5). Resonating with Varela's above distinction, Bohm noted that confusion of the two levels, theory and 'reality', is the cause of numerous problems, the least of which is our fragmented and politicized world of organizations as it has evolved under the Cartesian paradigm.

Bohm's (1980) view indicates that theories are not just innocent ways of looking; there is more to it than this, since the two levels interact, and theories thus become constructive of reality, particularly so since they always arise within a consensual domain of discourse through language. However, in the realm of therapy and organizational change, we do not often realize that theories are far from 'objective' ways of looking. We are not inclined to put objectivity in brackets. Clearly, enclosed within socially consensual domains, and through the distinctions they make, theories are active ways of 'bringing forth' their objects. Indeed, we act mostly subconsciously, through our tacit or explicit multiple theories; and through our actions, we create our multiple realities which in turn influence our theories, thus creating a self-fulfilling situation.

So, in fact, theories are not representations of the world at all; they are a way of worldmaking, of constructing *a* world, not *the* world. This point of view has also been eloquently clarified by psychotherapist Graham Barnes (1994) when he expressed his concerns about 'how to do therapy in theory'. His compelling answer is to view psychotherapy as a conversation. And conversation requires establishing a shared language among the participants viewed as autonomous entities engaged in an ongoing process of mutual structural coupling to accomplish social coordination of action. Barnes conceived a conversation as a complex braiding of language, body and emotion. However, for most therapists, the theory of psychotherapy becomes a way of seeing, thinking, speaking and acting, such that

> The theory as a language speaks through them. The theory creates its objects. The objects of the theory appear as the theory constructs them. The theory hides its constructive activity. The theory in itself becomes the objects. Thus the objects are the patients. The patients, as the objects of the theory, their diagnosis, therapy and cure, are products of the theory. (Barnes, 1994: 165)

The therapist whose diagnosis builds on the patient's dreams will induce dreaming in the patient. When resistance to change is part of the theory, resistance will occur.

The intricate problems and questions of psychotherapy as revealed by Barnes' and Okuyama's points of view and also Maturana's influence on family therapy (see Mingers, 1995) present a welcome alternative metaphor for the realm of organizational change. It may be relevant to ask change agents the same questions that Barnes asked of practitioners of psycho-therapy theory. He asked not only what we are doing with our theories, but also 'What are our theories doing through and to us?' These questions are not simple to answer. To ask 'Can we do without theories?' is like asking whether we can do without our fantasies. It is itself a theory of no-theory. By their very nature, we have to admit that mindlike activities are self-referential and locked into a minefield of circularities.

The Cybernetic Epistemology of Change

We must reduce the primacy of context-free, general theories, like most of the managerial change programmes claim to be, because, in doing and redoing change management, these theories will inevitably turn into top-down control from 'without', and, concomitantly, increase resistance to change. A revolutionary insight from second-order cybernetics is that instructive interventions will fail because an essentially organizationally closed system responds by compensating for the imposed disturbances in ways that are determined by its own structure, and that do not reflect the intentions of the intervenor. By contrast, involved in a pathological social system manifested by, for example, antagonistic conversations, the change catalyst can act as follows. He or she can help build, in a bottom-up manner, a local theory among its constituting participants, including him- or herself, to establish self-understanding and to induce new conversations to achieve new self-descriptions.

Here, modern cybernetics provides some general guidance. It contends that all humans are 'non-trivial, self-referential machines' and that the resulting autonomy means responsibility for one's self. In such an instance the ethical imperative is to 'act in such a way that the number of possibilities increases'. Furthermore, because of the embodied closed self-referential dynamics, logically, there even exists a 'fundamental impossibility of active intervention in another's operational space' (Bardmann, 1996: 211; von Foerster, 1993).

This resonates with Maturana's social theory, which starts with humans as autonomous, autopoietic (self-producing) unities essentially embodied in their structure-determined nervous systems. Though organizationally closed, these unities are interactively open through the plasticity of their structures. Maturana asserts that a social system, though not itself autopoietic, emerges as the *medium* through which the human autopoiesis is continually realized through recurrent conversations. Human components of the social system do this through *languaging*, involving language, body and emotions by developing a history of structural coupling. This will generally lead to considerable structural changes, so-called 'ontogenetic drift', somewhat equivalent to the concept of adaptation, though basically their own individual autonomy and integrity is maintained (Maturana and Varela, 1987). These insights are reinforced by the findings of the new sciences of complex dynamic systems.

The Science of Organized Complexity

Cybernetician Stafford Beer argued that, whereas management is the *profession* of effective organization, cybernetics is the *science* of effective organization (Beer, 1985: ix). The implication, of course, is that management has a lot to gain by taking to heart the laws and principles of 'communication and control' in complex systems, whether 'animal or machine' (quotes from the original definition of cybernetics by Norbert Wiener, 1961). Wiener's definition would still be a fair description for the new science of complexity, which has to do with pattern, order and structure. In short, the definition can be applied to 'organization' as it spontaneously emerges in complex dynamical systems characterized by non-linear recurrent interactions. Both cybernetics and the science of complexity can be viewed as parts of an overarching science of complex systems which has been evolving since the middle of the twentieth century (Broekstra, 1994).

The science of complexity recently gained popularity through the writings on complex adaptive systems as developed by the Santa Fe Institute (Kauffman, 1993; Langton, 1989, 1992; Lewin, 1992; Waldrop, 1992). It has also gained momentum owing to the work on self-organized criticality (better known as the sandpile metaphor) by those at the Brookhaven National Laboratory (Bak, 1996; Bak and Chen, 1991). Like the more simple systems of chaos theory, non-linear complex systems are known for their unpredictability. The weather is an example of a system in which many components interact in complex ways. The geophysics of earthquakes with their characteristic 'punctuated-equilibrium' behaviour presents another. The so-called 'butterfly' effect symbolizes the non-linear effects of sensitive dependence on initial conditions in such systems. Small local changes may at one time lead to catastrophic avalanches sweeping through the entire system; at another time nothing much happens.

Self-organization in complex dynamical systems may also lead to the spontaneous emergence of order, even if the system is a massively disordered system such as in random Boolean networks. This is the revolutionary domain of people like Stuart Kauffman (1993), who believes that Darwinian natural selection in evolution as the sole source of order has been heavily overrated and does not answer the question of how sudden order arose in the first place. The essence of the argument is that order is generated as an inevitable, natural product of the intrinsic dynamics of the system itself. As the compelling motto goes: 'Order is free.' Thus, whether we are interested in the sudden origin, development and disappearance of a depression spiral in the weather system, or in the popping-up of a thought in the brain, or in the characteristic flocking of birds, or the emergence and subsequent decline of civilizations, or the pattern of warfare frequencies in the world system (Byron, 1996), emerging ordered patterns can be observed all around us, and can only be understood properly from a holistic and evolutionary rather than a reductionist perspective.

Perhaps one of the most intriguing findings of complex systems science is the hypothesis of the *edge of chaos*, a state of a complex system which is poised between stability, or frozen order, and chaos, or complete disorder. The daring hypothesis of Kauffman is that natural systems have a tendency to move towards the edge of chaos, where they achieve maximum creativity, adaptivity and exquisite self-control – in short, maximum life. Likewise Per Bak (1996) has argued that large complex systems tend to self-organize into a poised, *critical state*. However, Bak has shown how a system can self-organize to a critical state, whereas Kauffman's systems require careful tuning. Nevertheless, all this emerges from the internal dynamics from within the total system itself, not from some external driving force. In this far-from-equilibrium critical state, the system is loosely coupled; a pattern of near-decomposability, as Nobel Prize winner Herbert Simon (1962) intuited a quarter of a century ago, when he aimed to provide an 'evolutionary explanation of hierarchy'. In these near-decomposable systems, Simon argued, interactions among subsystems are weak but not negligible.

A similar position is held by Kauffman (1993). His results on random Boolean networks seem to fit well with Simon's qualitative argument. With tight coupling between the components, any small change would sweep through the entire system causing chaos. In Bak's terms, it would be supercritical. With hardly any coupling, local changes would remain localized and the system remains more or less frozen into its existing order, that is, subcritical. This image provokes an excellent idea of what may happen in a social system-in-crisis, constituted as it is by a network of loosely coupled conversations; a state imagined to be analogous to a critical far-from-equilibrium state. The intriguing phenomenon of *organized criticality* (Bak, 1996) may apply in this poised state. An inverse power law may govern the extent of communications sweeping through the crisis-ridden social system: small ones (micro-conversations: people standing together in small groups) are very common; large ones (macro-conversations: big crisis meetings) are more rare; intermediate ones fall in between.

Self-organization and Emergence

For our purposes it is most pertinent that the new science of complexity stays close to the concrete phenomenology of complex dynamical systems and their rule-based behaviours, whether they be the brain, an ecosystem or a social organization. The complexity perspective follows a bottom-up, parallel-processing, distributed-control approach in which local interactions within populations of semi-autonomous entities are governed by a system of usually simple rules. When recursively applied to individual behaviours and interactions among the components of the system, unpredictable, global behavioural patterns may, under certain conditions, be observed and these appear lifelike. Local rules or principles embodied in the organization of the system generate global orders. In short, simple systems generate complex patterns. To use the Santa Fe credo propounded by Nobel Prize winner Murray Gell-Mann, we are able to observe 'surface complexity arising out of deep simplicity' (Lewin, 1992: 14).

Self-organization, self-reference and emergence are pivotal notions in these complex adaptive systems. Here, phenomena emerge from local neighbourhood interactions among individual components who have mostly only local knowing of their situation and who are born or socialized into some tacit system of rules. In computer simulations, the emphasis is basically on the specification of generative rules for the 'individual parts of a system, which are then 'turned loose', and allowed to interact with one another' (Langton, 1992). A compelling example is provided by the simulation of the complex phenomenon of birds' flocking behaviour. Each of these computerized birds, or boids, first studied by Craig Reynolds, was subject to only a small number of rules, such as each individual bird should try to match its speed with its immediate neighbours, and should avoid bumping into them and other obstacles in its path. The amazing thing is that, as the boids begin to move according to these simple rules, over time, through their self-organizing interactions, characteristic bird flocking patterns and movingly realistic encounters with obstacles emerge on the computer screen. In keeping with the observations of cybernetics, note that a lot of energy may be dissipated in the system, yet it is the recurring 'communicative' interactions among the boids that are the significant factor for dynamic order to emerge. In other words, self-organization presupposes a physical world made of matter and energy, a point that is often missed by social constructivists.

To develop a sense of how the system works as a whole, even in this simple example, we may already discern the importance of three levels that make up the whole organizing system, including the observer: one is the level of rules; the second is the level of the interactive system of discrete boids itself that is brought to life by recursively applying the rules to the local interactions and individual behaviour; finally, we have to discern the level of the observer describing, from a culturally embedded consensual language system, certain global emerging patterns in the complex system as a whole. We may assume that the birds themselves, focused on their local environment, have no notion of their global flocking behaviours. In reflexive human systems such as social organizations, where the observers may themselves be participants in the operation of their 'social flocking', this level of cognition, as I will call it, will in turn influence the other two levels by changing the rules, or the degree and nature of connectedness in the system, and so on.

Including the observer in the whole system of organizing is akin to the step taken by second-order cybernetics and results in the complexities of self-reference already discussed above. Furthermore, complex systems science has taught us the importance of the emergence of spontaneous organizational closure (Varela, 1979). This means that closed networks of recurrent interactions, of which autopoiesis in physical systems is a special case, are responsible for a complex social system's autonomous and conservative behaviour (Broekstra, 1997). It is to be remembered that these complex adaptive systems, along with their components, may be organizationally closed, but are interactively open. Kauffman (1993), for example, referred to the phenomenon of closure as 'catalytic closure'. It is very much related to the origin of strange attractors identified by chaos theory: global states in the state space of the whole system toward which the system is attracted, as manifested by the example of a whirlpool in a stream of water. In this state the system appears to resist perturbations, and acts so as to internally compensate for perturbations in maintaining its identity. Transformation is then viewed as a system moving to another part of the state space where it may display unexpected new and unintended behaviours. All of this sounds already familiar to cyberneticians.

I would like to build on this wealth of exciting new ideas about the dynamics of organizing and, if only metaphorically, achieve some new understandings for the field of corporate renewal. Going beyond metaphor, I would like to utilize this material in order to achieve fresh inroads to effective change. The complexity perspective will lead to a far deeper appreciation of the constitutive order-generating, order-maintaining and renewal capacities of social organizations than the standard approach which relies mostly on static conceptualizations. For example, a business organization is often described as an open system which copes with a turbulent environment by choosing an appropriate strategy, fitting its structure to align with the strategy and leveraging its core competencies and key resources, all of which presupposes clear cause and effect relationships. Understandably, upon implementation, resistance to change emerges as a nuisance to be forced out of the system.

Obviously, in this description there is no reference at all to the interlocking local activities of the organizational actors nor to the self-organizing circular socialization processes established by previous expectations and habituations. The complexity perspective basically regards strategies, structures and cultures as global descriptive constructs to be explained in the first place from the local recurrent conversational interactions of rules-driven individual human components of the system. As said, particularly in the complex realm of organizational transformation, the bottom-up methodology advocated by complex systems theory would require a focus on the re-specification of the rules, which, like genetic codes, govern individual behaviours and neighbourhood interactions of the human agents in the evolving system. This is what happens when, for example, people are put into a parallel, orthogonal organization of project teams in which they assume new roles, new relationships and new responsibilities. Engaged in new conversations, they start to construct new scripts, new identities of self, and shared and contested meanings (see Woodilla, this volume).

The Triune Architecture of Organizing

To capture the essence of the bottom-up organizing process in complex social systems, a simplified descriptive model of three interrelated levels is proposed (see Figure 9.1). The multilevel generative description is adapted from the Santa Fe scholar Chris Langton's description of the dynamics of emergent properties in complex adaptive systems (Lewin, 1992: 13).

Through the dynamics of vertical feedback interactions between the levels, the whole system is to be regarded as a three-in-one, or triune architecture of organizing. The essence of the structure is the epistemological distinction, discussed above, between the cognitive level of description and the experiential level of operational interactions. However, since both levels, cognition and social interaction, are interrelated in a feedback relationship of mutual specification, the duality of theory and (inter)action, subject and object, of knower and known tends to dissolve. It is implied that social reality is a social construction, indeed, that theory and practice form a unified whole. In fact, within this conceptual framework constructed by us observers, the nature of the relationships between the cognitive and phenomenological level may be postulated to constitute an autopoietic conceptual system of ideas and concepts interacting with actions/communications; that is, it is actively self-producing. Although social autopoiesis has problems of its own (Mingers, 1996), this conceptual meta-formulation comes closer to Luhman's (1986). The whole system acquires a self, and tends to maintain this self or identity against outside disturbances. In this way the whole triune system constitutes a dynamic socio-cognitive gestalt.

Looking at change in real social systems from the perspective of complex systems cybernetics, this distinction is also essential because a great deal of attention should go to the conversational exchange of messages in the system: the particular use and deconstruction of language, stories, rituals, myths and fantasies (Gabriel, 1995). To study the pathology of conversations in social organizations, we know from the work of Watzlawick et al. (1967) how important it is to look at both the content and relationship aspects enclosed in a single message. The model in Figure 9.1 explicitly recognizes these findings from the field of pragmatic communication, which, incidentally, relied heavily on insights from cybernetics. Watzlawick's fundamental axiom is that all behaviour is communication, and that it is impossible not to communicate. This implies that all organizational behaviour is conversation and, likewise, that, despite attempts of control-oriented

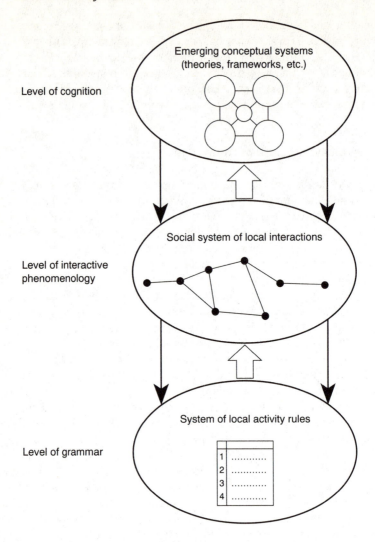

FIGURE 9.1   *The triune organization of the organizing process*

managers to avoid conversation within the organization, it is impossible not to converse in organizational contexts. As a result of this ignorance, schizophrenic organizations are a widespread phenomenon.

Operating principles of selectivity and self-sealing of particular behaviours and actions become apparent when we realize that the emerging social organization, produced and reproduced by the network of intended and unanticipated actions and interactions through a history of structural coupling of its components, in turn 'selects', that is, constrains or enables, only those behaviours of participants that are compatible with their individual structure-determined constitutions. As explained earlier, this mutual structuring of the social organization acts as a medium for human autopoietic components. The selectivity of behaviours and actions aids in explaining the conservative, organization-maintaining tendencies of social systems, that is, their organizational closure. Furthermore, this causal circularity of structuring and selectivity exhibited in social systems can also be understood as the operation of unobservable rules governing the selection of (inter)actions and generating the observable behaviours. For generative purposes it is therefore important to consider a separate level of rules (see Figure 9.1). Again, to a certain degree, rules and social interactive organization can be viewed as mutually specifying and reproducing systems (see also Mingers, 1996, for a comparison between Maturana's and Giddens's social theories). We will now briefly discuss the three levels in some more detail.

The Level of Grammar

The lowest level is the level of rules. Rules are interpreted broadly as all those directions which govern behavioural repertoires of the actors at the next higher level, and which govern the interactions between them. A simple kind of rule is: *If* (condition), *Then* (action).

We talk of rules as rules of the game. They may vary from specific organizational rules, guidelines and procedures to more general policies, strategies and systems. Rules may be explicit, but mostly are tacit (see Figure 9.2). Through socialization and habituation people are no longer aware of them, or would have difficulty explaining them. A useful distinction may also be between algorithmic and heuristic rules. Algorithmic rules are specific and variety-reducing: the 'dos' and 'don'ts' of the organization. Heuristic rules are more general and capable of generating variety; corporate values are a good example (see below).

Rules may be written or unwritten. Scott-Morgan (1994) argued that the most important rules that govern people's behaviour in organizations are unwritten, or tacit, and more often than not provide hidden barriers to change. He also suggested setting up conversations where people talk about specific business issues. To uncover the unwritten rules related to these issues, he advised focusing on what is being said about: (i) what is important to people; (ii) who is important to them; and (iii) how they go about getting what they want.

Although this naked truth about a ubiquitous organizational practice may come as a shock to organizational idealists, it resonates fascinatingly with the cyberneticians' recognition of a social system as the medium in which, most importantly, the autopoiesis of individuals is realized and maintained, and in which we can imagine that structural couplings are realized that minimize undesirable triggers and foster desirable ones. Scott-Morgan's position thus appears to reinforce the strongly biopsychological foundations, as advocated by second-order cybernetics, of the practice of organizational conversations. As Stafford Beer has pointed out, even at the level of institutions as a whole in their environments, the maintenance of their

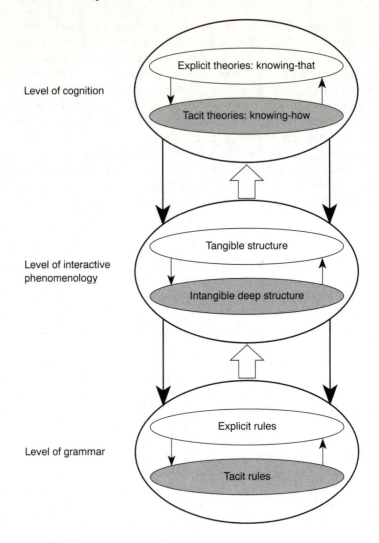

FIGURE 9.2   *The tacit and explicit organizations*

identity appears to be the most important thing. Indeed, 'being in the business of preserving its own organization' leads to a tendency to become 'pathologically autopoietic' when customers are subtly treated as obnoxious triggers (1979: 405).

Scott Morgan contended that unwritten rules are the crystallizations of perceptions that people hold of the organization's written rules and management actions. In other words, and as illustrated in Figure 9.1, they are the outcomes of dynamical processes of cognition at the highest level. The vertical downward arrows in Figure 9.1 are therefore also meant to indicate that the level of cognition and the level of rules are directly connected.

If *shared* by a community of actors, constituting a consensual domain, this level of rules underlying the system of local interactions at the next higher level may also be referred to as the *grammar* of the system. Karl Weick (1979) appropriately employed the term 'consensually validated grammar' as an essential ingredient for organizing interdependent actions. Finally, it should be noted that, in any company, despite a common set of rules, for example certain corporate values and norms, a set of different grammars may coexist. For instance, the rules governing behaviours and interactions in the production department will differ from those used in the marketing department. As a result they play different games.

The Level of Interactive Phenomenology

This represents the level of the dynamics of recurrent interactions among the social actors of a complex adaptive system, and their experiences. The essence of the behavioural relationships at the level of phenomenology is communication, in the broadest sense, verbal or non-verbal, between the actors of the system. The sum total of the communicative relations in action is called a conversation. As said, I will adhere to Maturana's point of view that conversations are a linking of language, bodyhood and emotions.

At this point it is important to stress that in explaining the autonomous behaviour of living systems, Maturana and Varela (1980) make an crucial distinction between *structure* and *organization*. Since, however, the latter term is so overworked, I have come to replace it by the term *deep structure* (Broekstra, 1996a). Structure, then, refers to the tangible, observable or explicit aspects of the social system of interaction, and deep structure to the intangible, unobservable or tacit aspects (see Figure 9.2). This is somewhat similar to the definition of deep structure adopted by Gersick (1991) where he discussed the punctuated-equilibrium paradigm of organizational trans-formation. In understanding change, Gersick refers to this 'most critical' concept of deep structure as the 'highly durable underlying order' which 'persists and limits change during equilibrium periods, and as what dis-assembles, reconfigures, and enforces wholesale transformation during revolutionary punctuations' (1991: 12–13; cf. Bak, 1996).

According to Maturana and Varela (1980), deep structure refers to the relations that essentially define a complex system as a whole entity, a unity, belonging to a particular class. It determines its identity. Deep structure is defined independent of the tangible properties of the components of the system; it has no connection with materiality. To give a static example, an object becomes a member of the class of chairs by virtue of certain relations between components that we refer to as legs, seat and back. The set of relations that determines the pattern that makes it a chair and not, say, a table is called the deep structure. What materials the components are made of is immaterial for this cognitive classification. The *structure* of the chair is formed by the actual relations between the concrete components that make the system a concrete entity in a given space: my worn-out leather easy chair in the study. Deep structure thus determines the properties of the system as a whole.

Going further than Maturana and Varela, who sometimes appear to employ the terms as merely descriptive, I attribute a more formative or generative role to the deep structure in that, in a sense, the tacit deep structure realizes the explicit structure. As already described above, in essentially far-from-equilibrium conditions, through self-organization and organizational closure, and through interaction of all levels, a social system consisting of basically autopoietic humans attains and maintains an identity of its own. This is highly reminiscent of Roberto Unger's (1987) intriguing concept of *formative context* constituted by the recurrent interactions of the 'imaginative schemas' (our cognitive level) of participants with their 'institutional frameworks' (our level of interaction). The formative context is an essentially tacit and resilient phenomenon which attributes a *false necessity* to social arrangements. Unger believes that society 'always stands at the edge of a cliff', and that, although obscured, social systems are therefore more or less arbitrary, and real opportunities exist for change (see also Blackler, 1992). This strongly resonates with the poised critical state thought to exist in self-organizing ecosystems. The false necessity becomes apparent when the system itself is considered to be a component in a period of stasis in a larger ecosystem in a state of self-organized criticality. For long periods of time it may falsely perceive itself to be in a stable situation, until it is hit by an inexplicable intermittent burst of catastrophic changes originating elsewhere in the ecosystem of organizations it is a part of, but erroneously thought it had grown immune to.

The approach to corporate renewal advocated here is heavily based on the insights of complex systems theory, which finds that self-organization of the system is a powerful driving force in the spontaneous emergence of relatively stable patterns of conversation. This phenomenon is thought to be due to a natural tendency of complex systems to achieve circularities of conversational interaction through organizational closure in their deep structure. It constitutes the basis for an explanation of their self-perpetuating capacity towards, even 'arbitrary' (Unger, 1987), autonomy and the maintenance of sometimes 'pathologically autopoietic' identity (Beer, 1979). This kind of closure is easily observed in social systems when we think of, for example, the dynamics of socialization and habituation, which includes the interaction with the level of cognition to be discussed below.

It is noticeable that – and here the whirlpool in a stream of water is a simple metaphor to keep in mind – whereas matter and energy may be abundantly dissipated at the level of structure, the focus of the attention should be directed to the mechanisms in the deep structure that cause the closure in the system to occur and that drive the characteristic pattern of a whirlpool. In the same vein, one could ask what deep pattern of relationships makes us observers call some social organization 'a bureaucracy' despite visible differences in services, people, systems, and so on, in its structural aspects. Humans are clearly deep-pattern recognizers. Likewise, by virtue of common deep structures, and despite widely different product offerings, technologies, structures and people, we are able to characterize business organizations, whether banks or supermarkets, uniquely as typical defenders, analysers or prospectors (Miles and Snow, 1978).

The Level of Cognition

There is no more terse definition of cognition than that of von Foerster, who paraphrased it as 'computing a reality', or, similarly, as Maturana and Varela would put it, 'bringing forth a reality' (see, for example, Brier, 1996). Considering that for von Foerster reality may also be equivalent to community, the intricate interlock between the previously discussed level of social interaction – we can say level 2 – and the level of cognition (level 3) becomes immediately apparent. Nevertheless, experience may be considered to be primary (level 2) and cognition secondary (level 3). The cognitive level is therefore analytically distinguished as the level of the observing system, that is, the observer (which may be a collectivity). As such, it is the consensual domain of descriptions and explanations.

In the Western world, the domain of knowledge would primarily mean *explicit* knowledge. However, cognition encompasses both explicit and tacit knowledge (see Figure 9.2). To Michael Polanyi we owe the distinction between tacit and explicit knowledge, which expresses that the body of our knowledge extends far beyond what we can express: 'We know more than we can tell' (1966: 4). This distinction and the dynamics of interchange between the two types of knowledge are, for example, applied in a seminal theory of organizational knowledge creation developed by the Japanese organization theorists Nonaka and Takeuchi. They rejected the typically Western inclination to define knowledge exclusively as explicit, something that can be put in 'words and numbers', and is transmittable in formal language. Tacit knowledge, they argued, although 'not easily visible and expressible', is a much more powerful category in explaining, for example, innovation in successful Japanese companies (1995: 8).

In brief, tacit knowledge is 'deeply rooted in an individual's action and experience, as well as in the ideals, values, or emotions he or she embraces' (Nonaka and Takeuchi, 1995: 9). It is therefore highly subjective and context-specific. Insights, intuitions and hunches, for example, are tacit knowledge. Nonaka and Takeuchi distinguished two dimensions of tacit knowledge, technical and cognitive. The technical dimension relates to skills and crafts, the *know-how* of a person, or, at the level of the organization, its competencies and capabilities embedded in the social interaction system. The cognitive dimension pertains to mental models, beliefs and perceptions reflecting 'our image of reality (what is) and our vision of the future (what ought to be)' (1995: 8). Beliefs, ideals, values, visions and emotions all belong to this category of tacit knowledge, which, with its 'soft and qualitative elements', Nonaka and Takeuchi believed to be 'crucial to an understanding of the Japanese view of knowledge' (1995: 8).

It is noteworthy that the tacit–explicit distinction is virtually compatible with Ryle's (1949), who distinguished between *knowing-how* and *knowing-that* in elaborating his concept of mind.

Tacit knowledge is also viewed as context-specific and relational, that is, socially constructed as it is generated dynamically at the level of the social interaction system. At this level, tacit knowledge is exchanged by the sharing of experience through the conversational processes of *dialogue* and imitation, a process known as socialization. Nonaka and Takeuchi asserted that, although not easily communicated, 'the key to acquiring tacit knowledge is experience' (1995: 63).

According to Nonaka and Takeuchi, systematized systems of concepts and explicit ideas emerge at the level of cognition through a complex process of knowledge conversion consisting of four stages (thought to be embedded at the level of cognition in Figure 9.2). These are: socialization (tacit to tacit), externalization (tacit to explicit: upward arrow), combination (explicit to explicit) and internalization (explicit to tacit: downward arrow). It should be noted that conversational instruments like metaphors, analogies and stories in general are liberally used in the socialization and externalization modes.

Looking now for a moment at the relationships between the three levels, we could say that the upward arrow from the level of the social interaction system to the level of cognition has a twofold meaning. First, it emphasizes the *emerging* character of knowledge, rooted in local experience, local tacit knowing, and externalized into explicit theories. These, in turn, may be ordered in a hierarchy of context-specific theories, like Drucker's (1994) 'theory of the business' at the bottom, and grand, comprehensive but context-free theories at the apex. This is contrary to the primacy of 'top-down' explicit, context-free theories. Second, the upward arrow symbolizes the process of *sense-making* (Weick, 1995) that continually goes on, at both the tacit and explicit level. The downward arrows from the level of cognition to the level of social interactions indicate the *action* or constructive perspective of knowledge or theories, as a generic term. This view is reinforced by splitting off the level of grammar, which can be thought of as the system of action rules that are implied by or generated by the level of cognition. Thus, contrary to the logical positivist belief, theories are highly normative in shaping social action.

Finally, the whole system of interactions between the levels stands for the self-perpetuating, or rather autopoietic, nature of the whole social-organizing process. The system self-organizes to attain the status of a self, such that theories about reality, action, social interaction and sense-making form an integrated whole with a specific identity, a socio-cognitive gestalt. As such it is hard to transform. Using Unger's (1987) terms, it attains the status of a false necessity. Thinking about it in this circular way, the dualities between subject and object, knower and known, observer and observation, understanding and action, theory and practice, body and mind, become more or less irrelevant, indeed, tend to evaporate.

The Tacit Organization

It now becomes quite useful to think in terms of a *tacit organization*, constituted by taking the three lower, tacit parts of each level of the organizing process together, and, likewise, the *explicit organization*, formed by the three upper, explicit parts in Figure 9.2 as two disjunct, but interrelated 'organizations'. This evokes the image of a deep organizing process taking place at a tacit level, which constitutes the unobservable and virtual living soul of the organizing process and a more visible organizing process, which is, so to speak, only the tip of the iceberg.

I believe this distinction has a lot of merit, considering that commonly managerial control, if not the whole of the managerial praxis, is directed at the interactively open explicit organization, which is subject to the imperative of economic rationality. By contrast, the tacit organization represents the organizationally closed, deep natural system, the autonomous generative source of organizational life. To use Gouldner's original distinction of rational versus natural system models (Thompson, 1967), a synthesis of two opposing approaches in organization theory is thus suggested. Also the dialectical conflict between, and the organizational dilemmas resulting from, the interlinked, but often incongruent tacit and explicit organization become quite apparent by this distinction.

Argyris and Schön's (1978) theory of organizational learning beautifully resonates with the distinction I propose to make between the tacit and explicit organization. First, reinforcing the importance of distinguishing a level of rules in the organizing process, they argued that a collectivity of people becomes organized when they create *rules*, such as those for decision-making, delegation and membership. Second, they also introduced the tacit dimension by asserting that 'rulemaking need not be a conscious, formal process. What is important is that member's behavior be rule-governed in the crucial respects. The rules themselves may remain tacit' (Argyris and Schön, 1978: 13). They gave some well-known illustrations of tacit rules governing behaviour: protect yourself unilaterally; protect others unilaterally; control the situation and the task (1978: 40). These rules are assumed to be embedded in what they repeatedly referred to as the 'behavioural world' (our level of social interaction), to be contrasted with the largely cognitive enterprise of organizational learning (level of cognition).

It is useful to pursue Argyris and Schön's (1978) ideas a little further. They argued that theories of action are either 'explicit,' called the *espoused theory* (embedded at level 3 in our explicit organization), or 'often tacit', the *theory-in-use* (embedded in our tacit organization, also at level 3). The latter, according to Argyris and Schön, is to be constructed from a description of actual behaviour. The organizational theory-in-use, they contended, may also 'remain tacit' because 'its incongruity with espoused theory is *undiscussable.* . . . Whatever the reason for tacitness, the largely tacit theory-in-use accounts for organizational identity and continuity' (1978: 15). This strongly supports what I have said above about the autonomous, identity-maintaining behaviour of the tacit organization. The suggested incongruity between the tacit and explicit organization is an important theme in the change methodology to be discussed below. Argyris and Schön's conception of double-loop learning, along with their belief that 'organizing is a reflexive inquiry' (1978: 17) and that in interventions an 'increase in control . . . in many cases, appears to reduce the present level of organizational effectiveness, while adding activities that make the system more rigid' (1978: 159), strongly resonates with the idea of symmetry-breaking through orthogonal conversations in the change methodology to be discussed below.

Naturally, transformational or second-order change should be directed primarily at the tacit organization to elicit, through symmetry-breaking, *deep change* of the whole system, rather than just a part of it. Transformation is holistic. As I have tried to indicate, alterations in conversational practices (sharing, dialogue and discussion) appear to be the keys to transformation of social practices. However, first-order or incremental problem-solving change mainly implies tinkering with the explicit organization (Argyris and Schön's [1978] single-loop learning). Needless to say, confusion between the two types of change processes spells disaster, as managers, perceiving the need for and aspiring to transformation, apply explicit theories in the form of business fads to the explicit organization while being unaware of the underlying generative tacit organization. The latter organization is the result of virtually tacit evolutionary processes taking place under the surface of appearances. It is the systemic cause of so-called 'resistance to change'.

The current approaches to second-order organizational change are in line with the Cartesian fallacy of defining the world in terms of problems that need to be solved, rather than in terms of awe for the outcomes of self-organizing evolutionary processes that we hardly understand (Broekstra, 1992). The preliminary insights from complex systems science may hopefully lead to a revolutionarily different understanding of the 'origins of order' and to a deeper respect for the positive implications of self-organizing evolution in complex social systems and in all natural systems. Further, a different approach to developing change methodologies may emerge which aligns rather than battles with the evolutionary tendencies of such systems. An attempt at developing a new strategic change methodology based on the above philosophy and epistemological framework will be summarized below.

A Company's Idea System: Values, Vision, Concepts

From a series of action research projects in diverse industries, I have developed an organizational renewal methodology which is anchored in the complex systems ideas unfolded above. As a part of this, a particularly useful guiding instrument in strategic conversations is a self-construction of the company's idea system thought to be embedded in its distributed mind.

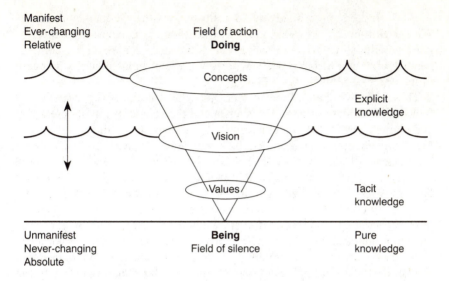

Manifest
Ever-changing
Relative

Field of action
Doing

Concepts

Explicit
knowledge

Vision

Values

Tacit
knowledge

Unmanifest
Never-changing
Absolute

Being
Field of silence

Pure
knowledge

FIGURE 9.3   *A company's idea system*

The representation of this in Figure 9.3 is to be thought of as a more refined elaboration of the level of cognition in Figure 9.2.

Adding a touch of romanticism, three levels can be distinguished, metaphorically representing the *body* (doing), *mind* (values, vision, concepts) and *soul* (being) of an organizational unit as a living system. The core of the framework is the mind enwrapped in the dialectic between *being* and *doing*, a distinction I owe to Richard Pascale (Goss et al., 1993). Before a company complies with its natural urges to continually engage in action, it is advised to contemplate its reasons for being. This should be a reflection on the authenticity of its self or identity, its core values and beliefs, and its sense of purpose acquired through a long history of structural coupling. Such a proposition appears to be of considerable value in the light of the findings of, for example, Collins and Porras (1994) on visionary companies. A similar view is held by Kotter and Heskett (1992), who found in their research on the relationship between culture and performance that high-performing companies have adaptive cultures where people have bought into a timeless philosophy or a particular set of core values, including those that pertain to continuous change.

One step deeper, beyond the relatively enduring core values representing a company's relative being, is a step into the metaphysical, the *corporate soul*, so to speak. It is a natural step to include in the framework a reference to the perennial wisdom of ancient philosophies that speak of an absolute state of stillness and unified wholeness, whether the unnameable is called Being, Tao or Self. It is described as the ultimate ground of self-reference, something which should appeal to a sense of consistency in modern systems thinkers. Indeed, in a highly lucid contribution, the German philosopher Werner Strombach drew the ultimate (meta)logical conclusion about systems thinking: that its core subject of 'wholeness can never be comprehended without a metaphysical anchorage of the phenomenon of wholeness in the order of being' (1983: 71).

The (collective) Self, as the ancient Upanishads assert, is supposed to be a transcendental state of complete silence and the source of infinite creativity and knowingness, which can be reached by appropriate meditation. Expanding the distinction of tacit and explicit knowledge, I have therefore added a third category of knowledge, that of *pure knowledge*, as the ultimate source of corporate wisdom into Figure 9.3. It also serves as a reminder that it may be quite effective to precede a period of 'brain-storming' the corporate mind by a brief period of 'brain-stilling' in order to shake off ordinary shallowness of thinking and reach deeper levels of silence. This is indeed a technique advocated by the modern Indian management scholar Chakraborty (1991), who advocates in his country a stronger reliance in modern business on the authentic core values of ancient Indian culture than is currently the case, given the prevailing enchantment by American and Japanese pop management cultures.

The inverted pyramid in Figure 9.3 also symbolizes the bottom-up evolutionary progression from relatively timeless and enduring point unity to the volatile and multiple diversity of the ecology of ideas and concepts in the more relative regions of the corporate cortex (Broekstra, 1996b). Embedded in the ecology of ideas of the distributed strategic mind three sublevels or stages are distinguished: the articulation of values, of vision and of concepts. These three sublevels themselves, recursively, map onto the whole triune architecture of Figure 9.1, representing the level of rules (values), the social-interaction system (vision, as its future envisioned state) and the cognitive level itself (concepts).

The idea is that the three sublevels stand for: (i) a connection of the social-organizational system with its past, through its authentic core *values* which constitute its genetic code or guiding principles; (ii) a connection to the future by an inspiring *values-based vision* representing a company's ambition or mission (in this way, the past is connected to the future); and (iii) bringing the future back to the present, the stage of articulating *concepts*, which implies the making of choices for courses of action. For this stage, I have been using a conceptual framework developed years ago, called the Consistency Model. It is a holistic, yet pragmatic way of elaborating the values-based vision into concepts, and for guiding choices with respect to products, markets, technologies, strategies, structures and people (Broekstra, 1984).

Finally, the wavy lines, getting stronger and going upward, indicate increasing volatility and readiness for change, and hence a capability for flexibility. The wavy line that forms the separation between tacit and explicit knowledge, as indicated by the vertical arrow, may normally be way up in the diagram. This is the usual case of a virtually *closed* corporate mind, where values, vision and even most concepts have fallen (if they were ever explicitly known) into dark subconscious oblivion. This was the case at Ford Motor Company in the early 1980s. In a state of deep crisis, it turned to a wrenching reflection on its authentic values and guiding principles. These were already espoused as 'spiritual principles' by its founding father, Henry Ford, in the early part of the twentieth century. Having dusted them off, the management at Ford breathed new life into them in order to reinvigorate the company (Collins and Porras, 1994).

The idea is, of course, that inner (tacit) conversations through meditation and outer (explicit) conversations through sharing, dialogue and discussion bring the separation line downwards, symbolizing enhanced awareness and articulation of a company's core values, vision and concepts. In fact, both Collins and Porras (1994) and Kotter and Heskett (1992) have found that those visionary or adaptive companies that are rooted in a deep awareness of their enduring core values actively preserve their core. By virtue of such awareness these companies have developed a strong sense of purpose and are able to achieve great things. Having the stability of enhanced awareness apparently brings forth the confidence to be also the most active in stimulating progress, as if manifesting an internal drive to stay ahead of the world's turbulence. Similar to personal life, an attitude of self-referral due to a deep experience of Self is deemed to be more effective and powerful than one of other-referral, where one is continually seeking the approval of others and is influenced by fleeting circumstances. The ultimate other-referral is the 'fully saturated self' that has 'become no self at all', the apocalyptic description of the postmodern predicament (Gergen, 1991: 7). Other-referral is essentially fear-based, and the deeper cause of the need for controlling others.

The VVC (Values, Visions and Concepts) Renewal Methodology

Most companies on the verge of renewal do not just have a *problem* which, if properly diagnosed and analysed for its causes, could be solved by creating straightforward solutions. Diagnosis is always 'theory-laden'. There are always multiple interpretations of descriptions of reality involved, probably as many as there are coalitions. If this is ignored, what is essentially an intricate *problem situation* can become pathologically distorted by political game-playing among the actors in the social system who hide their games behind pseudo-cognitive reasoning. It may be better to disregard 'the problem', since problems are never solved at the level at which they seem to occur.

The approach followed here is decidedly different. It is founded on the living-systems philosophy outlined above. Hence, it appreciates the operation of a life-giving generative context, the tacit organization, and the distributed nature of the corporate mind. Furthermore, in keeping with cybernetics' ethical imperative to always increase the number of possibilities, it assumes that the world is always full of business opportunities. The core assignment faced by corporate renewal is, in principle, to match these potential *opportunities* with the organization's potential *capabilities* through a shared *values-based vision*. To achieve this coherent strategic focus and intent, as well as widespread commitment, it is suggested that strategic conversations are used to organize and articulate the company's idea system. In short, get everyone responsible for the system in the room.

What follows is a brief description of the VVC methodology that has evolved from action research and from consulting and which is oriented towards helping companies enhance their institutional leadership by self-renewal. It may be noted that, in spirit, there is an interesting parallel with the form of action research called *appreciative inquiry* (Cooperrider and Srivastva, 1987). Moreover, the recent publication of Emery and Purser's (1996) book on the Search Conference showed that an open-systems planning methodology for community action is surprisingly close to the independently developed VVC methodology. A synthesis of both methodologies is a subject of further research.

- Step 1. *Contextual appreciation*, requiring a raising of awareness, the creation of context, making contact with what's going on in the world and assessing the need for transformational renewal. This step is used to induce meaning, explore shared ideals, and mobilize energy.
- Step 2. *Systems appreciation* reliant on the articulation of authentic *core values*. Dialogues are produced on why people think the company exists and on what it stands for. People are explicitly asked to come up with stories, myths of striking events, or tales of heroic deeds from the past of the company. These conversations usually provide inspiration and liberate psychic energy, which can be applied to nudge the sometimes 'frozen' system further towards a critical state.
- Step 3. *Values-based visioning*, whereby, on the basis of the core values, the company's *vision* is carefully formulated as a future self-definition. I found a modified version of the concept of the *driving force* (Tregoe et al., 1989) as the centre of gravity in the value-creation process to be a helpful tool to link values consistently with vision. The vision usually unfolds as a short story rather than as a catchy motherhood slogan.
- Step 4. *Concept formation*, through which a unified system of *concepts* is developed; basically a set of codes of how to get to where the vision points. It is unfolded with the help of a conceptual framework (Broekstra, 1984) emphasizing consistency. Much more detailed work emerges now, such as the formulation of strategies, product–market matrices, value chains, systems, strengths and weaknesses profiles, and so forth, all tested against the values-based vision that provides the necessary focus. People are now ready for making choices. (Although this description is brought about in a linear way, naturally, backtracking and criss-

crossing occur quite often, making it a far more complex and, at times, emotionally wrenching process.)

- Step 5. *Action projects*, whereby in all cases of organizational renewal, and following the conceptual stage, so-called 'breakthrough projects' are formulated to induce new behaviours. I believe that to get things moving the tacit organization should be left unaffected at first. As Michael Beer and his colleagues (1990) argued, manifestations of the tacit organization such as structures and systems are the last thing to change. So, from the start of the whole process, people work explicitly in a parallel, orthogonal organization of multi-functional teams. These orthogonal conversations are focused on getting things done, on results, whilst at the same time learning to play with new behaviours. As Beer (1990) argued, being placed in an '*ad hoc* organization' of new roles, responsibilities and relationships, people learn the rules of a new game, new patterns of social interaction and develop new organizational capabilities. A new deep structure is thus gradually evolved and experimented with, outside the 'false necessity' of the old system, in protected niches which eventually, it is hoped, 'predate' the old tacit organization. Nonaka and Takeuchi (1995) suggested a similar set-up with what they called a 'hypertext organization'.
- Step 6. *Closure*, based on the gestaltist argument that when a cycle of new experiences of raised awareness, energy mobilization, action and contact has been accomplished, it is important that the cycle is closed. This closure represents a moment for drawing meaning from the process, settling any unfinished business, and preparing for the next stage of continual renewal (Nevis, 1987).

Conclusions

The VVC renewal methodology relies essentially on the idea of the organization as a conversation. It assumes that organizing occurs in processes of sharing, dialogue and discussion of ideas, whether tacit or explicit, and that these create reality and meaning. The conversations are not *about* the social relationships; they *are* the relationships. The organizing process is continually reproduced and constituted in a loosely coupled network of many micro-conversations and builds on local knowing. The latter is particularly important to realize since in most companies people at the local level, almost to the point of social saturation (Gergen, 1991), are immersed in communications with the organization's outside environment – even more so than with those within. This conversation overload in itself continues to blur the boundaries between the organization and its environment and continually threatens to cause internal disorientation, and, in time, an identity drift.

The corporate strategic mind is a distributed process, driven, as it were, by a virtual formative social context, the tacit organization. Rather than being obsessed by control, the managerial focus should be on dialogue and self-organization. It should be immersed in creating coherent institutional leadership, a process which I characterize as *un*management. Organizing the conversations founded on a values-based vision shared at the individual level creates a coherent direction for the organization as a whole, an internalized shared focus. The conversations of organizing, in a self-referential way, create flexibility.

The VVC methodology recognizes, builds on and, indeed, respects the social system's qualities of self-organization and emergence. Acquiring a new organizational identity thus becomes a matter for inclusion by those constituting the system, fostering active participation in bringing forth new consensual domains of language and action. Thus, the spiritual core of the methodology operates from an evolutionary perspective, thereby attempting to work *with* evolution rather than against it.

10   Metaphor, Language and Meaning

Didier Cazal and Dawn Inns

In this chapter we critically assess some of the principal claims that have been made about metaphor in organizational analysis. We then present our own assessment of the value of metaphor in the study of organizations. Throughout the chapter, we are operating with a definition of metaphor given by Cuddon. To him, metaphor is 'A figure of speech in which one thing is described in terms of another' (1991: 542).

Claims About the Value of Metaphor in Organizational Analysis

We feel that claims about the value of metaphor in organizational analysis can be divided into three broad types: those concerning its role in the structuration of organization theory; those concerning metaphor and the discursive texture of organizations; and those concerning metaphor as an ethnographic tool.

The Structuration of Organization Theory

It has been argued that metaphor can shed some different light on the theoretical developments in organizational analysis. In this way the classical pitfall of a 'historical' presentation of schools of thought in organization theory is bypassed. In this latter view, schools follow one another throughout history, from the rational school, to the school of human relations, followed by the contingency school and ultimately the cultural school. Knowledge is assumed to be developed during a continuous and cumulative process which constitutes progress: each school capitalizes on the attainments of former ones, by criticizing or completing them, so that the evolution of knowledge is achieved.

   Such an allegedly historical presentation clearly yields to an evolutionary and linear view of theoretical developments in organizational analysis which has long been criticized by historians and philosophers of sciences (see also Burrell, this volume). It eventually appears to be supported by an organismic metaphor: knowledge is conceived like an organism with its own progress, learning and change (Schlanger, 1983: 147). As underlined by Schlanger (1971), such a Lamarckian conception of evolution typically dates from the nineteenth century.

In sum, presenting the field of organizational analysis in terms of metaphors provides an expanded view because it is then portrayed as a heterogeneous field composed of a number of schools which rely on different world views. Moreover, such a presentation avoids any normative assessment of these schools, for instance in terms of 'newer', thus 'better'.

Metaphors and the Discursive Texture of Organizations

Another claim is that the use of metaphor acknowledges the importance of language in organizations and organizational analysis. For instance, according to Morgan, it 'provides us with an effective means of dealing with [the] complexity, the ambiguity and the paradoxical nature of organizations' so that 'we can read the same situation from multiple perspectives in a critical and informed way' (1986: 322).

This view is relevant to organizational analysts as well as practitioners. Morgan's argument is that people and organizations tend to act or think according to implicit metaphors of, for example, action, others and organizations – and then 'to get trapped by the images they hold of themselves' so that the basic problem is 'that genuine change requires an ability to see and challenge these self-images in some way' (1993: 288). The issue is, then, not to replace the prevalent hidden metaphor by another one, more efficient or relevant than the former. What is at stake is to highlight this metaphor, to emphasize its merits and limits, and to show how alternative metaphors can give complementary insights.

In short, a major contribution of metaphors to organization theory, as viewed by those such as Morgan, is that they enhance our ability to develop multiple interpretations. Morgan advocates 'a style of critical thinking that recognises how analysis and management are always based on an interpretative process that can take many forms according to the paradigms, images, or metaphors that are used to frame inquiry' (1988: 239). In this respect, Morgan has brought a valuable contribution to organizational analysis.

Metaphor as an Ethnographic Tool

It has been claimed that metaphor can be a useful tool in ethnographic research. The ethnographic approach to research starts from the belief that meanings are not given but are actively constructed by participants through interaction and negotiation. We should therefore recognize that 'The world is not already there, waiting for us to reflect it' (Cooper and Burrell, 1988: 100).

Organization theorists, in common with other social scientists, have the central aim of understanding events, perceptions, actions and situations from the participants' point of view, and of conveying these to readers removed from the setting described. They are therefore involved in the active processes of interpretation and representation of reality. From an ethnographic perspective, this involves three stages.

First, the researcher must gain access to the meanings given by participants to events in a specific context. Qualitative research is judged on how accurately the researcher has been able to penetrate these meanings. Easterby-Smith and his colleagues sum this up in the form of a question: 'Has the researcher gained full access to the knowledge and meanings of informants?' (1991: 41). Second, ethnography involves drawing together the perceptions and feelings of participants and arranging these into some kind of order; prioritizing and sorting what is central to an understanding of a situation from what is peripheral or incidental. This is what Rapport calls 'the considered ordering of experience, and the conscious production of meaning' (1994: 19). Third, the researcher must represent these experiences and meanings to readers of texts in a manner which retains the intensity of participants' perceptions but is comprehensible to readers removed from the context.

In the search for methodological tools which enable the researcher to meet these demanding ethnographic requirements, it has been claimed that metaphor offers great potential. This potential has been recognized by various organizational researchers who have explored the utility of metaphor in relation to the three steps of research described above. These are: gaining access to the meanings given by participants to events in a given context; analysing and imposing structure on research material; and conveying meaning to readers.

In relation to the first step, Srivastva and Barrett (1988) reveal how a focus on metaphors used by members of a group can give the researcher insights to hidden, barely conscious feelings which the participants have about being in the group. The use of different dominant metaphors at different times by group members can also show the different stages in a group's maturity. Similarly, it has been claimed that metaphors can reveal thoughts and perceptions that are difficult to articulate. These lie below the level of conscious, rational thought but are intuitive, embryonic understandings which may foreshadow deeper comprehension. As Inns and Jones have argued: 'Metaphors suggest themselves for reasons which may not at first be apparent. It is important to explore and capture these intuitive impressions' (1996: 120). As regards the second step, Miles and Huberman (1994) claim that metaphor is useful in analysing research because metaphor acts as a 'decentering device', enabling researchers to see beyond their existing conceptual frameworks and models. Turning to the third step, it appears that metaphor can be used to convey meaning to readers in a text. Morgan's (1986) work is still a landmark attempt at presenting information using a variety of metaphoric perspectives but there are several other examples, including Cohen et al. (1972) and Hedberg et al. (1976). In the same vein, Miles and Huberman (1994) argue that metaphors are useful to researchers because they act as 'data-reducing devices', compactly conveying many connotations and ideas to the reader.

Critical Assessment of Claims

On the basis of the aforementioned claims, metaphor appears to be a powerful tool for organizational analysis at the theoretical as well as the methodological level. But we feel these claims leave some critical questions unanswered and that they ignore some major reservations made by philosophers to an unbounded use of metaphor. A reasonable and well-tempered use of metaphor in organizational analysis clearly requires an examination of these points.

Implicit Metaphors

Alvesson (1993b) addresses criticism to metaphorical approaches to organizations, especially the one initiated by Morgan's 1986 and 1993 work. He argues that 'metaphors normally give a broad and imprecise picture of a phenomenon, unless they are structured in a particular way' (Alvesson, 1993b: 115). The result is that the same metaphor may eventually map onto very different, even competing, approaches to organizations. For example, the culture metaphor, far from conjuring up a unitary image, may lead to a variety of conceptions of the organization. As has been underlined in a number of recent works (for example, Frost et al., 1991; Martin, 1992), it may open up at least three perspectives: one that focuses on consensus through integration; one that takes a differentiation perspective and emphasizes conflicts between subgroups; and one that takes a fragmentation perspective underlining the inherent basic ambiguity which prevails in organizations.

Having identified the way in which metaphors encourage broad and imprecise interpretations, Alvesson goes on to introduce the notion of second-order metaphors. He argues that to some extent the use of a metaphor is informed and guided by another framework, the 'hidden' metaphor. For instance, the culture metaphor can lead to different and even contradictory conceptions because it can rely upon a number of second-order metaphors.

Though we cannot but agree with the starting point for Alvesson's criticism, the conclusions he draws do not fully meet our expectations. The notion of second-order metaphor only shifts the emphasis to another level. Acknowledging that the same name may be utilized for a variety of contents, or that a single concept can be apprehended from different viewpoints, would be simpler and more economic. Clearly, to take Alvesson's own examples, culture is not an object but an already elaborated representation and 'organism in itself functions more as a label or an umbrella concept' (1993b: 118). Culture and organism would be more properly considered as concepts, elaborated in other fields: cultural anthropology and biology (see also Gaill, 1987; Schlanger, 1971). Such a use of the metaphor in organizational theory is conditioned by a prior theoretical elaboration and this may then imply a further elaboration in the 'importing' field. Though Alvesson employs the term 'metaphorical concepts', he does not seem to draw all the implications from the conceptual nature of some metaphors.

Two other criticisms can be made, with some caution, because they are aimed at the potential rather than explicit driftings in Alvesson's approach. First, one may wonder why there could not be third-order metaphors, which may lead – though he repels such a temptation (Alvesson, 1993b: 130) – to an endless recursive game. More simply stated, why should second-order metaphors be less ambiguous, thus less guided and informed by higher level metaphors, than first-order metaphors? According to which criteria can a metaphor be said to be less broad and fuzzy than another? Alvesson acknowledges that 'if all seeing is metaphorical, then this must be also valid for metaphors in themselves' (1993b: 118), and, we would add, for metaphors, whatever their order, if we follow his line of argument.

We do, however, concur with Alvesson when he writes: 'A critical and constructive purpose of interpretation of metaphors is to examine the more basic assumptions of a particular conceptualization of a phenomenon and bring these more clearly to the "surface".' It also invites us 'to go beyond the explicit or surface metaphors used, and look for the underlying image' (Alvesson, 1993b: 117). But some questions remain unanswered: How can basic assumptions be uncovered? What is beneath the underlying image? Should not the various uses he makes of the term 'surface' be metaphorical and thus cover some underlying epistemological assumption? These driftings might derive from him approaching the metaphor as the core unit of analysis.

Second, a more important risk is to view the organization only as a mere text to be deciphered. This position is supported by Morgan, who sees 'organizational reality as a kind of "living text" that is simultaneously "written" and "read" ' (1993: 284). Here the distance between relativism, as it is advocated by Morgan, and nihilism appears at least short. Even to be consistent with the spirit of such an approach, one may wonder which authority (author-ity, as Martin [1992] writes it) the researcher would be vested with in order to unveil games he or she is engaged in, and to reveal the meaning which eludes others. Where or when should interpretation stop, and how does interpretation have to be interpreted?

Critique of Metaphor as Theory

Morgan contends that our 'images or metaphors *are* theories or conceptual frameworks. Practice is never theory-free, for it is always guided by an image of what one is trying to do' (1980: 336). The critical question here is: Must such theories be assimilated with scientific theories? The meaning of 'theory', as this term is employed by Morgan, has thus to be questioned.

Such an approach to theory seems to be shared by, or borrowed from, Lakoff and Johnson: 'our ordinary conceptual system, in terms of which we both think and act, is fundamentally metaphorical in nature' (1980: 3). According to Morgan, 'The real issue is whether or not we are aware of the theory guiding our action' (1980: 336), but this leads to the question of whether our representations, even explicit (considered as such and not as taken for granted), systematically form a theory. The term 'discourse' might well be more appropriate; theory would then be a particular discourse, ruled by specific social standards and academic norms.

While we agree that metaphors provide new insights, we deny that they produce any knowledge by themselves and thus that they can be equated to, or directly generate, any theory. May the various bodies of knowledge relying upon the same metaphor be considered as equivalent? Is it reasonable to assume that there is a unified conception of the machine or of the organism, thus enabling us to find a single, or even only homogeneous, mechanistic or organismic approach to organizations? In this respect, metaphors appear to be an original tool for classifying various theories of organizations, but they do not encapsulate the knowledge provided. Metaphors help in organizing theories of organization, but the latter cannot be merely deduced from, nor reduced to, their underlying metaphor.

What Morgan means by 'theory' might in fact be 'conception' or 'representation'. In this regard, metaphors deserve interest because of the statements they may encourage. In the case of the machine metaphor, this is based on our observing that a machine is made of various specialized parts, organized in a specific manner, and so on. The critical issue here is to what extent such an attribution is knowingly made, on the one hand, and strictly determined by the sole metaphor, on the other. The use of organismic metaphors clearly leads to different views, for instance, in the framework of population ecology of organizations and in that of human relations. In the first case, the metaphor (with a Darwinian perspective) is the explicit starting point for the research programme and the theorization, but in the second case, it is only implicit.

In essence, then, a theory is not merely a set of conceptions or representations, nor is it contained in a single conception. In linguistic terms, it is closer to semantics (articulated statements made of signs, whose meaning is conferred by this articulation) than to semiology (a set of signs, possessing a meaning by themselves, and consequently whose articulation does not actually matter) (see, for example, Ricoeur, 1978). Such a weak conception of theory is obvious with the puzzle metaphor used by Morgan; in this instance knowledge and even theory would simply be the juxtaposition of various components.

Limitations on the Creative Potential of Metaphors

There are three further problems that can be levelled at Morgan's (1986) line of argument in relation to the creative potential of metaphors. In the first place, the bodies of knowledge Morgan presents as based upon the same metaphor are highly heterogeneous, so that the same metaphor apparently results in a variety of theories, sometimes contradictory. In the second place, according to the principle he calls the metaphor's injunction, a given metaphor inevitably leads to a single and well-determined pattern of action. Finally, one can wonder whether a metaphor provides any fixed meaning.

Taking the first of these problems, the bodies of knowledge covered by a single metaphor appear as highly heterogeneous, and one may even doubt that the schools of thought presented by Morgan are actually based upon a unified conception of the metaphorized object. For instance, Fayol, Taylor and Weber are regarded equally as representative writers of the mechanical approach. Critical differences regarding their own purpose, background, conception, proposals and contribution (even misinterpreted) are then underscored. In relation to the second problem, and as was earlier remarked, one can also doubt that most theories are based on a single metaphor. For instance, motivation theories are typically seen as being informed by the organism metaphor (for example, Morgan, 1986: 42–3). However, theories such as Maslow's hierarchy of needs (at least as presented in most organizational behaviour textbooks) have something mechanical about them, in all likelihood inherited from behaviourism. Hence, needs are hierarchized once and for all; higher level needs are activated in a mechanical manner; humans are literally driven by their needs. This point is critical: 'metaphors give us *systematic* ways of thinking about how we can or should act in a given situation' (Morgan, 1986: 331; emphasis added). In other words, 'each metaphor has *its own injunction* or directive: a mode of understanding suggests a mode of action' (1986: 334; emphasis added). This bias in Morgan's reasoning clearly appears when he invites us to 'follow the implications of a powerful image to *its logical conclusion*' (1986: 336; emphasis added). What Morgan calls the injunction of metaphor thus seems highly deterministic: the metaphor used (knowingly or not) would seem to command systematic ways of thinking and then literally dictate the actions to be undertaken. This stance seems rather contradictory with his conception of organizations as ambiguous, since the interpretation made through metaphors is highly unequivocal. It also brings us to the third problem concerning the creative potential of metaphors which is that it is doubtful that they bring any meaning by themselves, or more precisely bring a meaning independent of the conceptual framework, or the issue of concern, for which they are used. Consequently, one might hypothesize that metaphors require interpretation, before being themselves a tool for interpretation of some object or situation.

The Ambiguity of Metaphor

The ambiguity of metaphor raises questions about the 'use' of metaphoric analysis as an ethnographic tool. Yet, in contrast to studies of the use of metaphor in poetry, which emphasize how metaphor draws attention to the ambiguity of language and meaning, the study of metaphor in organizational theory has largely presented metaphor as a rational, reductionist tool that can be usefully employed to aid organizational analysis (Inns and Jones, 1996).

We would now like to explore the claim that metaphor can be used in organization analysis as an ethnographic tool from a Lacanian standpoint. Jacques Lacan has investigated metaphor in relation to the *stability of meaning in language*. His ideas, whilst not directly concerned with organizational research, nevertheless explore the functioning of metaphor and its ambiguity and highlight the difficulty of approaching metaphor as an analytical tool.

Lacan argues that metaphors reveal the instability of meaning in language. This instability, we can infer, leads to a difficulty in, first, fully understanding meanings given by organizational participants, and, second, conveying these meanings to readers of organizational behaviour texts. To ensure that the three stages of ethnographic research described earlier are achieved, there should be a thread of consistency in how language and words are used and understood across participants, researchers and the readers of texts. Such a stability of meaning, which might reside in linguistic terms, has, however, been rejected by Lacan, who argues that the relation of word to concept, or meaning to sign, is much more fluid and problematic, so that: 'Meaning shifts around, and metaphor is the name of the process by which it does so' (Sarup, 1993: 47). In short, metaphoric usage shows how events are perceived and interpreted in multiple ways according to various associations made which renders meaning hard to grasp. Metaphor, therefore, allows for and draws attention to 'the proliferation of meaning' in language (Sarup, 1993: 47). Lacan's work draws on both Freud and Saussure to understand the process of metaphor, and it is useful to investigate briefly their ideas and trace how Lacan builds on this psychoanalytic and linguistic heritage.

Lacan uses both Freud's and Saussure's ideas because he sees the metaphoric process as governing both the conscious and unconscious mind and language. Central to his argument is the idea of movement and the fluidity of meaning. Metaphor, like metonymy, draws attention to the relations, connections and links between terms and concepts in a linguistic system. This is because metaphor involves a *transfer* or *carrying* of meaning from one domain to another. This unexpected transfer produces a new meaning created by the juxtaposition of two realms which are usually kept separate. The claim that metaphor is primarily about movement is also supported by tracing the Greek roots of the word: *metaphora*, transport; and *metaphorein*, to carry (Lemaire, 1977: 192).

This argument has two main implications. First, because meaning does not reside firmly in a concept or word, it can be carried from one domain to another via links of association and similarity. In the new domain it is partly transformed by the new context. Second, the associations made when using a metaphor are not only socially defined but are also individual and idiosyncratic and can only be understood in relation to a personal code of meaning and a specific context. This makes the researcher's task of understanding and conveying the interpretation of reality difficult and elusive.

Lacan's use of Freud and Saussure's work in order to justify his treatment of metaphor does not stop here, however. For example, he draws heavily on Freud's *The Interpretation of Dreams* (1991). Here, Freud argues that the unconscious can be accessed in part via the analysis of dreams. This is because dreams provide symbolic representations of unconscious desires. In order to be represented in images and to avoid the censorship of the rational mind, the dream thoughts must undergo transition. The two processes by which this transition occurs are *condensation* and *displacement*. Condensation refers to the compression of ideas and associations into images or symbols which must subsequently be unpacked to discover their wealth of meaning. Displacement is the process which allows desire to avoid the censorship of the rational mind. Thoughts and emotions are represented in a disguised form and must be interpreted. Displacement involves the transference of meaning from an original sign or signifier to another signifier which then stands in for the original one.

Lacan relates Freud's process of *condensation* to metaphor and the process of *displacement* to metonymy (Lemaire, 1977). He argues that the same processes direct conscious thought and language in the same way that they direct unconscious thought. He articulates the implications of this. These are that meaning is elusive because it can be transferred from one signifier to another, and that condensed images and associations can only be decoded with reference to a personal code of meaning.

Lacan assigned similar importance to Saussure's work and his criticism of representation theory (Culler, 1985). Representation theory states that a sign or 'signifier' in language (that is, a word, sound or image) is clearly linked to a 'signified' (that is, a concept or idea). Saussure rejected this and Lacan builds on this rejection. More generally, Saussure introduced at least three controversial ideas into the field of linguistics (Culler, 1985). These are fundamental to an understanding of Lacan's ideas on metaphor. First, meaning is not inherent and stable in linguistic terms but is a function of relations between terms. Words refer back or forward to other parts of a phrase and to other concepts so that 'Language is not a nomenclature that expresses pre-existing meaning but a structure of differential signifiers and signifieds, which contrast and combine with one another to produce effects of meaning' (Saussure, cited in Culler, 1985: 119). Second, the attachment of meaning to certain signs is for the most part arbitrary. Saussure argues that different languages divide up the world into various concepts and signs and that our perception of the 'external' world could be otherwise. This argument is supported by Leach, who remarks: 'The world is a representation of our language categories, not vice versa' (1972: 47). Third, if the world is a representation of language categories, this means that language is imbued with socially defined values. Meaning is socially created, determines perception and changes over time (Culler, 1985).

If Lacan is correct, the implications of Freud and Saussure's work are as follows: metaphor involves the condensation of associations, images and ideas and a transfer of meaning across domains. These associations may only be fully understood with reference to a personal code of meaning in a specific context; furthermore meaning does not reside in terms and words but in the juxtaposition of various elements. These elements can be assembled and reassembled in many different ways. This leads on to a further argument related to the ambiguity of metaphor: the relational nature of metaphor.

Metaphor and Connections

The function of metaphor seems to be not only to give new perceptive insights, but also to lead continually to other associations. Metaphor shows how meaning is not contained in a sign but refers endlessly to other signs, concepts and ideas – creating what Lacan describes as a 'chain of signifiers' (1977: 154). To quote Sarup: 'Meaning will never stay quite the same from context to context; the signified will be altered by the various *chains of signifiers* in which it is entangled' (1993: 34; emphasis added). Thus, Lacan argues that meaning can be attached to different signifiers which are then attached to each other through links of similarity and substitution. These links and transfers of emotion occur through the processes of metaphor and metonymy and result in a 'carrying over' or 'transportation' of meaning across domains.

The process of metaphor is, then, central to Lacan's view of human experience and, together with metonymy, is the basic process by which both the conscious and unconscious mind operate. Metaphor is fundamental to an understanding of how meaning is elusive and displaced onto different signifiers (that is, words, sounds or images) which combine and refer to each other in relations of similarity and substitution. This leads to Lacan's notion of the 'floating' nature of meaning whereby the 'possibility of signifying something other than what is being said determines language's autonomy from meaning' (Lemaire, 1977: 42).

The implications of Lacan's work on metaphor are particularly pertinent to ethnographic organizational research. Earlier, we said that ethnographic research involves a transfer of meaning across different people: from the participant of an event; to the researcher who interprets the 'text' of the participant's discourse; to the reader who faces the written-up report of the research. We argued that for a chain of meaning to be unbroken, there must be consistency of meaning and understanding across these stages. Lacan's (1977) deep pessimism about the instability of meaning in language would lead him to claim that such a consistency of meaning is impossible. We feel that his work can be tempered with some optimism but that it is useful in highlighting difficulties.

To take the first step in the research process, Lacan denies that the individual subject (in our case the participant of an organizational event) is consciously aware of why he or she is choosing to use certain expressions. According to Lacan, there is a 'subtext' beneath conscious discourse which the conscious subject is not able to control in terms of what he or she conceals or reveals. Expressions suggest themselves for reasons that the individual may not be aware of and the researcher, without access to a personal code, may not be able to accurately interpret the precise meaning of the metaphoric expressions used.

The impact of metaphor means that there may be a 'pseudo-gestalt' (Inns and Jones, 1996). However, unless a metaphor is unpacked for the compact images and associations contained in it, the meaning of a metaphoric expression may not be accurately apprehended by the researcher. In addition, tracing expressions through a 'chain of signifiers' meaningful to the participant must also be difficult and takes a degree of time that the researcher may not have. The researcher must spend a significant amount of time in the setting to have access to Cicourel's 'situational-context-specific' language (1968:160). Some metaphoric expressions used by participants will relate to socially constructed meanings in a given setting. These can only be understood with reference to the particular context and this takes an in-depth knowledge of the setting on the part of the researcher.

The second stage in ethnographic research concerns how the organizational researcher interprets the 'text' of the participants and imposes an order or framework on it. The positivist branch of social science would imply that we can keep the researcher largely outside of the account. Positivistic methodology refrains from admitting, as Geertz does, that what might be being put forward in a piece of social scientific writing is 'our own constructions of other people's constructions of what they and their compatriots are up to' (Geertz, 1973, cited in Rapport, 1994: 9). Researchers select information to include and facts to leave out and present findings using metaphoric expressions. The metaphoric expression that a researcher uses to put forward the information will include a value system, or 'world view', that may not be made apparent or explicit in the writing.

Finally, the instability of meaning, which Lacan draws attention to, reveals the difficulty of the third stage in the ethnographic process; the last stage at which consistency of meaning can break down. This third stage is the text, which the reader confronts and which stands between the reader and the writer. Sartre (1972) discusses how reading is an act of collaboration between the reader and the writer. The meaning of the text cannot be dictated by the writer. Choice of expressions and order of words, what is left out and what is included, can influence perception, but ultimately the reader is as active as the writer in constructing meaning from a text. Each reader will interpret the text, not only influenced by the writer's choice of expressions and values, but also with their own associations, chains of meaning and '(ways of) reading' (Sarup, 1993: 43).

The Value of Metaphor

Our assessing the value of metaphor in organizational analysis stems from our critical assessment of the writers explored in this chapter. We will now further explore the implications for organizational analysis, taking into account the relational nature of metaphor. We will also consider the value of drawing upon Lacan's treatment of metaphor in relation to how humans ascribe meaning to events. Then, in the concluding part of the chapter, we open out the discussion to focus on the value of metaphor as both a language and creative resource.

The Relational Nature of Metaphor

The relational nature of metaphor has been discussed in a number of contexts. For example, Lakoff and Johnson (1980) talk about metaphors in terms of 'experiential gestalt', a position loaded with implications that thus far have not been sufficiently taken into account. Metaphors do have creative power, but not by themselves; rather, it lies in the statements they give access to, and in the webs of significance they are caught in. They put into contact areas in disconnected fields. Similarly, Lévy has suggested that thinking is relational because there is always some previous knowledge, whether it is 'materialized, institutionalized, or internalized' (1990: 27–9). Thinking develops through dialogue and exchange – dialogue and exchange that may be assisted by metaphor. Transfers of concepts or theoretical statements have often been at the root of theoretical developments and thus may create new areas for thinking of unexplored issues. For instance, Darwin borrowed from Malthus's theory in order to elaborate his theory of evolution. In short, the fecundity of metaphors comes from the access they open up to webs of arguments, associated meanings and statements, which are internalized and communicated (both through common sense, social-ization, cultural imaginary of the time, and learning), and materialized (conveyed by material means, like paper, tapes, discs or institutions), interpreted and appropriated.

Metaphors could also be conceived as superficial, but revealing, 'labels' (a term employed by Ricoeur, 1978) for various discourses, which are then made available in a field other than the one they originated from. They inform and guide explorations in a new field, rather than conceal other metaphors. New meanings are created by the interaction of the imported statements into the new field, not by a second-order metaphor which would encapsulate and convey some allegedly universal and ultimate proper meaning (see Ricoeur, 1978, for a similar line of argument). In a similar sense, Weick (1979: 47–51) regards metaphor as one tactic for thinking about 'organizing'. He underlines the way that various authors have expli-citly resorted to metaphors (anarchies, seesaws, space stations, garbage can, marketplace, savage tribe . . .) and thus have enriched organization theory, because 'each metaphor has articulated some property of organizations which might otherwise have gone unnoticed', and he judges 'this articulation as crucial' (Weick, 1979: 47). What matters most in metaphorization is less the sole concept which would be simply transferred, but the theoretical patterns it originally supports amongst others and then activates within another framework, by interaction with the issues, problematics or objects of concern.

Lacan's Treatment of Metaphor

Although Lacan's work presents a pessimistic view of the ability to fully grasp meaning, it could also be interpreted as offering some support for the value of metaphor which has been listed in other works. It seems that metaphor is basic to how individuals make sense of events in a *collective and individual* way. As Giambattista Vico says (cited in Ragland-Sullivan, 1986), metaphors we today take for granted, such as 'mouth of a river', 'head of a pin', are the result of our ancestors' use of the imperfect collective structures of language to express individual sense perceptions. In this respect, metaphors are a point of contact between socially defined meanings in a particular context and individually created meanings and show individuals using 'relatively stable collective forms for the making and expressing of diverse and possibly idiosyncratic and private meanings' (Rapport, 1994: 24). They are one of the keys to studying how humans ascribe meaning to events and to the world by working on the basis of similarities, association and substitution. The value of metaphor, which can be inferred from Lacan's work but which is rejected by him in his extreme anti-humanist stance, is that metaphor shows us that 'it is still the individual subject which remains active in its interpretations' (Rapport, 1994: 41).

Lacan's work also shows another benefit from the analysis of metaphor. This relates to the way that languages have divided the world up into discrete entities – words and signs. The world can be divided up in other ways, as a study of other languages shows. Metaphor, as Lacan implies, may recover forgotten links or associations or create new ones, thus opening up new areas of perception, and helping to close the gap between what is experienced and what is said. However, the meanings may not be easily grasped and brought to the surface.

Further examination of Lacan's work on metaphor seems to support findings on the use of metaphor in poetry (Inns and Jones, 1996). These reveal that metaphor may appear to give a gestalt understanding of a subject and unite emotional and rational insights, but that by its ambiguous nature it points to the complexity of meaning. The ambiguity is due in part to what Sarup refers to as the 'double-bind' of metaphor: it 'states one thing but requires you to understand something different' (1993:47). This complexity and multi-layered nature of meaning is the reason for the intensity of the impact of poetry. Lacan supports this when he says: 'One has only to listen to poetry . . . for a polyphony to be heard, for it to become clear that all discourse is aligned along the several staves of a score' (Lacan, 1977: 54).

These strata of meaning, embedded in metaphor and in the proliferation of meaning that metaphor draws attention to, make the organizational research-er's role very difficult. Poetry does not try to make the meanings and implications of a text explicit but organizational analysis is more compelled by its goals of achieving improvement and progress to produce a coherent analysis of behaviour.

Metaphor offers promise as a focus of study of how meanings are generated but reveals the extreme difficulty of this. The instability of meaning, illustrated by metaphor, erodes any firm security in understanding discourse and points to the elusive, ambiguous, interconnected and fluid nature of meaning. It also emphasizes the elusiveness of the way that metaphor works. Metaphor works by implicit comparisons and links and it may be that trying to make the links explicit destroys much of its power. Lacan's work highlights these difficulties. In so doing, it proves that the researcher, as well as the participant and the reader, cannot escape the ambiguity of language and the elusiveness of meaning. This does not mean that analysing social behaviour and discourse is an impossible enterprise, but that it demands great depth of analysis and time, thereby supporting the argument for in-depth case studies. It also requires an acknowledgement that organizational researchers are involved as much as anything in games of rhetoric; that they do anything but produce 'plain texts' – they are 'mixed up in the "sharp practice" of rhetoric' (Rapport, 1994).

The Value of Metaphor as a Language and Creative Resource

In relation to metaphor's value as a language and creative resource, Schlanger (1983, 1988) considers metaphor as a major force in scientific invention. The notion of invention appears more relevant than that of discovery, which implies the pre-existence of laws and rules to be borne into light. For instance, Einstein invented the laws of relativity rather than discovered them. Consequently, creativity is a critical issue to the advance-ment of sciences, particularly, we feel, for organization studies.

Despite their fecundity, metaphorical patterns do not have a direct cognitive use, in the sense that they deliver no knowledge. They permit us to unlock new issues or new elaborations of issues, but they do not give the answers (Schlanger, 1971: 258). Here the gap with the claims reviewed above is patent: metaphorization leads the way for new perspectives, but it does not in itself directly provide or generate knowledge; this makes it both fecund and dangerous. In the words of Passeron (1991: 145–6), organiza-tional analysts like Morgan yield to the trap of 'mimetic short-cut', which supersedes the meaning of descriptive statements to a prime or ultimate signification, and his approach proceeds from those invitations which ingenuously lead the reader as well as the author to the appropriation of a ready-made intelligibility. Moreover, these patterns do not even have normative properties, and it is improper to draw from them any inference about what human conduct should be at any level (Schlanger, 1971: 259). The metaphor's injunction postulated by Morgan thus appears not only unduly restrictive and unrealistic but also unfounded in epistemological terms.

We contend that the very interest of metaphorization lies in its heuristic character. This character is often overestimated, and, through lack of proper examination/extrapolation, unbounded creativity is raised to the status of the very core of a metaphorical approach to organizations, whereas it might merely be its preamble. The metaphor is more properly viewed as less a matter of representation than of language, or repertory: metaphorization only permits us to visualize and enunciate, to extend and enrich the area to deal with (Schlanger, 1988: 86). Seeing and expressing do not come down to thinking; they are only a preliminary step. We must therefore understand that the role of metaphor is expressive rather than cognitive, or in the words of Weick: 'metaphors enable people to predicate characteristics that are unnameable' (1979: 48). Seen in this light, metaphors do not produce knowledge but are a condition of it (Schlanger, 1983: 190).

If the recourse to metaphors is considered as a language, a number of difficulties most metaphorical approaches are tainted with are overcome. The interest shifts from the metaphor itself to its function; so that the approach is reversed and the unit for explanation is located not in the isolated image and its transposition, but in a complex constellation of meaning (Schlanger, 1971: 59). This can be quite illuminating. For example, if we look at the language of the organism, it is both a constant and variable historical feature; for a long time one has resorted to this language in order to explain, amongst other things, social reality, but not always in the same manner, nor in the same respect, so that the recourse (the universal) must here be distinguished from the use (the contingent) (Schlanger, 1983: 193). Similarly, even the apparently self-evident metaphor of the machine cannot be correctly apprehended outside the historical context it originated from. In the same respect, its opposition with the metaphor of the organism is a traditional but (thus) misleading opposition (Canguilhem, 1965), because in the nineteenth century both were figures of organizing, thus of harmony (Schlanger, 1971: 59). As Ricoeur (1978: 297) has pointed out, they therefore turn out to be not mere realities but themes, and the attention must then shift from their representational power to their 'argumentative plasticity' (Schlanger, 1971: 49).

The expressive function of metaphor leads us to our final point. This is that we should be mindful that the recourse to metaphors is often based on their having a rhetorical or argumentative role. As Weick has pointed out, 'metaphors are closer to perceived experience and therefore are more vivid emotionally, sensorially and cognitively' (1979: 48). Drawing on a wide repertory, that of ordinary language, specialist language or dominant cognitive language, or, more generally speaking, on a kind of 'cultural imaginary' (the clockwork, the balance . . .), metaphorical patterns appear as enlightening, even though partial and distorted (Schlanger, 1983: 202). Thinking requires naming, and metaphors offer opportunities to organize the description and the interpretation of a set of meanings. Such a role is also of utmost importance, because a new model must gain the attention and assent of its audience. A metaphor, because it provides the means of expressing something new, might then be effective in theoretical innovation as well as in the communication strategy of this innovation. Consequently the use of metaphors for a creative purpose does not eliminate the need for further discussion of their ability to elaborate theory. Failure to do so may well mean that metaphor remains a rhetorical ornament, and finds it difficult to shake off the commonly held image of its being an aesthetic embellishment.

11   Organizational Analysis as Discourse Analysis: A Critique

Mike Reed

This chapter evaluates the contribution of Foucauldian discourse analysis to our understanding of organization. The argument is divided into three broad segments. First, a general overview describes the major ontological and analytical features of Foucauldian discourse analysis and the manner in which it has been carried into organizational analysis in recent years. Second, a thematic component highlights three major research areas where discourse analysis has been extremely influential in contemporary organizational analysis; that is, in relation to organizational subjectivities or identities ('technologies of the self'), organizational surveillance and control ('technologies of discipline') and organizational change ('technologies of government'). And third, the chapter concludes by identifying the crucial features of Foucauldian discourse analysis which severely limit its analytical and explanatory significance.

The exposition and critique are grounded in realist social and organization theory (Archer, 1995; Layder, 1997; Reed, 1997) and both the underlying ontological and epistemological commitments entailed in critical realism and their implications for 'doing' discourse analysis in organization studies will be discussed in more detail below. Hence, it is important to recognize that this evaluation of the relatively brief and controversial 'career' of discourse analysis in organization studies is formulated from a radically different vision of what the study of organization is about and how it should be carried through than that articulated by Foucauldian organization theorists.

Enter Foucault

As Cousins and Hussain have persuasively argued: 'Foucault's concern is not to produce a general theory of discourse. . . . His use of the term discourse may be taken to be tactical. It may be thought of as an attempt to avoid treating knowledges in terms of "ideas" ' (1984: 78). Subsequently, they suggest that Foucault's tactical use of the concept of discourse turns on his aim of making historical evidence about the material and social practices through which social life exhibits certain patterns or regularities intelligible in terms of *particular problems*. In this respect, Foucault abjures any intention of treating discursive formations as cultural expressions or representations of general movements in history and society which can be encapsulated in 'totalizing' theoretical explanations. Instead, the former must be treated as consisting of and constituted by *material and socio-linguistic practices* which support a common theme, what Foucault in his later works will call a 'strategy, a common institutional, administrative or political drift and pattern' (Cousins and Hussain, 1984: 85). On this interpretation, Foucault (1972, 1979) is promoting discursive formations as sets of patterned or ordered practices that identify certain objects and specify their conditions of existence so that we can speak, read, write and reason about them in a coherent and relevant way. They cannot be reduced to their linguistic and symbolic elements alone; rather, they must be seen as configurations of statements, techniques, instruments, interventions and norms held loosely together by a body of anonymous historical rules directed to the practical exercise of power and control in specific organizational sites such as asylums, prisons and hospitals. Such practices provide the 'conditions of possibility' for some discursive formations, such as the discourse of enterprise (du Gay, 1996; du Gay and Salaman, 1992; du Gay et al., 1996), to establish a privileged position within certain historical and temporal contexts. At the same time, this position of cultural and ideological privilege is always open to challenge by alternative discursive formations, such as public service, professionalism, community or citizenship (Reed, 1996), which struggle to displace and replace dominant discourses and the techniques of government which they require.

Foucault's tactical formulation and usage of 'discourse' has a number of crucial implications for organizational analysis which are not always fully recognized by its *cognoscenti* (du Gay et al., 1996). First, it is a highly *materialistic* conception which refuses to prioritize or isolate – for analytical or explanatory purposes – the linguistic, rhetorical, symbolic and communicative components of discursive formations from their physical, technical, organizational and political elements. Second, it treats discourse as *constitutive* of social reality; that is, both the process of discursive formation and the social relations which it instantiates are regarded as determinants of whatever coherence and meaning concepts and entities such as 'society', 'power' or 'organization' manage to sustain and convey (Dryberg, 1997; Fairclough and Wodak, 1997; Mumby and Clair, 1997). Third, it symbiotically ties the construction, articulation and reformulation of discourse to the exercise of power and control in micro-level sites of 'dividing practices' which become organizational nodes in a web of relations through which individual minds and bodies are normalized and disciplined (Barry et al., 1996; Cousins and Hussain, 1984; Dumm 1996; Garland, 1990; O'Neil, 1986). It is an inherently *political* conception of discourse in that it ties the formation of systems of knowledge and belief into the matrices of power relations and practices that they inhabit. Fourth, it promotes an *'agentless'* conception of discursive formation in which the role of specific agents – individual and/or collective – and forms of agency is simply reduced to that of nodal points in the intersection of various discourses which act as 'ciphers' for the 'messages' that the latter convey (Layder, 1997: 130–2). Fifth, it tends towards a *localized, even de-institutionalized*, form of discourse/organizational analysis in which any concern with wider structural issues and the more durable forms of domination which they represent is rejected in favour of a more 'bottom-up' or ascending, rather than descending, analysis of power networks or webs (Dryberg, 1997; Foucault, 1980: 78–165; Rosenau, 1992). Each of these defining characteristics requires further elaboration and clarification, given the 'fateful consequences' which they entail for the manner in which Foucault's discourse analysis has been transposed into organization studies.

Foucault's (1972) conception is highly materialistic in that he insists that the concepts of discourse and discursive formation must retain the full range of socio-historically contingent linguistic, cultural, technical and organizational resources which actively constitute fields of knowledge and the practices they instantiate. As Fairclough argues,

> for Foucault, discourse analysis is not to be equated with linguistic analysis, nor discourse with language. Discourse analysis is concerned . . . with specifying socio-historically variable discursive formations (sometimes referred to as 'discourses'), systems of rules which make it possible for certain statements but not others to occur at particular times, places and institutional locations. (1992: 40)

Considered in these terms, that which a discourse marginalizes, indeed excludes, is as, if not more, important, from both an explanatory and political viewpoint, as that which it includes as legitimate objects of knowledge (as issues for investigation) and governmental practice (as problems for intervention). Thus, the system of rules and conditions that make certain discursive formations viable, while marginalizing others, is the outcome of a complex interaction between material and ideational practices that define the terrain on which the objects and subjects of social life emerge.

Nevertheless, there is no doubt that Foucault sees discourse as *constitutive* of socio-organizational reality. It generates, reproduces and transforms the very stuff of our lives as sentient and social beings. Discourse does not just signify and represent socio-organizational reality; it defines the structure and content of that reality. We are made by discourse; it makes our world for us. As he argues in *Birth of the Clinic*:

> we are doomed historically to history, to the patient construction of discourses about discourses, and to the task of hearing what has already been said. . . . The clinic – constantly praised for its empiricism, the modesty of its attention, and the care with which it silently lets things surface to the observing gaze without disturbing them with discourse – owes its real importance to the fact that it is a reorganization in depth, not only of medical discourse, but of the very possibility of a discourse about disease. (1976: xvi–xix)

Thus, for Foucault, the clinic, as an identifiable organizational reality, is the product of 'a new "carving up of things" and the principle of their verbalization in a form which we have been accustomed to recognizing as the language of a "positive science" ' (Foucault, 1976: xvii). Consequently, the discourse of positive science consists of a complex configuration of systematic linkages between linguistic and material practices that constitute 'the clinic' as a recognizable and viable organizational form dedicated to the treatment of objectively determined disease: 'The structure in which space, language, and death are articulated – what is known, in fact, as the anatomo-clinical method – constitutes the historical condition of a medicine that is given and accepted as positive' (Foucault, 1976: 196). It is these funda-mental structures of linguistically and culturally determined human experi-ence, such as the clinic, the asylum or the prison, which construct subjects and their subjectivity in sustainable institutional forms. Discourse attains ontological and methodological primacy within Foucault's universe because it determines the strategies and rules by which we can speak about and act on a domain of objects, including ourselves, in such a way that certain possibilities and outcomes are realized rather than others.

At the same time, discourse is necessarily tied into relations of power and control. Systems of knowledge and the 'truths' they instantiate are mutually related to modalities of power through which human populations are disciplined and managed (Cooper, 1992; Foucault, 1979). Institutions and organizations can only be analysed by focusing on the discursive practices through which they are constituted as structures of power and control: 'Discourse is not simply that which translates struggles or systems of domination, but is the thing for which and by which there is struggle: *discourse is the power which is to be seized*' (Foucault, 1984: 110; emphasis added). It defines and codifies the nature of the 'human subject' by preconstituting the linguistic and cultural categories through which such subjects become objects to be acted on by various governmental technolo-gies directed to the normalization and regulation of social behaviour. By literally 'talking subjects into existence' and objectifying the underlying conditions of possibility for their treatment, discursive formations constitute the critical resources and practices which must be secured and controlled in any struggle for power and domination.

This reflects Foucault's *ascending*, rather than descending, approach to the analysis of power relations and processes. Insofar as it establishes an ontological and methodological warrant for prioritizing the *micro-mechanisms and practices* that shape 'how things work at the level of ongoing subjugation, at the level of those continuous and uninterrupted processes which subject our bodies, govern our gestures, dictate our behav-iours' (Foucault, 1980: 97), it asserts that 'power is employed and exercised through a net-like organization' (Foucault, 1980: 98). In turn, this encour-ages a 'turning away' from 'the regulated and legitimate forms of power in their *central locations, with the general mechanisms through which they operate, and the continual effects of these*' (Foucault, 1980: 96; emphasis added). Instead, Foucault's approach focuses on 'the micropowers dispersed within different locales throughout the social body' (Dean, 1994: 156) as they develop and implement a diversity of assembled strategies and technologies concerned with 'the formation of the real in a governable, programmable, form' (Dean, 1994: 159). Foucauldian discourse analysis, therefore, is predicated on a capillary conception of power – as a finely stranded, 'hair-like' spider's web – which rejects the structural determinism it sees as inherent in juridical or sovereign conceptions of power (Foucault, 1980: 88–91).

Again, this is consistent with Foucault's demand for an 'agentless' conception of power/knowledge discourse in which 'analysis should not concern itself with power at the level of conscious intention or decision . . . it should not attempt to consider *power from its internal point of view* and that it should refrain from posing the labyrinthine and unanswerable question: Who then has power and what has he in mind?' (Foucault, 1980: 97; emphasis added). This entails a refusal to recognize, much less analyse, power/knowledge discourses, and the organizational practices and structures which they constitute, as the direct expression of strategies of control and domination pursued by identifiable individuals, social groups, classes and movements within a wider historical and institutional context. Rather, they must be treated as the highly provisional, localized and contingent expressions of a multiplicity of forces, energies, materials and interventions consistent with an overarching framework of ontological imperatives and methodological protocols that rejects any conception of social reality as a hierarchically structured and layered entity.

Finally, each of the preceding building blocks in Foucault's ontology and methodology for analysing discursive formations and their associated disciplinary regimes inevitably pushes him towards a highly localized, even de-institutionalized, view of the processes and practices by which the former are constituted. Consistently, his attention is focused on the necessarily fragmented, diverse, localized and contradictory nature and operation of discourses – such as medical science, penology and psychology – as they reveal their inherent limitations, inconsistencies and uncertainties as congenitally failing attempts to subdue, order and contain an inherently recalcitrant and uncontrollable social reality. Nevertheless, while there is recurring reference to recalcitrance, resistance, ambiguity and failure in Foucault's work (see his contributions to Burchell et al., 1991), the overriding impression one is left with is 'of people being helplessly subjected to immovable systems of power . . . he gives the impression that resistance is generally contained by power and poses no threat' (Fairclough, 1992: 57; also see Garland, 1990). He is clear in his outright rejection of an overarching socio-historical logic of action, such as Weberian rationalization or Marxian accumulation, lying behind the myriad power/knowledge discourses and disciplinary regimes characteristic of modernity. Yet, the all-pervading sense of a ubiquitous and determining 'will to power', as it finds direct articulation in the discursive formations of the natural and human sciences – and their governmental/disciplinary progeny – is very difficult, if not impossible, to shake off in 'Foucaultland'. We escape Weber's iron cage of bureaucratic rationalization and Marx's immutable laws of capitalist development only to be trapped, indeed trap ourselves, within a Foucauldian disciplinary society where we become incarcerated within a total organizational world in which we play no conscious part or active role in making but which completely dominates all aspects of our normalized and regularized lives (Burrell, 1988, 1997). In place of Hegel's 'cunning of history', which always works behind people's backs, we have Foucault's 'history of the present' in which we are condemned to reconstruct the discursive formations and re-enact the disciplinary regimes within which we imprison ourselves.

These, then, are the key features of Foucault's conception and approach. Discourse emerges as an assemblage of material, political, technological and cultural factors which can only be properly appreciated as an inherently ambiguous, but nonetheless immensely powerful and ubiquitous, process that pervades and dominates our being and action. As such, it

> serves to *undermine* conventional distinctions between 'thought' and 'action', 'language' and 'practice'. The term refers *both* to the production of knowledge through language and representation and the way that knowledge is institutionalized, shaping social practices and cultural technologies and setting new practices and technologies into play. (du Gay et al., 1996: 265; emphasis added)

In such circumstances 'organization' becomes the arena or site for a multiplicity of dividing practices – instantiated and legitimated by a range of, often competing, discursive formations in which individuals participate – through which our identities, potentialities and fates are ineradicably fashioned and regulated. The implications of this for the study of organizing and organizations are discussed in the following sections in relation to three major research areas which have developed in recent years.

Technologies of the Self

The discursive construction of organizational subjectivities and identities has emerged as one of the most popular and influential areas of research and analysis in recent years (Casey 1995; Clark et al., 1994; Knights and Morgan 1991; Michael, 1996; Thompson and Ackroyd, 1995; Willmott 1994). In part, this reflects an increasing disillusionment with objectivist and structuralist approaches which seem to trade on highly reductionistic and deterministic theories of 'the subject' (Clegg, 1994; Collinson, 1994; du Gay, 1996; Gergen, 1991; Willmott 1990). At another level, a growing interest in the theme of the 'organizational self' seems to gel with a broader concern with the micro-level processes and networks through which the everyday practical work of ordering social reality and assembling social order is accomplished (Cooper and Law, 1995; Michael, 1996; Reed, 1997). Both these developments have reinforced the relevance of Foucault to organizational analysis insofar as they emphasize the importance of tracing 'the *dispersion of identity* across networks, or rather how networks come to be "condensed" or "congealed" at nodes that we specify as human identities' (Michael, 1996: 78; emphasis added). Instead of Weber's disenchanted specialist without spirit, Merton's overintegrated bureaucratic personality and Whyte's socially conformist organization man, we are left with Gergen's (1991) 'saturated postmodern self' – a much more unstable and decentred self, condemned to cope with, and add to, the chaos of multiple realities and its endemic ontological and moral relativism the only way that 'it' knows how; that is, by completely accepting and internalizing 'the loss of identifiable essences, the increasing sensitivity to the social construction of reality, the erosion of authority, the growing disregard for rational coherence, and the emergence of ironic self-reflection (Gergen, 1991: 16). Thus, the decentred postmodern organizational subject and the multiple identities which s/he takes on are seen as the product of various discourses and techniques which fabricate, indeed literally 'make up', the linguistic, technological and ethical forms within and from which 'the self' becomes a viable, yet highly precarious, socio-psychological project.

Much of the recent work in this area directly draws on Foucault's conception and analysis of discursive formations. Three studies exemplify the way in which his approach has become increasingly influential in contemporary organizational analysis: Kondo's *Crafting Selves* (1990), Casey's *Work, Self and Society* (1995) and du Gay's *Consumption and Identity at Work* (1996). Each will be discussed in some detail to illustrate the key features of a Foucauldian approach to organizational subjectivity and identity.

Kondo's study of identity formation in a small, family-owned Japanese factory emphasizes that the

> subject becomes a site for the play of difference, a site for the play of shifting and potentially conflicting meanings. The 'identity' of the subject is multiple, produced within discourse, and potentially contradictory, and though there can be 'a temporary retrospective fixing' of meaning and identity, no ready form of coherence can be posited in advance. The unitary subject is no longer unified . . . identities are not essential wholes, but subject-positions – shifting nodal points within often conflict-ridden fields of meaning. (Kondo, 1990: 36–46)

Given this overriding emphasis on identity as a dynamic arena of contradiction and conflict – as a linguistic, cognitive and cultural terrain where various discourses temporarily intersect and crystallize in specific ways – Kondo's analysis inevitably moves on to the discursive strategies and practices through which paternalistic conceptions of the company provide the wider organizational setting in which people's construction of 'their-selves' can occur. In particular, she highlights the continuous struggles over discursive meaning, subjectivity and identity that shape the organizational terrain on which some sense of 'self' can be crafted and maintained at 'the multiple, mobile points of potential resistance moving through any regime of power' (Kondo, 1990: 225). Thus, work customs, gender roles, authority relationships and family connections within the factory all become inter-woven within a tableau of institutional and everyday discourses that shape and constrain organizational life.

The Foucauldian lineage becomes most evident when Kondo deals with the political and disciplinary aspects of the discourses through which multiple and unstable 'selves' are created and maintained. She analyses the problematic emergence of selfhood as the 'product of a complex negotiation, taking place within specific, but shifting, contexts, where power and meaning, "personal" and "political", are inseparable' (Kondo, 1990: 24). By making issues of power, discipline and control central to the discursive construction of organizational subjectivity and identity, she suggests that

> the intertwining of meaning and power creates sets of institutions and disciplinary practices: from the structure of the company, to the designation of people who work there as different selves – *shacho* [company president], artisans, part-timers – to everyday interactions. . . . Power/meaning *creates* selves at the workplace, and consequently, no one can be 'without power'. (Kondo, 1990: 221)

But this intertwining of discourse and power generates constraints as well as opportunities; it establishes a matrix of organizational practices and relations that become 'vehicles for the disciplinary production of selves. Selves everywhere are crafted through coercions and disciplines, which offer culturally, historically specific pathways to self-realization as well as dom-ination' (Kondo, 1990: 305). Consequently, the company she researched is represented as an institutional embodiment of disciplined organizational subjects discovering fulfilment *in the very act of disciplining and being disciplined*. In true Foucauldian fashion, discursive multiplicity, ambiguity and contradiction are theoretically and empirically aligned with conflict, discipline and constraint in an inherently messy and complicated organiza-tional 'reality' which ensures that the formulation, communication and legitimation of organizational identity *is never beyond the gaze and reach of power*.

Casey's (1995) analysis is more sensitive to macro-level institutionalized structures of domination and control, but nonetheless resonates with Kondo's emphasis on the multiple contexts in which individuals and groups fashion some workable conceptions of themselves as 'employees'. Her ethnographic research on cultural re-engineering within a high-tech, North American multinational corporation reveals a similar drive towards paternal-ism, familialism and integration, but in a historical, cultural and political context in which individualism, competition and meritocracy are the domi-nant motifs. However, the latter no longer provide adequate cultural and ideological foundations for the emerging decentred or virtual workplace and the company-specific 'para-professionalism'; the latter have radically undermined traditional discourses of occupational specialization and the organizational structures they created. Thus, for Casey, with the increasing linguistic and political dominance of

> discursive (including knowledge) means of production, occupational distinctive-
> ness . . . no longer matters. . . . Replacing occupation as a primary locus of class
> and self-identification in the corporate workplace is team and knowledge. . . .
> Relationship to a product, to team-family members and to the company displaces
> identification with occupation and its historic repository of skills, knowledges and
> allegiances. (Casey, 1995: 108–9)

This putative paradigm shift from 'occupation' to 'organization' is grounded in a Foucauldian understanding of the individual as constituted by the significatory and representational practices through which 'the self' is fabricated. Thus, discourse is treated as that

> historically contingent body of regularised practices of language that are con-
> doned by a society. These practices make possible certain statements and
> communicational practices while disallowing others. A discourse is made up of
> rules and procedures, the empirical 'discursive' object or idea, that constructs and
> legitimates the way we see things and talk about them. (Casey, 1995: 20)

For Casey, the major discursive shift which is taking place in post-industrial capitalist society is from bureaucratic rationality and professional morality towards a new discourse of production. Within the latter, the primary narrative of organizational cohesion and identity becomes a 'designer culture' that signifies and legitimates a much more polarized corporate workplace and internalized forms of surveillance and control. 'Smart tech-nologies' and 'network structures' are anchored in a post-industrial corpor-ate culture and organizing discourse in which 'corporatized selves become sufficiently repressed to effectively weaken and dissolve the capacity for serious criticism or dissent' (Casey, 1995: 150–1). Thus, the ideal corporate member is a 'colluded self: dependent, over-agreeable, compulsive in dedication and diligence, passionate about the product and the company. The colluded self is comforted by primary narcissistic gratifications of identifi-cation with a workplace family free of the older attractions of occupation-and class-based solidarities' (Casey, 1995: 191). As a product of a new corporate discourse centred on the transmutation of 'occupational' differ-entiation and integration into 'organizational' homogenization – based on the enterprise, the team and the task – the 'colluded corporate self' is an inherently contradictory and unstable identity based on simulated myths of community, consensus, family and solidarity. Nevertheless, the concept of the 'designer employee' and the technologies through which it is translated into practical terms – through techniques such as cultural re-engineering, quality management, autonomous work teams, just-in-time production sys-tems and employee involvement programmes – have done their work. They have created a new 'corporate religiosity' that disguises and contains the

tensions, conflicts and rigidities inherent in organizational structures characteristic of 'designer capitalism'.

Du Gay's ethnographic research on the construction of new forms of
work-based subjectivity and identity in four multiple retail organizations
takes its ontological and analytical cue from Foucault's conception of
discourse as that loose configuration of linguistic and material practices
through which 'subjects' are produced as objects to be 'worked on' and 'represented' in ways appropriate to a given type of disciplinary regime – such
as 'enterprise' (du Gay, 1996: 40–50). This approach is contrasted with
structurally oriented neo-Weberian and Marxian approaches in which subjectivity is treated as an epiphenomenon of underlying economic and social
forces or simply ignored altogether. In either case, work-based subjectivities
and identities are regarded as the unproblematic, unified and integrated
outcomes of social conditioning. Ideal typical forms of work orientations –
such as the 'instrumental worker' – are simply 'read off' from structural
factors without any attention to the discursive practices through which they
are produced as *inherently* unstable, unfinished and unbounded representations of complex and contradictory 'realities' (du Gay, 1996: 9–38).

Du Gay suggests that the dominant managerial discourses of the 1980s
and 1990s – the 'enterprise culture' and the 'excellent firm' – had to be
translated into practical, operational terms through the application of a series
of material and linguistic techniques which would transform 'old' work-
based subjectivities and identities grounded in industrial bureaucracy into
'new' ways of thinking, feeling and acting based on the market and its
natural entrepreneurial qualities. The discourse of enterprise and the project
of excellence can be seen as the most recent articulation of a trajectory of
managerial thought and practice stretching over most of the present century
(Barley and Kunda, 1992; Jacques, 1996). Yet they also signified and
signalled a qualitative shift away from the corporate culture of rational
bureaucracy towards a disciplinary regime founded on the *internalization* of
self-regulation, calculation and control in which externally imposed authority and discipline becomes *much less significant* (also see Reed, 1998).
Consequently, the new work-based subjectivities and identities are focused
on the cultivation of 'enterprising selves' who calculate about themselves
and work upon themselves in order to better themselves (du Gay, 1996:
56–64).

Within the firm, du Gay (1996: 75–95) argues, the most dramatic
discursive expression of the 'enterprising self' is to be found in the 'culture
of the customer' which pervades contemporary corporate capitalism. Within
this culture,

> an active, 'enterprising' consumer is placed at the moral centre of the market-
> based universe. What counts as 'good', or 'virtuous', in this universe is judged by
> reference to the apparent needs, desires and projected preferences of the 'sover-
> eign consumer' . . . the character of the customer . . . is also linked to a

transformation in programmes and technologies for regulating the internal world of the private business enterprise. (du Gay, 1996: 77; emphasis added)

These programmes and technologies are driven by the need to ensure that all employees become dedicated to, indeed obsessed with, satisfying the requirements of the customer. They subject themselves to a new type of discursive and organizational rule that demands total conformity with its dictates within and outside the boundaries of the business enterprise. Moreover, this requires a remoulding of organizational identity around the highly complex and taxing emotional and symbolic work needed to keep the 'sovereign customer' happy. The discourse of 'repressive tolerance' and 'impersonal functionality' characteristic of Weberian rational bureaucracy is replaced by a discourse of 'symbolic seduction' and 'personalized consumption' characteristic of the excellent business enterprise. Within the latter, 'the function of surveillance in consumer culture is now placed in the hands of the market, social surveillance gives way to "auto-surveillance" ' (du Gay, 1996: 79).

However, as with Kondo and Casey, du Gay's research clearly indicates that this conversion from bureaucratic functionary to enterprising entrepreneur is far from complete: there are *always* limits to the control which any new discursive formation and its technological instrumentation can achieve. The re-imagining of organizational identities in the retail firms reveals a process in which the programmatic aspirations of senior managers are translated into new ways for 'employees to be made up' in a highly partial, ambiguous and contested manner (for a similar story in health service organizations, see Reed, 1995). The tactics and discursive routines which senior managers enact – such as quality management, customer awareness and team-working – are necessarily contextual, relational and pragmatic; they cannot and will not realize their full potential because they are forced to adapt to constantly changing circumstance and constraint. As such, the re-imaginization of organizational identities and the retooling of organizational control systems are fated to deliver far less than they promise. But they do establish the ideological and political bridgeheads into processes of organizational change that will redefine the vocabularies of motive and action shaping contemporary organizational life.

Each of the studies reviewed above stands testimony to a Foucauldian conception of discourse which

challenges traditional models that view the self as a stable entity. . . . From this perspective, then, a 'self' is the result of contending discourses: 'selves' are a distinct product growing out of social interaction. The self, no less than institutions or other social structures, is a social product and is therefore historically and culturally contingent, emerging from the ongoing struggle that characterizes social reality. (Phillips and Hardy, 1997: 168)

Technologies of Discipline

As the previous section has illustrated, Foucauldian discourse analysis raises a number of key issues about the *internal world* of the contemporary business corporation. In particular, it focuses attention on the ways in which 'organizational reality' is defined and represented in a discursive and technological form appropriate to certain modes of managerial intervention rather than others. By conceptually and cognitively ordering 'organizational reality' and by mobilizing the knowledge which this generates, discursive formations establish the linguistic and cultural framework for the regimes of surveillance and control that regulate everyday organizational life. As du Gay argues, in Foucauldian fashion, 'power works *in and through subjectivity*. Different governmental rationalities – attempts to invent and exercise different types of rule – are closely linked to conceptions and attributes of those to be governed . . . particular rationalities of government involve the construction of specific ways for people to be' (1996: 54; emphasis added).

Recent research on intra-organizational disciplinary regimes from a Foucauldian perspective has concentrated on the network of discursive and technical practices through which all aspects of an employee's existence – physical, mental and behavioural – are subject to *continuous* surveillance and control (Alvesson, 1993a, 1996; Clegg, 1994; Grey, 1994; Jacques, 1996; Knights and Vurdubakis, 1994; Newton, 1994; Sewell and Wilkinson, 1992; Townley, 1994; Zuboff, 1988). Thus, the internal disciplinary world of the modern employee is structured by a range of interrelated practices which ensure that the meanings, motives and recipes for action are tightly circumscribed and regularized. Jacques (1996: 98–110) provides a useful historical and analytical overview of the spatial, classificatory, observational and technical systems through which modern organizational subjects are produced and controlled. Taken together, he argues, these systems establish a much 'gentler' and 'therapeutic' disciplinary regime than that prevailing under more openly coercive and bureaucratized control systems based on the constant threat of physical and/or mental punishment and externally imposed administrative regulation.

Indeed, this research suggests that the normative shift towards the 'enterprising self' has been accompanied by a corresponding structural shift in disciplinary regimes away from conventional bureaucratic surveillance and control towards 'panopticon control' (Barker, 1993; Burris, 1993; Kallinikos, 1994; Lyon, 1994; Nohria and Berkley, 1994; Reed, 1998; Sewell 1996). This seems to entail a much greater emphasis on more advanced information and communication technologies coupled to the development of more sophisticated discursive control practices. Taken together, these are seen to make continuous, intensive surveillance and internalized normative discipline realistic possibilities; the internal disciplinary world of the most advanced capitalist corporations becomes less and less like Weber's 'iron cage' of bureaucratic rationality and control in which institutionalized mechanisms of externally imposed administrative power and domination take on 'a life of their own' (Turner, 1996: 11–14). Instead, the latter are superseded by a loosely coordinated series of technical and cultural practices through which 'discipline organizes an analytical space' (Foucault, 1979: 143). This facilitates the emergence and diffusion of a form of disciplinary power that 'is omnipresent as it is manifest and produced in each moment. . . . The focus on order with accompanying surveillance and education shifts control away from the explicit exercise of power through force and coercion and places it in the routine practices of everyday life' (Deetz, 1992: 37–8).

Several commentators have questioned the viability of this analysis of 'control shifts' – both in relation to its overall validity as a description and explanation of a general trajectory in disciplinary technologies (Lyon, 1994; Reed 1998; Webster 1995) and in terms of its particular relevance to the dynamics of intraorganizational control regimes (Alvesson, 1996; Barker, 1993; Thompson and Ackroyd, 1995). It is also true to say that a rather more careful and cautious use of Foucauldian analysis has been advocated by a number of commentators so that 'the role of the pressures acting on the subjectivity of the individual, caught up in the web of a disciplinary system, to manage themselves, *thereby reinforcing a project of instrumental rationalization*' (Sewell, 1996: 793; added emphasis), can be properly mapped and understood. Nevertheless, insofar as one can draw any overall conclusion, no matter how tentative, recent work conducted within a Foucauldian perspective must be seen as anticipating the more widespread diffusion of a form of *skeletal* 'panopticon control' within organizations. The latter provides *a metaphor of and theory for* a form of disciplinary technology in which a network of micro-level spatial, observational, informational and administrative techniques, allied to an overlapping set of discourses of the organizational subject, pervades our everyday organizational existence in a ubiquitous manner. In turn, this new, internalized, indirect and imaginized circuit of panopticon surveillance and control is linked to the rise of modern rationalities and technologies of government which complement and reinforce the discursive innovations reviewed in the previous section.

Technologies of Government

In Foucault's terms, government, or 'governmentality', is concerned with the 'ensemble formed by the institutions, procedures, analyses and reflections, the calculations and tactics that allow the exercise of this very specific albeit complex form of power, which has as its target population, as its principal form of knowledge political economy, and as its essential technical means apparatuses of security' (Foucault, 1991: 102). He suggests that we live in an era of 'governmentality' first developed in the eighteenth century, subsequently refined and extended during the nineteenth and twentieth centuries with the consolidation of the administrative state in the shape of the police, pastoral care in quasi-state institutions such as asylums, prisons and hospitals, and the diplomatic-industrial complex. The relation between expertise and politics stands at the core of 'governmentality' in that the latter depends on the historical accretion of a range of 'professional' discourses which have engendered the development of public bodies facilitating 'action or control-at-a-distance' (Barry et al., 1996; Cooper, 1992; Gane and Johnson, 1993). Thus, in Foucault's view, both the discourses/technologies of the organizational subject and control are closely related to changes in middle-range and macro-level governmental agencies which 'install and empower a variety of "professionals", investing them with authority to act as experts in the devices of social rule' (Rose, 1996: 40). These discourses of professional expertise and power provide an intellectual and technical machinery through which various programmes of government can be practically enacted at the 'organizational coalface'.

More recent analysis of government conduct suggests that, as in the case with the self and the organization, it has become more 'reflexive', 'liberal' and 'pluralized' in line with the increasing influence of market rationality as an overarching moral and political imperative (Rose, 1996). A new relation between discourses of expertise and discourses of politics has been developed which implies that the state is devolving aspects of its previously centralized administrative domination into a complex network of decentralized meso- and micro-level technologies – such as trusts, quangos, agencies, utilities and alliances – which have 'reconfigured flows of accountability and responsibility in fundamental ways' (Rose, 1996: 56; also see Hoggett, 1991). This move towards 'centralized decentralization', it is argued, has major implications for the government of capitalist corporations to the extent that they enhance the diversity of regulatory mechanisms through which government is practised. Simultaneously, they increase the political and managerial importance of indirect, organizational-level, mechanisms that coordinate macro-level governmental policies and programmes with micro-level localized activities (Miller and Rose, 1990).

However, what we might call 'Foucault's curse' strikes again; for the discourse and practice of governmentality – that is, the alignment of centralized policies/programmes, driven by an ascendant market rationality, with decentralized organizational practice, as encapsulated in the discourse of enterprise and excellence – is doomed to failure, or at best highly partial success. The increasing dependence of governmentality on professional expertise, the considerably enhanced self-regulatory capacities of enterprising organizational subjects and the increasing influence of panopticon-style disciplinary regimes seem to coalesce into technologies of government which seek to translate ideas into action and thought into reality in a much more systematic and subtle way. But they always have to contend and come to terms with the dynamics of an independent, recalcitrant and 'messy' local world of negotiated organizational order in which avoidance, manipulation and resistance are ever-present contingencies (Reed, 1995). It is this *endemic* analytical and empirical tension, not to say contradiction, between the political *project* of panopticon power and control – that is, complete, all-embracing self-discipline and regulation – and a social ontology which consistently emphasizes the inherent ambiguity, uncertainty and openness of organizational life, which stands at the centre of Foucauldian discourse analysis in organization studies. The underlying theoretical foundations of this tension are discussed and evaluated in the following section.

Critique

There are four issues which are central to any evaluation of Foucauldian discourse analysis: first, the basic conception of *power*; second, the implications of this conceptualization for the way in which organizational *surveillance and control* are analysed; third, the extent to which the analyses of both power and control are parasitic upon deeper assumptions about the *'agency/structure'* relationship; finally, the *ontological precepts* which inform the approach as a whole. This discussion will suggest that Foucauldian discourse analysis exhibits a number of deficiencies which undermine its potential 'explanatory payoff' in the study of organization. It is further suggested that these failings can only be rectified by the development of a realist conception of discourse/organizational analysis.

As we have already seen, Foucauldian discourse analysis is anchored in a conception of power as an inherently productive and creative game or field consisting of a constantly shifting web of coalitions and alliances which 'nobody' possesses or dominates. Consequently, Foucault's nominalist conception of power is based on 'the fundamental *circular* structure of power as the limit in time and space . . . power is not a game one can choose to play or withdraw from, but is the *very nature of the game itself*' (Dryberg, 1997: 91; emphasis added). By treating power as the conceptual vehicle for conveying his commitment to the *fundamental* undecidability and contingency of 'social reality', Foucault rejects any attempt to search for the 'origins' or 'causes' of such a phenomenon in an already objectified or institutionally constituted 'structure' or 'agency'. Instead, power/knowledge discourses are conceptualized and studied as processes that constitute and configure the subject's identity and reality as a social being. Discourses of power/knowledge, such as 'strategy discourse' (Knights and Morgan, 1991), locate and define individuals within a network of linguistic and material practices through which they come to see 'the truth' of who they are and what they are.

However, this nominalist/discursive view of power runs into major explanatory problems when asked to account for the existence and significance of more durable and constraining forms of power as conveyed in the Weberian concept of domination or the Gramscian notion of hegemony. The structured organizational and institutional context within which the linguistic and material practices associated with the exercise of disciplinary power are deployed is virtually missing from Foucault's ontology and epistemology. As Layder has argued: 'Although disciplinary power targets the body, it does so under the auspices of a structured organizational context and this begs the question of how, and to what extent, it is related to other aspects of social organization' (1997: 158). In this respect, Foucault and his followers are guilty of 'conceptually overdosing' on the ontological and explanatory 'high' which they get from a nominalist/discursive conception of power/knowledge discourses. The latter presupposes too much, in the sense of assuming that there is no, temporally and historically, *pre-existing* structuring of the situationally specific processes and practices through which organizational selves and control regimes are discursively constructed. It also presupposes too little in the sense of being ontologically and theoretically deaf to the institutionalized forms of domination which make the *continuous* exercise of disciplinary power, at the micro and/or meso levels of social organization, feasible as a realizable political aspiration – much less as a realized political outcome.

Thus, Foucauldian discourse analysis is necessarily tied into a conception of power that cannot hold the explanatory load that it's required to bear – that is, to provide a sustainable theoretical basis on which panopticon control can be regarded as an, at least potentially, achievable political project. Neither can it provide the theoretical means for linking an ascending analysis of micro-level power/knowledge discourses to a descending analysis of the macro-level systems of governmentality and structures of domination in which the former are situated – however disjointed the alignment between them may be in practice. The crucial relationship between localized *circuits* of power, generated by the everyday operation of disciplinary discourse, and the matrix of institutionalized *structures* of power in which they are embedded cannot be adequately theorized, much less researched, by means of a circular conception of power which remains deaf to its hierarchical contextualization (Reed, 1997).

The analysis of the changing forms of organizational surveillance and control also exhibits a number of problems. Insofar as Foucauldian discourse analysis identifies a general movement towards internalized and indirect, as opposed to externalized and direct, forms of organizational surveillance and control, then it can only sustain this prognosis by presuming a level of institutional structuring which is inconsistent with its own ontological and theoretical premises. If power/knowledge discourses are as open, dispersed, fragmented and ambiguous as Foucault suggests, then how does any particular discursive formation – such as 'enterprise', 'excellence' or 'designer culture' – achieve the level of institutional legitimation and range of organizational enactment presumed in the notion of disciplinary or 'panopticon' power? Even in its embryonic or skeletal form, the latter implies a stabilized regime of sufficient durability and scope to sustain a level of interorganizational generalizability denied by the very ontological and analytical premises on which it rests. But this durability and scope only becomes a practical political project *if* discursive formations and their associated disciplinary practices can sustain a level of institutional embeddedness and organizational interrelatedness inconsistent with the micro-level reductionism which Foucauldian discourse analysis tends to favour (Alvesson, 1996: 104–13; Layder, 1997: 147–63). Institutional analysis is rather like Banquo, the ghost at the feast in *Macbeth*: a theoretical apparition which appears and reappears at set times, but is only ever seen by Macbeth/Foucault himself. Once seen, the ghost is banished to the nether reaches of the narrative, called upon only to supply the very faintest allusion to the historical and structural context in which the tragedy unfolds.

This inability to provide a coherent ontological and theoretical rationale for disciplinary power/panopticon control as a *generalizable* political project/governmental rationality owes much to the inadequate treatment of the 'agency/structure' relationship within Foucauldian discourse analysis. The latter's rejection of any analytical differentiation between social action and structural constraint paradoxically leads to a form of explanatory determinism or 'totalism' in which social actors become the products, rather than the creators, of the discursive formations in which they are trapped (Reed, 1997). This 'backdoor determinism' arises from the assumption that the production and reproduction of discursive formations, as systems of thought which inform material practices, has a logic of its own *independent* of the social action through which it is made possible (Alvesson and Deetz, 1996: 205–11). As a result, the potential for people to influence, much less control, the construction and reconstruction of the discourses which define *their* lived realities, identities and potentialities is virtually extinguished by a *sui generis* process of discursive reproduction in which they become the biological and cultural 'raw material' to be 'worked on and through' by the latter's constitutive practices. We become enterprising and/or calculating and/or colluding and/or disciplining 'selves' because we are the subjects/objects of discursive formations 'which each have their own history, their own trajectory, their own techniques and tactics' (Foucault, 1980: 99).

By denying any ontological and/or analytical differentiation between creative agency and structural constraint, Foucauldian discourse analysis ends up with an explanatory logic that is unable to distinguish between 'open doors' and 'brick walls', and the complex interaction between them in different temporal and spatial locales (Smith, 1991). A failure to recognize that discursive practices are differentially constrained by the material and structural realities in which they are enacted is compounded by a further failure to accord social agency/enactment sufficient explanatory weight as a vital contributor to the social construction and reconstruction of discursive formations. As a result, the complex socio-historical interaction between agency and structure, as it shapes and reshapes our systems of thought and material practices, disappears from view to be replaced by a form of discursive determinism that 'flattens' and simplifies our social reality in such a way that it is denuded of scale, continuity and durability (Reed, 1997; Sayer, 1997).

This brings us to the final issue of ontology. Each of the previously discussed problems encountered in Foucauldian discourse analysis – power, disciplinary power and agency/structure – has its roots in a radical onto-logical constructivism which presumes that 'language creates an imagined ontology and a structure for rendering intelligible how and why constituents of the ontology are related' (Gergen, 1994: 8). In one sense, it is onto-logically mute or neutral in that it asserts that 'whatever is, simply is' (Gergen, 1994: 72). What is is the product of discourse; reality is literally talked and manufactured into existence through the local linguistic and material conventions which 'capture reality as it is' (Gergen, 1994: 73). Each discursive community constructs and reconstructs its conceptions of reality and communicates these by means of various sociolinguistic prac-tices, rituals and patterns. Disagreements over these constructions can only be settled from within the cognitive, linguistic and cultural boundaries constituted by and through such discursive formations. There is literally nothing 'outside' discourse but more discourse; as a discursive product, 'organization' must entail a multiplicity of discursive perspectives that constitute the very stuff of the realities which they permit. The relationship between these discourses and the realities they represent is essentially *arbitrary* – even, indeed particularly, in relation to the biological, physical and natural properties which they denote as 'significant' entities which have to be acted on in some ways rather than others (Sayer, 1997; also see the earlier discussion of Foucault's view of the relationship between medial discourse and the birth of the clinic). There are no logical and/or natural necessities which have to be the way they are for the world to be the way it is; all reality, natural and social alike, is discursively contingent.

Yet, in another sense Foucauldian constructivism *is anything* but onto-logically mute or neutral. By advocating a puritanical commitment to a nominalist and processual ontology, it rules out any possibility of con-ceptualizing the social world as consisting of entities – including discourse itself – with essential properties that are indispensable for that entity being configured in one way and not another (Sayer, 1997). The radical social constructionism on which Foucauldian discourse analysis rests *denies itself* the very opportunity to understand and explain the generative properties which make social practices and forms – such as discursive formations – what they are and equip them to do what they do. This is a highly complex and difficult task to carry through, but there is no chance of bringing it off if discourse analysis remains wedded to an ontology in which discourse is treated *as nothing more than a social construction*.

In this respect, radical social constructionism has a number of debilitating explanatory consequences. By treating social and natural reality as in a *constant* state of movement and flux and by defining this processual ontology entirely in discursive terms, Foucauldian discourse analysis cannot begin to understand, much less explain, *how our material and social constructions are constrained and facilitated by the relatively stable and intransitive properties of the very materials and agents through which they are made possible*. As social constructions, organizations, disciplinary regimes or discursive formations are the objective effects and ontological referents of relatively stable and durable material relations and circum-stances which allow the former to come into existence as constituent features of social reality. The relationship between a discourse and that which it represents is not entirely arbitrary and independent of its anchoring in an extant set of material and social conditions: landlords and tenants, masters and servants, owners and workers can only be what they are as a result of the objectified material conditions and institutionalized social relations which inhere in respective systems of property distribution, social stratification and economic production. The discourses which assemble, represent and per-form or enact these institutional structures – market, status and class – locate and constrain social actors within a framework of linguistic rules and social relations defining who they are and what they can do. Of course, actors will strive to reinterpret and renegotiate their scope for action, but this occurs *within* a pre-existing *structure* of material, social and discursive relations which simply cannot be ignored or redefined out of existence through 're-imaginization' or 're-enchantment'. The complex *interaction* between agency and structure requires full recognition as the vital source of explana-tory coherence in organizational analysis, but this is lacking within Foucauldian discourse analysis because of its underlying commitment to a social ontology in which they become conflated into a 'flattened-out' view of the world (Reed, 1997).

Foucauldian discourse analysis emphasizes the representational aspects of discourse to the virtual exclusion of any other aspects of discursive forma-tion as a constrained social action. In stark contrast, realism stresses the *performative* aspect of discourse (Sayer, 1997): it's what a discourse *does*, rather than what it represents and how it represents it, which is the crucial explanatory issue for a realist ontology/epistemology. In this respect, the latter rejects the extreme constructivist ontology on which Foucauldian discourse analysis rests as being *congenitally unable to account for its own problematic*. The social construction of discursive formations and its material and political effects can only be properly described and explained if we reject the non-relational and constructivist ontology on which the Foucauldian approach relies for its descriptive and explanatory rationale. In this way, realism shifts the direction of discourse analysis away from a single-minded focus on the symbolic representation and communication of 'constructed worlds' towards a much wider concern with the political economy of discursive formation and its long-term institutional effects.

Realism and Discourse Analysis

As Gergen (1994: 75) correctly points out, realism is based on the core ontological assumption that social reality consists of real structures which exist and act independently of the pattern of events that they generate. It posits a world of material and social objects or mechanisms possessing powers or capacities which generate or cause both natural and social phenomena to behave in certain ways rather than others. If this realist ontology is accepted, then it becomes possible to treat discourses as generative mechanisms or properties possessing certain 'performative potentials' – that is, the innate potential to structure social action in certain ways – which may or may not be enacted within a particular organizational setting. Whether or not this underlying potential is realized in practice will depend on a range of situational contingencies, but it will be critically dependent on the capacity and intentionality – that is, the 'agency' – of the social actors acting within that organizational situation to act as agents for the potential which these generative mechanisms or structures contain. If discourses are regarded in this fashion, then it opens up all sorts of vital theoretical and empirical questions about who are the agents with the particular powers to shape the discursive formations structuring social interaction in specific organizational contexts and what are their links with more stable and durable domination structures based on class, gender, ethnicity, race or whatever – questions which the Foucauldian 'take' on discourse/organizational analysis is unable to ask, much less answer, because its ontology refuses to recognize that the world consists of natural and social objects possessing essential or in-built capacities for acting on and through that world which cannot be reduced to the, self-disciplining, discursive constructions of enterprising or calculating selves.

Thus, realism firmly rejects the Foucauldian domain assumption that 'there is *no ground* beyond the discursive realm to prevent the collapse of structures' (Dryberg, 1997, emphasis added). Indeed, the breathtaking ontological hubris conveyed by such a view simply defies any kind of theoretical repair short of a fundamental rethinking of the way in which the study of discourse has been imported into organizational studies through the medium of Foucauldian analysis. Undecidability is not a given ontological fact of social reality; discourses are not arbitrarily constructed sociolinguistic forms which bear a totally contingent relationship to the objective effects which they generate and represent. Power is not simply, or even primarily, grounded in discursive production; it is as much, if not more, to do with realizing and sustaining the 'structuring potential' entailed in the material and social relations on which the latter depends for its existence and legitimacy. It is not, as Foucault asserts, impossible to possess and control power: power can be and is generated and controlled by agents and structures as they struggle to impose their interests and/or logics on others at the level of everyday interaction and institutionalized politics.

Conclusion

This chapter has provided a critical overview of the Foucauldian approach to organizational analysis. The argument has indicated that Foucault's form of discourse analysis exhibits a number of debilitating explanatory weaknesses which cannot be repaired by remaining locked within the ontological universe and analytical framework which it specifies. It has also been suggested, albeit somewhat briefly, that a realist approach to discourse/ organizational analysis provides the most promising way of moving out of the explanatory cul-de-sac into which Foucauldian analysis has driven organization studies. Only in this way, so it has been argued, can the analysis of discursive formation and performance make its full contribution to our understanding and explanation of contemporary organizational reality and its transformative potential.

Part IV

A CONCLUDING DISCOURSE

12   Discourse, Organizations and Paradox

Richard Dunford and Ian Palmer

In the introductory chapter to this book Grant, Keenoy and Oswick conclude with a discussion of the role of paradox in understanding discourse and the need for a 'highly reflexive approach' to the study of organizational discourse. In this closing chapter we develop this proposition by identifying the extent to which attempts to analyse discourse are complicated by the paradoxical nature of the phenomena one seeks to understand. The analysis is in two parts. First, we identify six paradoxes which are represented among the chapters in this book. Second, we identify six different strategies of engagement which a researcher can utilize in addressing these paradoxes.

Paradoxes in Talk and Action

Two broad paradoxes can be identified that involve the relationship between talk and action. These are, first, that talk both enables and constrains action, and, second, that talk is action.

Paradox 1: *Talk Enables and Constrains Action*

This paradox focuses on the distinction between talk and action, but juxtaposes these two concepts in terms of the differential effects of talk on action. The paradox accepts that the primary direction of influence is from talk to action. However, and as we shall show, the paradox itself is actually located within the nature of this 'influence'.

Talk can achieve closure on meaning and thereby enable action. This is because some understanding has been established concerning such things as the objectives of action and, in some cases, the appropriate or legitimate means for achieving those outcomes. In clarifying these issues, other options are likely to be explicitly or implicitly delegitimated as appropriate action. For example, stories can be part of an official rhetoric that demands a unified voice. Indeed, a story may be a key component of corporate mythology such that it is not to be tampered with. It may be, in Salzer-Mörling's terms (Chapter 6), 'a singular and exclusive statement . . . one voice, one logic, one moral'.

This situation is not as straightforward as it initially suggests because meaning may be subject to resistance, contest and interpretation – a point clearly illustrated by Hardy et al. (Chapter 4) and Reed (Chapter 11). While talk embodies power, it is through talk that resources are constituted which are broadly available to social actors to utilize for their own purposes. By way of example, take an organization where senior management adhere to the notion of corporate image as being the pre-eminent logic underlying their decisions about resource allocation within the organization. At the same time, it is likely that others with distinct agendas may seek to co-opt the already legitimated discourse to support actions contrary to initial intentions of senior management.

As discussed by Hardy et al. (Chapter 4), talk helps to constitute individual identities. These identities influence how individuals are perceived. This in turn influences how the appropriateness, legitimacy and significance of their actions are evaluated. As such, it is enabling to the extent that the constructed identity is consistent with the intent of the actor. Conversely, it is constraining to the extent that a central part of the construction of identity is the formation of a view as to what actions (both topics and parameters) are appropriate for that actor.

Talk also helps to constitute collective identities and in so doing can enable collective action. This, though, is no guarantee of consensus, for while talk helps to constitute a common issue of concern, it is at the same time more clearly defining a territory upon which grounds for disagreement can be articulated. Hence, talk may enable collective action yet be constrained by a multiplicity of interpretations as to the meaning of the action. Alternatively, once talk constitutes a community of interest, a forum exists within which divergent opinions can be circulated in a way that is not possible amongst fragmented players.

Paradox 2: *Talk is Action*

The paradox 'talk is action' focuses on the distinction between talk conceived of as an alternative to action and talk as a form of action. In what Marshak (Chapter 1) describes as 'folk models' of talk, talk (both spoken and written) is represented as an alternative to action. What is more, it is represented as inferior to action. It is acknowledged as, at best, perhaps having a role as a precursor to action. Even then, like the entertainment that precedes a major sporting event, it may have an acknowledged place, but no-one confuses it with the real action, that is, the event that follows. From this perspective there is a linear relationship from talk to action to outcome (on the perils of linearity, see Burrell, Chapter 8).

Less charitably, talk is seen as an impediment to action, soaking up precious time that could otherwise be used productively, that is, in 'doing something'. The frustration associated with this position is clearly expressed by John Donne in 'The Canonization' when he protests, 'For God's sake, hold your tongue, and let me love.'

Talk is commonly treated as antithetical to action. This contrasts with the social constructionist position where, in Marshak's terms (Chapter 1), 'the real action is the talk'. From this perspective, talk and action are not discrete categories. Talk is integral to action at several levels. First, it is itself a form of action, albeit not a very active form – our cultural image of 'action man' or 'action woman' is of a triathlete, not of someone who is a skilled communicator. Second, talk may facilitate subsequent forms of action through establishing common understandings as to what is required, by whom, where and when. The context-free action is, if not an impossibility, something which has little connection to instrumental notions of actions. Third, and as shown by Hardy et al. (Chapter 4), talk may facilitate subsequent action through its contribution to relationship-forming, a contribution in which the activity of talk can have an effect independent of the content of the talk. Fourth, talk may facilitate subsequent action through generating 'emotional energy' (Westley, 1990, cited in Hardy et al., Chapter 4). Equally, the absence of emotional 'buy-in' may impede action. Again, the point is well made by Hardy et al (Chapter 4), who argue that individual action is based not so much on the result of rational calculation as on the emotional energies that are generated as individuals move from situation to situation. Fifth, actions do not produce their own meanings; talk is central to establishing meaning – even within instrumental accounts, notions of what constitutes 'success' are not internal to the action but are provided by associated 'talk'. Within this perspective, talk and action do not have a linear relationship. Rather, and as Marshak explains (Chapter 1), talk and action 'are linked in self-referencing cycles of meaning and experience'.

Paradox in Stories and Sense-Making

Three broad paradoxes can be identified that are associated with stories and sense-making. These are, first, that stories create and destroy meaning; second, that organizational stories are unique and general; and third, that non-sense is sense.

Paradox 3: *Stories Create and Destroy Meaning*

In this instance the paradox focuses upon the way in which organizational stories are implicated in the construction and deconstruction of meaning. This can occur in a number of ways.

First, the more complex and potentially unintelligible people's lived experiences become, the greater the significance of stories as ways of making experience meaningful (Boje and Dennehy, 1993, cited in Gabriel, Chapter 5). In a complex and ambiguous situation stories are concise ways in which people establish meaning – but these meanings are always partial and in a process of becoming intelligible.

Second, and as asserted by Gabriel (Chapter 5), stories destroy meaning when they 'disintegrate into clichés'. The power of the story is depleted because the more the story is told, the less is its ability to establish meaning in fluid and constantly changing organizational situations. Thus, the constancy associated with the story can be a source of comfort and insight into appropriate actions, but the very changeability of contexts provides the instability in the efficacy of the story over time. As new meanings are established through new stories, the legitimacy of older ones and their associated meanings is at one and the same time brought into question.

Paradox 4: *Organizational Stories Are Unique and General*

This paradox identifies the way in which organizational stories are unique in the sense that each has its own combination of players and contexts. However, unique elements in the story are likely to be far fewer than implied by the tellers of the story. That which is regarded as unique may contain core elements which reflect common themes across many organizations.

Perceived uniqueness is a quality that is deliberately sought by those who wish to establish a belief in the coherence, distinctiveness and 'specialness' of an individual organization. The uniqueness quality is thus part of official rhetoric. Uniqueness bestows a sense of privilege on those associated with the organization. In the case of Ikea, and as described by Salzer-Mörling (Chapter 6), the unique quality is portrayed as that of the rebel, challenging the establishment's taken-for-granted assumptions as to how to do business. But the 'rebel' is clearly a general story applicable to many organizations that compete in a way that is counter to the dominant logic of the industry, for example, Wal Mart, Southeast Airlines and Dell Computer (D'Aveni, 1994).

Paradox 5: *Non-Sense is Sense*

The paradox 'non-sense is sense' establishes the way in which non-sense is not the absence of sense. From a social constructionist position, non-sense is constituted through sense-making processes. To quote from Wallemacq and Sims (Chapter 7): 'Non-sense is not a failure of the sense-making process. It is a part of it; it is a categorization that permits sense to be made, even of "non-sense".'

The same sort of logic is found in the argument put forward by Mangham (Chapter 3). To him, emotions are rational. Whereas it is commonly perceived that emotions in organizations should be separated from processes that require rational actions and judgement, Mangham proposes that 'practical reasoning alone is not sufficient for practical wisdom'. Rather, such wisdom 'is likely to be deeply informed by emotion'. For example, displays of emotion may signal the existence of an important issue needing attention within an organization. From this perspective, rather than emotion being part of a non-logical realm, emotions are simultaneously cognitive and physiological, and the distinction between emotional and rational thought is fundamentally flawed.

Paradox in Conversation

Paradox 6: *Organization is Conversation*

Here we identify a major paradox – that organization is conversation. That is to say, conversation does not just occur about organizations; conversations constitute organizations. Organization is not independent of conversation.

Organizational 'being' is the foundation for organizational 'doing'. That is, a clear collective awareness of a company's core values and vision can provide the basis for future activities. What Broekstra (Chapter 9) describes as 'networked conversational processes' is presented as being central to this. As he explains, the ability for coherent organizing to occur depends upon 'the myriad of loosely coupled micro-conversations going on endlessly every day'. Similarly, the ability to engage in organizational change is the ability to change the conversation.

Internal conversations become even more important where people are extensively involved in communication outside the organization. To Broekstra such a situation may produce 'conversation overload' from which disorientation may follow unless the players involved have a clear sense of their organization's strategic intent. The paradox is that conversations are a way of both describing and enacting social relationships.

Paradoxes and Reflexivity

What is clear from the foregoing is that understanding organizational discourse requires an understanding of its paradoxical nature. We agree with Grant, Keenoy and Oswick, who in their Introduction argue that researchers need to adopt a reflexive approach to enable them to become critically aware of these paradoxes. This approach is one which a number of organization theorists have suggested is a way of coming to terms with the different ontological and epistemological assumptions which underpin organization theory (Gergen and Gergen, 1991; Jackson and Willmott, 1987; Krippendorff, 1991; Linstead, 1994; Palmer and Dunford, 1996) – after all theory-building is itself 'a discursive enterprise' (Poole and Van de Ven, 1989: 564).

A reflexive approach entails 'the ability to be critical or suspicious of our own intellectual assumptions' (Hassard, 1993: 12). We suggest that organizational analysts should understand the extent to which their own theoretical and methodological approaches address the contradictory, paradoxical elements of discourse which emerge in their work. This position recognizes that, for the most part, researchers adopt an everyday or pragmatic philosophy in relation to their activities (Dyson, cited in Fuchs and Ward, 1994a). As such, it is a stance that does not encourage them to reflect upon the extent to which their research is sensitive to the play of paradoxical or contradictory positions which might conceal blind spots in relation to their research outcomes and findings (Fuchs and Ward, 1994b).

In practical terms, then, adopting a reflexive position requires researchers to become aware of their current mode of engagement with different discursive paradoxes. Such an inquiry also enables them to consider the validity of this mode of engagement through attention to alternative modes. In the following section we suggest that there are a variety of strategies of engagement with paradox which researchers may employ, each of which has differing outcomes.

Strategies of Engagement

We will outline initially four strategies of engagement with paradox as described by Poole and Van de Ven (1989). We then extend their framework by identifying two additional strategies of engagement.

One strategy of engagement is to accept the paradox, live with it and endeavour to use it constructively. By juxtaposing different parts of the paradox, organization theorists can stimulate new thoughts and perspectives (Poole and Van de Ven, 1989). In this perspective, paradoxes can be used to question current assumptions and purposes (Beam, 1994). Paradoxes can be cultivated to enable new, creative outcomes to emerge (Stroh and Miller, 1994). For example, in relation to the paradoxes noted above, one may accept that 'talk' both enables and constrains 'action'. This paradox can be used constructively by ensuring that alternative courses of action are not prematurely closed off because they are not 'conceivable' within the language being used to frame the situation.

The next three strategies of engagement entail different ways through which researchers try to resolve paradoxes. The second strategy is one which involves trying to resolve paradox by clarifying the level of analysis at which it is experienced (Poole and Van de Ven, 1989). For example, as Beardsley observed: 'Discourse that works at more than one level of meaning may, of course, be inconsistent at one level but consistent at another' (1950: 289). Hence, paradoxes 'may be self-contradictory on the level of designation, but they have a consistent higher-level meaning' (Beardsley, 1950: 291). This 'solution' to the paradox is what philosophers call the 'Simple Theory of Types', which suggests that 'all entities divide into a hierarchy of types, starting with individual entities, moving to properties of individual entities, then to properties of properties of individual entities, and so on' (Kahane, 1973: 312). In this way paradox can be understood as resultant from different hierarchies of meaning such as micro/macro, individual/society, and so on (Poole and Van de Ven, 1989). The paradox is 'resolved' by noting that its different component parts operate on multiple levels. For instance, the paradox that 'organizational stories are unique and general' is treated as being resolvable by recognizing that a story may be unique at one level, that of a single organization (for example, Salzer-Mörling's Ikea story), but at another level, such as the general population of organizations, the story is a general one about organizational development and the role of the 'rebel' founder.

The third strategy of engagement entails resolving paradox by separating the periods of time in which different parts of the paradox hold true (Poole and Van de Ven, 1989). Hence, whilst the paradox may be 'true', its elements can be distinguished in terms of their sequence over time. Using this technique, it could be argued that the paradox 'stories create and destroy meaning' might be resolved. To illustrate this process, one could show how as new stories emerge over time, older stories and the meanings they convey are brought into question, especially when they are treated as clichés within the organization. In this way, the creation of meaning and the destruction of meaning occur simultaneously through the story-telling process.

A fourth strategy of engagement relies on synthesis of opposing parts of the paradox through the identification of the conceptual flaws which underpin the assumptions on which the paradox is based (Poole and Van de Ven, 1989; see also Stroh and Miller, 1994). In this approach, the synthesis is achieved by disputing the inherent logic underlying the paradox, or by questioning its basic assumptions. When this technique is applied to the paradox that 'organization is conversation', it is argued that the paradox is shown to be based upon a flawed assumption. The flaw is that the paradox only exists if conversation and organization are seen as alternative forms of human interaction. If, however, it is argued that organization is fundamentally a pattern of human interaction, then conversation as a major medium for that interaction is directly involved in the social construction of organized relationships. Thus, the paradox only exists if the concept of organization is reified.

Moving on to the fifth strategy of engagement, this involves what we term a 'supremacy position' (Palmer and Dunford, 1996). It is a strategy that involves 'living with' the paradox, but assigning priority to one side of it. This priority is attached on the basis of an assertion of the inherent strength of one side of the paradox. For example, with the paradox 'talk is action', the analyst may recognize the existence of the paradox, but claim that action which goes beyond 'talk' is more powerful than action which is only talk.

The sixth and final strategy of engagement is what we term a 'relevance position'. This is one where the analyst accepts the existence of the paradox, but rates it in terms of its fundamental importance to practice. For example, some analysts have treated various paradoxes as relatively unimportant by viewing them as arising from an ambiguity of language or of using language in trivial ways (Mackie, 1973). In this situation the question asked concerns not the existence of the paradox, nor whether it can be resolved, but simply whether it is worth bothering with in terms of engaging with it. This entails reflection by the analyst upon the standards of evaluation (Cohen and Ben-Ari, 1993) which he or she applies when judging the relevance of specific paradoxes. Such standards might also be associated with the effect which the paradox is perceived to have, or, to paraphrase Lyotard (1984), its 'performativity'. In this respect the relevance or strength of the paradox may not be pregiven but rather related to the disposition of the analyst (Townley, 1994). Thus, the paradox 'non-sense is sense' may be accepted, but its relevance disputed. The paradox is treated as more appropriate to the world of semantics than to the world of practice.

Conclusion

The range of chapters presented in this volume indicates the diversity of material relevant to the analysis of discourse in organizations. Such diversity need not impair the identification or development of core issues within the field. By way of example, this chapter has shown that the existence and treatment of paradox is at the centre of organizational discourse and thus many of the contributions to the book.

The chapter has sought to demonstrate that a range of 'solutions' may be applied to the paradoxes we have identified. We have presented a particular solution in relation to each paradox, in order to illustrate particular strategies of engagement. In doing so, we make no claims that the illustrated strategy is the only one that could have been applied to the given paradox. Our aim has been to encourage organizational analysts to adopt a reflexive position. Such an approach would equip them with an awareness of alternative strategies of engagement, thereby helping them to re-examine the assumptions they make about the study of discourse in organizations.

References

Acker, J. (1992) *Gendering Organizational Analysis.* Thousand Oaks, CA: Sage.

Allaire, Y. and Firsirotu, M.E. (1984) 'Theories of organizational culture', *Organization Studies*, 5(3): 193–226.

Alvesson, M. (1993a) 'Cultural-ideological modes of management control', in S. Deetz (ed.), *Communication Yearbook*, Vol. 16. Thousand Oaks, CA: Sage.

Alvesson, M. (1993b) 'The play of metaphors', in J. Hassard and M. Parker (eds), *Postmodernism and Organization.* London: Sage.

Alvesson, M. (1994) 'Talking in organizations: managing identity and impressions in an advertising agency', *Organization Studies*, 15(4): 535–63.

Alvesson, M. (1995) 'The meaning and meaninglessness of postmodernism: some ironic remarks', *Organization Studies*, 16(6): 1047–75.

Alvesson, M. (1996) *Communication, Power and Organization.* Berlin: Walter de Gruyter.

Alvesson, M. and Berg, P.O. (1988) *Företagskultur och organisationssymbolism.* Lund: Studentlitteratur.

Alvesson, M. and Deetz, S. (1996) 'Critical theory and postmodernist approaches to organizational studies', in S. Clegg, C. Hardy and W. Nord (eds), *Handbook of Organization Studies.* London: Sage.

Alvesson, M. and Willmott, H. (eds) (1992) *Critical Management Studies.* London: Sage.

Anderson, M., Cuff, E. and Lee, J. (1978) 'The recommencement of a meeting as a member's accomplishment', in J. Schenkein (ed.), *Studies in the Organization of Conversation Interaction.* New York: Academic Press.

Archer, M. (1995) *Realist Social Theory: The Morphogenetic Approach.* Cambridge: Cambridge University Press.

Argyris, C. (1982) *Reasoning, Learning and Action.* San Francisco: Jossey-Bass.

Argyris, C. (1990) *Overcoming Organizational Defenses.* Boston: Allyn & Bacon.

Argyris, C. (1993) *Knowledge for Action.* San Francisco: Jossey-Bass.

Argyris, C. and Schön, D.A. (1974) *Theory in Practice.* San Francisco: Jossey-Bass.

Argyris, C. and Schön, D.A. (1978) *Organizational Learning: A Theory of Action Perspective.* Reading, MA: Addison-Wesley.

Aristotle (1963) *Poetics.* London: Dent.

Aristotle (1984) *The Rhetoric.* Princeton, NJ: Princeton University Press.

Atkinson, J.M. and Heritage, J. (eds) (1984) *Structures of Social Action: Studies in Conversation Analysis.* Cambridge: Cambridge University Press.

Austin, J. (1962) *How to Do Things with Words.* Oxford: Oxford University Press.

Averill, J. (1982) *Anger and Aggression: An Essay on Emotion.* New York: Springer-Verlag.

Bach, K. and Harnish, R. (1979) *Linguistic Communication and Speech Acts.* Cambridge, MA: MIT Press.

Baier, A.C. (1991) *A Progress of Sentiments: Reflections on Hume's Treatise.* Cambridge, MA: Harvard University Press.

Bak, P. (1996) *How Nature Works: The Science of Self-Organized Criticality.* New York: Springer-Verlag.

Bak, P. and Chen, K. (1991) 'Self-organized criticality', *Scientific American*, 264(1): 46–54.

Bakhtin, M. (1986) *Speech Genres and Other Late Essays*. Austin: University of Texas Press.

Bardmann, T.M. (1996) 'Social work: profession without qualities', *Systems Research*, 13(3): 205–13.

Barker, J (1993) 'Tightening the iron cage: concertive control in self-managing teams', *Administrative Science Quarterly*, 38: 408–37.

Barley, S. and Kunda, G. (1992) 'Design and devotion: surges of rational and normative ideologies of control in managerial discourses', *Administrative Science Quarterly*, 37: 363–99.

Barnes, G. (1994) *Justice, Love and Wisdom: Linking Psychotherapy to Second-Order Cybernetics*. Zagreb: Medicinska Naklada.

Barnett, G.A. (1988) 'Communication and organisational culture', in G.A. Barnett and G.M. Goldhaber (eds), *Handbook of Organisational Communication*. Norwood, NJ: Ablex.

Barry, A., Osborne, T. and Rose, N. (1996) *Foucault and Political Reason: Liberalism, Neo-Liberalism and Rationalities of Government*. London: University College London Press.

Barry, D. and Elmes, M. (1997) 'Strategy retold: toward a narrative view of strategic discourse', *Academy of Management Review*, 22(2): 429–52.

Barthes, R. (1974) *S/Z*. New York: Hill & Wang.

Bataille, G. (1985) *Death and Sensuality*. San Francisco: City Lights.

Baudrillard, J., (1983a) *In the Shadow of the Silent Majorities*. New York: Semiotext(e).

Baudrillard, J. (1983b) *Simulations*. New York: Semiotext(e).

Baumann, B. (1975) *Imaginative Participation*. The Hague: Martinus Nijhoff.

Beam, H.H. (1994) 'Review: Charles Handy, *The Age of Paradox*', *Academy of Management Executive*, 8(2): 94–6.

Beardsley, M.C. (1950) *Practical Logic*. Englewood Cliffs, NJ: Prentice Hall.

Beer, M., Eisenstatt, R.E. and Spector, B. (1990) *The Critical Path to Corporate Renewal*. Boston: Harvard Business School Press.

Beer, S. (1979) *The Heart of Enterprise*. Chichester: Wiley.

Beer, S. (1985) *Diagnosing the System for Organizations*. Chichester: Wiley.

Benedict, R. (1931) 'Folklore', in *The Encyclopaedia of the Social Sciences*, Vol. VI. New York: Longman.

Benjamin, W. (1968) 'The storyteller: Reflections on the works of Nikolai Leskov', in *Illuminations*. London: Jonathan Cape.

Berger, J. (1967) *Ways of Seeing*. Harmondsworth: Penguin.

Berger, P. and Luckmann, T.L. (1966) *The Social Construction of Knowledge: A Treatise on the Sociology of Knowledge*. Garden City, NY: Doubleday.

Berger, P. and Luckmann, T.L. (1967) *The Social Construction of Reality*. London: Penguin.

Bergquist, W. (1993) *The Postmodern Organization: Mastering the Art of Irreversible Change*. San Francisco: Jossey-Bass.

Bettelheim, B. (1976) *The Uses of Enchantment*. London: Thames & Hudson.

Bittner, E. (1965) 'The concept of organization', *Social Research*, 32: 239–55.

Blackler, F. (1992) 'Formative contexts and activity systems: postmodern approaches to the management of change', in M. Reed and M. Hughes (eds), *Rethinking Organization: New Directions in Organization Theory and Analysis*. London: Sage. pp. 273–94.

Blum, L. (1980) *Friendship, Altruism and Morality*. London: Routledge & Kegan Paul.

Bly, R. (1990) *Iron John: A Book about Men*. New York: Addison Wesley.

Boden, D. (1994) *The Business of Talk: Organizations in Action*. Cambridge: Polity.

Boden, D. and Zimmerman, D. (eds) (1991) *Talk and Social Structure*. Berkeley, CA: University of California Press.

Bogen, D. (1992) 'The organization of talk', *Qualitative Sociology*, 15(3): 273–95.

Bogue, R. (1989) *Deleuze and Guattari*. London: Routledge.

Bohm, D. (1980) *Wholeness and the Implicate Order*. London: Ark.

Bohm, D. (1989) *On Dialogue*. Ojai, CA: Ojai Institute.

Boje, D.M. (1991) 'The storytelling organization: a study of performance in an office supply firm', *Administrative Science Quarterly*, 36: 106–26.

Boje, D.M. (1994) 'Organisational storytelling: the struggles of pre-modern, modern and postmodern organisational learning discourses', *Management Learning*, 25(3): 433–62.

Boje, D.M. (1995) 'Stories of the storytelling organization: a postmodern analysis of Disney as *Tamara*-Land', *Academy of Management Journal*, 38(4): 997–1035.

Boje, D.M. and Dennehy, R.F. (1993) *Managing in the Postmodern World: America's Revolution against Exploitation*. Dubuque, IA: Kendall-Hunt.

Bormann, E.G. (1983) 'Symbolic convergence', in L. Putnam and M. Pacanowsky (eds), *Communications and Organizations*. Beverley Hills, CA: Sage.

Bourdieu, P. (1977) *Outline of a Theory of Practice*. Cambridge: Cambridge University Press.

Bourgeois, V.W. and Pinder, C.C. (1983) 'Contrasting philosophical perspectives in administrative science: a reply to Morgan', *Administrative Science Quarterly*, 28: 608–13.

Bowles, M.L. (1989) 'Myth, meaning and work organization', *Organization Studies*, 10(3): 405–21.

Bowles, M.L. (1990) 'Recognizing deep structures in organizations', *Organization Studies*, 11(3): 395–412.

Boyce, M.E. (1995) 'Collective centring and collective sense-making in the stories and storytelling of one organization', *Organization Studies*, 16(1): 107–37.

Boyce, M.E. (1996) 'Organisational story and storytelling: a critical review', *Journal of Organisational Change Management*, 9(5): 5–26.

Bradbury, M. (1977) *The History Man*. London: Arrow Books.

Brech, E.F.L. (1953) *Principles and Practice of Management*. London: Longman.

Brier, S. (1996) 'From second-order cybernetics to cyber-semiotics', *Systems Research*, 13(3): 214–27.

Broekstra, G. (1984) 'Management by matching: a Consistency Model for organizational assessment and change', in R. Trappl (ed.), *Cybernetics and Systems Research '84*. Amsterdam: Elsevier Science Publishers.

Broekstra, G. (1992) 'Toward a theory of organizational change: the Chaos Hypothesis', in R. Trappl (ed.), *Cybernetics and Systems Research '92*. Singapore: World Scientific.

Broekstra, G. (1994) 'Problems of chaotic simplicity', in R. Trappl (ed.), *Cybernetics and Systems '94*. Singapore: World Scientific.

Broekstra, G. (1996a) 'A complexity perspective of organizing', in R. Trappl (ed.), *Cybernetics and Systems '96*. Vienna: Austrian Society of Cybernetic Studies.

Broekstra, G. (1996b) 'The triune-brain evolution of the living organization', in D. Grant and C. Oswick (eds), *Metaphor and Organizations*. London: Sage.

Broekstra, G. (1997) 'Organizations are closed systems', *Systemica: Journal of the Dutch Systems Group*, 11: 43–63.

Broms, H. and Gahmberg, H. (1983) 'Communication to self in organizations and cultures', *Administrative Science Quarterly*, 28: 482–95.

Brown, G. and Yule, G. (1983) *Discourse Analysis*. Cambridge: Cambridge University Press.

Brown, J.S. and Duguid, P. (1991) 'Organizational learning and communities-of-practice: toward a unified view of working, learning and Innovation', *Organization Science*, 2(1): 40–57.

Brown, P. and Levinson, S. (1987) *Politeness: Some Universals in Language Use.* Cambridge: Cambridge University Press.

Bruner, J. and Feldman, C.F. (1990) 'Metaphors of consciousness and cognition in the history of psychology', in D.E. Leary (ed.), *Metaphors in the History of Psychology*, Cambridge: Cambridge University Press.

Budd, M. (1995) *Values of Art: Pictures, Poetry and Music.* London: Penguin.

Burchell, G., Gordon, C. and Miller, P. (eds) (1991) *The Foucault Effect: Studies in Governmentality.* Hemel Hempstead: Harvester Wheatsheaf.

Burrell, G. (1988) 'Modernism, postmodernism and organizational analysis 2: the contribution of Michel Foucault', *Organization Studies*, 9(2): 221–35.

Burrell, G. (1997) *Pandemonium: Towards a Retro-Organization Theory.* London: Sage.

Burrell G. and Dale, K. (1998) 'Modernism, postmodernism and organizational analysis: the contribution of Deleuze and Guattari'. Unpublished paper, University of Warwick.

Burris, B. (1993) *Technology at Work.* Albany, NY: State University of New York Press.

Button, G. and Lee, J. (eds) (1987) *Talk and Social Organisation.* Clevedon: Multilingual Matters.

Byron, M.P. (1996) 'Crisis-driven evolutionary learning'. PhD dissertation, University of Michigan, Ann Arbor.

Callon, M. and Latour, B. (1981) 'Unscrewing the big leviathan: how actors macro-structure reality and how sociologists help them to do so', in K. Knorr-Cetina and A.V. Cicourel (eds), *Advances in Social Theory and Methodology.* Boston: Routledge & Kegan Paul.

Cameron, D. (ed.) (1990) *The Feminist Critique of Language: A Reader.* London: Routledge.

Campbell, J. (1975) 'Folkloristic commentary' to *The Complete Grimm's Fairy Tales.* London: Routledge.

Canguilhem, G. (ed.) (1965) 'Machine et organisme', in *La connaissance de la vie.* Paris: Vrin.

Capra, F. (1982) *The Turning Point.* New York: Simon & Schuster.

Capra, F. (1996) *The Web of Life.* New York: Anchor Books.

Case, P. (1995) 'Representations of talk at work: performatives and "Performability" ', *Management Learning*, 26(4): 423–44.

Casey, C. (1995) *Work, Self and Society: After Industrialism.* London: Routledge.

Chakraborty, S.K. (1991) *Management by Values: Towards Cultural Congruence.* Delhi: Oxford University Press.

Child, J. (1964) *British Management Thought.* London: Unwin.

Chomsky, N. (1957) *Syntactic Structures.* The Hague: Mouton.

Cicourel, A. (1968) *The Social Organisation of Juvenile Justice.* London: Wiley.

Clair, R. (1993) 'The use of framing devices to sequester organizational narratives: hegemony and harrassment', *Communication Monographs*, 60: 113–36.

Clark, B.R. (1972) 'The organizational saga in higher education', *Administrative Science Quarterly*, 17: 178–84.

Clark, H., Chandler, J. and Barry, J. (1994) *Organisation and Identities.* London: Chapman & Hall.

Clark, T. and Salaman, G. (1996a) 'The use of metaphor in the client–consultant relationship: a study of management consultants', in C. Oswick and D. Grant (eds), *Organisational Development: Metaphorical Explorations.* London: Pitman.

Clark, T. and Salaman, G. (1996b) 'Telling tales: management consultancy as the art of storytelling', in D. Grant and C. Oswick (eds), *Metaphor and Organizations*. London: Sage.

Clegg, S.R. (1975) *Power, Rule and Domination*. London: Routledge & Kegan Paul.

Clegg, S.R. (1989) *Frameworks of Power*. London: Sage.

Clegg, S.R. (1994), 'Power relations and the constitution of the resistant subject', in J. Jermier, D. Knights and W. Nord (eds), *Resistance and Power in Organizations*. London: Routledge.

Clifford, J. and Marcus, G.E. (eds) (1986) *Writing Culture: The Poetics and Politics of Ethnography*. Berkeley, CA: University of California Press.

Cobb, S. (1993) 'Empowerment and mediation: a narrative perspective', *Negotiation Journal*, 9(3): 245–61.

Cobb, S. and Rifkin, J. (1991) 'Neutrality as a discursive practice: the construction and transformation of narratives in community mediation', *Studies in Law, Politics, and Society*, 11: 69–91.

Cohen, E. and Ben-Ari, E. (1993) 'Hard choices: a sociological perspective on value incommensurability', *Human Studies*, 16: 267–97.

Cohen, M.D., March, J.G. and Olsen, J.P. (1972) 'A garbage can model of organizational choice', *Administrative Science Quarterly*, 17(1): 1–25.

Collins, J.C. and Porras, J.I. (1994) *Built to Last: Successful Habits of Visionary Companies*. New York: Harper Business.

Collins, R. (1981) 'On the microfoundations of macrosociology', *American Journal of Sociology*, 86(5): 984–1013.

Collinson, D.L. (1988) ' "Engineering Humour": Masculinity, joking and conflict in shop-floor relations', *Organization Studies*, 9(2): 181–99.

Collinson, D.L. (1994) 'Strategies of resistance: power, knowledge and subjectivity in the workplace', in J. Jermier, W. Nord, and D. Knights (eds), *Resistance and Power in Organizations*. London: Routledge.

Colum, P. (1975) 'Introduction' to *The Complete Grimm's Fairy Tales*. London: Routledge.

Combes, C., Grant, D., Keenoy, T. and Oswick, C. (eds) (1996) *Organizational Discourse: Talk, Text, and Tropes*. London: KMCP.

Cooper, R (1992) 'Formal organization as representation: remote control, displacement and abbreviation', in M. Reed and M. Hughes (eds), *Rethinking Organization: New Directions in Organization Theory and Analysis*. London: Sage.

Cooper, R. and Burrell, G. (1988) 'Modernism, postmodernism and organizational analysis: an introduction', *Organization Studies*, 9(1): 91–112.

Cooper, R. and Law, J. (1995) 'Organization: distal and proximal views', in S. Bacharach, P. Gagliardi and B. Mundell (eds), *Research in the Sociology of Organizations, Vol. 13: Studies of Organizations in the European Tradition*. Greenwich, CT: JAI Press.

Cooperrider, D.L. and Srivastva, S. (1987) 'Appreciative inquiry in organizational life', *Research in Organizational Change and Development*, 1: 129–69.

Cousins, M. and Hussain, A. (1984) *Michel Foucault*. London: Macmillan.

Crisp, R. (1996) *How Should One Live? Essays on the Virtues*. Oxford: Clarendon Press.

Crouch, A. and Basch J. (1997) 'The structure of strategic thinking: a lexical content analysis', *Journal of Applied Management Studies*, 6(1): 13–38.

Cuddon, J.A. (1991) *The Penguin Dictionary of Literary Terms and Literary Theory*. London: Penguin.

Cuff, E. and Sharrock, W. (1985) 'Meetings', in T.A. van Dijk (ed.), *Handbook of Discourse Analysis: Discourse and Dialogue*, Vol. 3. London: Academic Press.

Culler, J. (1985) *Saussure*. London: Fontana.

Czarniawska-Joerges, B. (1992) *Exploring Complex Organizations: A Cultural Perspective*. Newbury Park, CA: Sage.

Czarniawska-Joerges, B. (1993) *The Three-Dimensional Organization: A Constructionist View*. Lund: Studentlitteratur.

Czarniawska-Joerges, B. (1996) 'Autobiographical acts and organizational identities', in S. Linstead, R. Grafton-Small and P. Jeffcutt (eds), *Understanding Management*. London: Sage.

Czarniawska-Joerges, B. and Joerges, B. (1990) 'Linguistic artifacts at service of organizational control', in P. Gagliardi (ed.), *Symbols and Artifacts: Views of the Corporate Landscape*. Berlin: Walker de Gruyter.

Daft, R. and Wiginton, J. (1979) 'Language and organization', *Academy of Management Review*, 4(2): 179–91.

Dale, K. (1997) 'Identity in a culture of dissection: body, self and knowledge', in R. Munro and K. Hetherington (eds), *Ideas of Difference: Social Spaces and the Labour of Division*. Sociological Review Monograph Series, Oxford: Blackwell.

Dale K. and Burrell, G. (1995) 'Organization studies and the anatomizing urge', *Warwick Business School Research Papers No. 195*. University of Warwick.

Dalton, K. (1993) 'The performance of narrative and self in conversational storytelling: a multidisciplinary approach'. Unpublished PhD thesis, University of Bath.

D'Aveni, R.A. (1994) *Hypercompetition: Managing the Dynamics of Strategic Maneuvering*. New York: Free Press.

Davidson, M.P. (1992) *The Consumerist Manifesto: Advertising in Postmodern Times*. London: Routledge.

Dean, M. (1994) *Critical and Effective Histories: Foucault's Methods and Historical Sociology*. London: Routledge.

Deetz, S. (1992) 'Disciplinary power in the modern corporation', in M. Alvesson and H. Willmott (eds), *Critical Management Studies*. London: Sage.

Deetz, S. (1995) *Transforming Communication, Transforming Business: Building Responsive and Responsible Workplaces*. Cresskill, NJ: Hampton Press.

Deetz, S. and Mumby, D. (1985) 'Metaphors, information and power', in B. Ruben, (ed.), *Information and Behavior 1*. New Brunswick, NJ: Transaction Press.

Deleuze, G. and Guattari, F. (1984) *Anti-Oedipus*. London: Athlone.

Deleuze, G. and Guattari, F. (1986) *Nomadology,*. New York: Semiotext(e).

Deleuze, G. and Guattari, F. (1988) *A Thousand Plateaus*. London: Athlone.

Deleuze, G. and Parnet, C. (1987) *Dialogues*. London: Athlone.

Derrida, J. (1978) *Writing and Difference*. Chicago: University of Chicago Press.

Derrida, J. (1982) *Margins of Philosophy*. Chicago: University of Chicago Press.

Donnellon, A. (1994) 'Team work: linguistic models of negotiating differences', *Research on Negotiations in Organizations*, 4: 71–123.

Donnellon, A. (1996) *Team Talk: The Power of Language in Team Dynamics*. Boston, MA: Harvard Business School Press.

Dorson, R.M. (1969) 'Theories of myth and the folklorist', in H.A. Murray (ed.), *Myth and Mythmaking*. Boston: Beacon Press.

Dougherty, D. (1995) 'Managing your core incompetencies for corporate venturing', *Entrepreneurship Theory and Practice*, 19(3): 113–35.

Douglas, M. (1973) *Natural Symbols*. New York: Pantheon Books.

Downing, S.J. (1997) 'Learning the plot: emotional momentum in search of dramatic logic', *Management Learning*, 28(1): 27–44.

Drake, B. and Moberg, B. (1986) 'Communicating influence attempts in dyads: linguistic sedatives and palliatives', *Academy of Management Review*, 11(3): 567–84.

Drew, P. and Heritage, J. (eds) (1992) *Talk at Work*. Cambridge: Cambridge University Press.

Drew, P. and Sorjonen, M. (1997) 'Institutional dialogue', in T.A. van Dijk (ed.), *Discourse as Structure and Process*, Vol. 2. London: Sage.

Drucker, P.F. (1994) 'The theory of the business', *Harvard Business Review*, September–October: 95–104.

Dryberg, T (1997) *The Circular Structure of Power: Politics, Identity and Community*, London: Verso.

du Gay, P. (1996) *Consumption and Identity at Work*. London: Sage.

du Gay, P. and Salaman, G. (1992) 'The cult[ure] of the customer', *Journal of Management Studies*, 29(5): 615–34.

du Gay, P., Salaman, G. and Rees, B. (1996) 'The conduct of management and the management of conduct: contemporary managerial discourse and the constitution of the "Competent Manager" ', *Journal of Management Studies*, 33(3): 263–82.

Dumm, T. (1996) *Michel Foucault and the Politics of Freedom*. Thousand Oaks, CA: Sage.

Dundes, A. (1965) *The Study of Folklore*. Englewood Cliffs, NJ: Prentice Hall.

Dundes, A. (1980) *Interpreting Folklore*. Bloomington: Indiana University Press.

Dunne, M. and Ng, S.H. (1994) 'Simultaneous speech in small group conversation: all-together now AND one-at-a time?', *Journal of Language and Social Psychology*, 13(1): 45–71.

Dunphy, D., Bullard, C. and Crossing, E. (1989) 'Validation of the general enquirer Harvard IV dictionary', in C. Zull, R. Weber and P. Mohler (eds), *Computer Aided Text Classification for the Social Sciences: The General Enquirer III*. Mannheim: Zentrum für Methoden und Analysen.

Durkheim, É. (1995) *The Elementary Forms of Religious Life*. New York: Free Press.

Dutton, J.E. and Ashford, S.J. (1993) 'Selling issues to top management', *Academy of Management Review,* 18(3): 397–428.

Dutton, J.E. and Dukerich, J.M. (1991) 'Keeping an eye on the mirror: image and identity in organizational adaptation', *Academy of Management Journal*, 34(3): 517–54.

Dutton, J.E. and Penner, W.J. (1993) 'The importance of organizational identity for strategic agenda building', in J. Hendry and G. Johnson (eds), *Strategic Thinking*. London: Wiley.

Easterby-Smith, M., Thorpe, R. and Lowe, A. (1991) *Management Research: An Introduction*. London: Sage.

Edelsky, C. (1981) 'Who's got the floor?', *Language and Society*, 10: 383–421.

Eisenberg, E.M. and Goodall, H.L. (1993) *Organizational Communication: Balancing Creativity and Constraint*. New York: St Martin's Press.

Ekman, P. and Oster, H. (1979) 'Facial expression of emotion', *Annual Review of Psychology*, 30(4): 527–44.

Elmes, M.B. and Kasouf, Chickery, J. (1995) 'Knowledge workers and organisational learning: narratives from biotechnology', *Management Learning*, 26(4): 403–22.

Emery, M. and Purser, R.E. (1996) *The Search Conference*. San Francisco: Jossey-Bass.

Erickson, F. and Shultz, J. (1982) *The Counselor as Gatekeeper: Social Interaction Interviews*. New York: Academic Press.

Escobar, A. (1995) *Encountering Development: The Making and Unmaking of the Third World*. Princeton, NJ: Princeton University Press.

Euripides (1973) *The Bacchae and other Plays*. Harmondsworth: Penguin.

Fairclough, N. (1992) *Discourse and Social Change*. Cambridge: Polity.

Fairclough, N. (1995) *Critical Discourse Analysis: Papers in the Critical Study of Language*. London: Longman.

Fairclough, N. and Wodak, R. (1997) 'Critical discourse analysis', in T.A. van Dijk (ed.), *Discourse as Social Interaction*. London: Sage.

Fairhurst, G.T. and Sarr R.A. (1996) *The Art of Framing: Managing the Language of Leadership*. San Francisco: Jossey-Bass.

Fayol, H. (1949) *General and Industrial Management*. London: Pitman.

Feldman, M. (1989) *Order Without Design*. Stanford, CA: Stanford University Press.

Fineman, S. (ed.) (1993) *Emotion in Organizations*. London: Sage.

Fineman, S. (1994) 'Organizing and emotion: towards a social construction', in J. Hassard and M. Parker (eds), *Towards a New Theory of Organizations*. London: Sage.

Fineman, S. (1996a) 'Emotion and organizing', in S. Clegg, C. Hardy and W. Nord (eds), *Handbook of Organization Studies*. London: Sage.

Fineman. S. (1996b) 'Emotional Subtexts in Corporate Greening', *Organization Studies*, 17(3): 479–500.

Fineman, S. and Gabriel, Y. (1996) *Experiencing Organizations*. London: Sage.

Finocchario, M.A. (1990) 'Varieties of rhetoric in science', *History of the Human Sciences*, 3: 177–93.

Fishman, P. (1983) 'Interaction, the work women do', in B. Thorne, C. Kramarae and N. Henley (eds), *Language, Gender and Society*. New York: Harper & Row.

Flesch, R. (ed.) (1959) *The Book of Unusual Quotations*. London: Cassell.

Follett, M.P. (1941) *Dynamic Administration*. London: Pitman.

Ford, J. and Ford, L. (1995) 'The role of conversations in producing intentional change in organizations', *Academy of Management Review*, 20(3): 541–70.

Foucault, M. (1972) *The Archeology of Knowledge*. London: Tavistock.

Foucault, M. (1976) *The Birth of the Clinic*. London: Tavistock.

Foucault, M. (1979) *The History of Sexuality*, Vol. 1. Harmondsworth: Penguin.

Foucault, M. (1980) *Power/Knowledge*. New York: Pantheon.

Foucault, M. (1984) 'On the genealogy of ethics: an overview of work in progress', in P. Rabinow (ed.), *The Foucault Reader*. Harmondsworth: Penguin.

Foucault, M. (1991) 'Governmentality', in G. Burchell, C. Gordon and P. Miller, (eds), *The Foucault Effect: Studies in Governmentality*. Chicago: University of Chicago Press.

Freud, S. (1991) *The Interpretation of Dreams*. London: Penguin.

Frost, P.J., Moore, L.F., Louis, M.R., Lundberg, C.C. and Martin, J. (eds) (1991) *Reframing Organizational Culture*. Newbury Park, CA: Sage.

Frye, C.N. (1990) *Anatomy of Criticism*. Harmondsworth: Penguin.

Fuchs, S. and Ward, S. (1994a) 'What is deconstruction, and where and when does it take place? Making facts in science, building cases in law', *American Sociological Review*, 59(4): 481–500.

Fuchs, S. and Ward, S. (1994b) 'The sociology and paradoxes of deconstruction: a reply to Agger', *American Sociological Review*, 59(4): 506–10.

Funkenstein, A. (1993) 'The incomprehensible catastrophe: memory and narrative', in R. Josselson and A. Lieblich (eds), *The Narrative Study of Lives*. Newbury Park, CA: Sage.

Gabriel, Y. (1991a) 'Turning facts into stories and stories into facts', *Human Relations*, 44(8): 857–75.

Gabriel, Y. (1991b) 'On organisational stories and myths: Why it is easier to slay a dragon than to kill a myth', *International Sociology*, 6(4): 427–42.

Gabriel, Y. (1991c) 'Organizations and their discontents: a psychoanalytic contribution to the study of corporate culture', *Journal of Applied Behavioral Science*, 27: 318–36.

Gabriel, Y. (1992) 'Heroes, villains, fools and magic wands: computers in organisational folklore', *International Journal of Information Resource Management*, 3(1): 3–12.

Gabriel, Y. (1995) 'The unmanaged organization: stories, fantasies, subjectivity', *Organization Studies*, 16(3): 477–501.

Gabriel, Y. (1997a) 'Meeting God: when organisational members come face to face with the supreme leader', *Human Relations*, 50(4): 316–42.

Gabriel, Y. (1997b) 'The use of stories in organizational research', in G. Symon and C. Cassell (eds), *Qualitative Methods in Organizational Research*. London: Sage.

Gabriel, Y. and Lang, T. (1995) *The Unmanageable Consumer: Contemporary Consumption and Its Fragmentation*. London: Sage.

Gaill, F. (1987) 'Organisme', in I. Stengers (ed.), *D'une science a l'autre: des concepts nomades*. Paris: Seuil.

Gane, M. and Johnson, T. (eds) (1993) *Foucault's New Domains*. London: Routledge.

Garfinkel, H. (1967) *Studies in Ethnomethodology*. Englewood Cliffs, NJ: Prentice Hall.

Garfinkel, H. (1974) 'The origins of the term "ethnomethodology" ', in R. Turner, (ed.), *Ethnomethodology: Selected Readings*. Harmondsworth: Penguin.

Garland, D. (1990) *Punishment and Society: A Study in Social Theory*. Oxford: Clarendon Press.

Gee, J. (1990) *Social Linguistics and Literacies: Ideology in Discourses*. Bristol, PA: Falmer Press.

Geertz, C. (1973) *The Interpretation of Cultures*. London: Hutchinson.

Geertz, C. (1988) *Works and Lives: The Anthropologist as Author*. Stanford, CA: Stanford University Press.

Georges, R. (1969) 'Toward an understanding of story-telling events', *Journal of American Folklore*, 82: 314–28.

Georges, R. (1980) 'A folklorist's view of story-telling', *Humanities in Society*, 3(4): 317–26.

Georges, R. (1981) 'Do narrators really digress? A reconsideration of "audience asides" in narrating', *Western Folklore*, 40: 245–52.

Gergen, K.J. (1991) *The Saturated Self: Dilemmas of Identity in Contemporary Life*. New York: Basic Books.

Gergen, K.J. (1992) 'Organization theory in the postmodern era', in M. Reed and M. Hughes (eds), *Rethinking Organization: New Directions in Organization Theory and Analysis*. London: Sage.

Gergen, K.J. (1994) *Realities and Representations: Soundings in Social Construction*. Cambridge, MA: Harvard University Press.

Gergen, K.J., and Gergen, M.M. (1991) 'Toward reflexive methodologies', in F. Steier (ed.), *Research and Reflexivity*. London: Sage.

Gersick, C.J.G. (1991) 'Revolutionary change theories: a multilevel exploration of the punctuated equilibrium paradigm', *Academy of Management Review*, 16(1): 10–36.

Gherardi, S. (1995) *Gender, Symbolism and Organizational Cultures*. Thousand Oaks, CA: Sage.

Giddens, A. (1979) *Central Problems in Social Theory: Action, Structure and Contradication in Social Analysis*. Berkeley: University of California Press.

Giddens, A. (1984) *The Constitution of Society*. Berkeley: University of California Press.

Giddens, A. (1991) *Modernity and Self-Identity*. Cambridge: Polity.

Gilbert, G.N. and Mulkay, M. (1984) *Opening Pandora's Box: A Sociological Analysis of Scientists' Discourse*. Cambridge: Cambridge University Press.

Glanville, R. (1996) 'Heinz von Foerster, a Festschrift', *Systems Research*, Special Issue, 13(3).

Goffman, E. (1967) *Interactional Ritual: Essays on Face to Face Behavior*. Garden City, NY: Anchor/Doubleday.

Goffman, E. (1974) *Frame Analysis*. Cambridge, MA: Harvard University Press.

Goffman, E. (1983) 'The interaction order: American Sociological Association, 1982 presidential address', *American Sociological Review*, 48(1): 1–17.

Goffman, E. (1990) *The Presentation of Self in Everyday Life*. London: Penguin.

Goodchild, P. (1996) *Deleuze and Guattari: An Introduction to the Politics of Desire*. London: Sage.

Goss, T., Pascale, R. and Athos, A. (1993) 'The reinvention roller coaster: risking the present for a powerful future', *Harvard Business Review*, 38(3): 97–108.

Gowler, D. and Legge, K. (1983) 'The meaning of management and the management of meaning: a view from social anthropology', in M.J. Earl (ed.), *Perspectives on Management*. Oxford: Oxford University Press.

Gramsci, A. (1971) *Selections from the Prison Notebooks*. London: Lawrence & Wishart.

Grant, D. and Oswick, C. (eds) (1996) *Metaphor and Organizations*. London: Sage.

Grey, C. (1994) 'Career as a project of the self and labour process discipline', *Sociology*, 28(2): 479–97.

Grice, H.P. (1957) 'Meaning', *Philosophical Review*, 67: 53.

Grimshaw, A.D. (1989) *Collegial Discourse*. Norwood, NJ: Ablex.

Grimshaw, A.D., Feld, S. and Jenness, D. (1994) 'The multiple analysis project: background, history, problems, data', in A. Grimshaw (ed.), *What's Going on Here? Complementary Studies of Professional Talk*. Norwood, NJ: Ablex.

Gronn, P. (1983) 'Talk as the work: the accomplishment of school administration', *Administrative Science Quarterly*, 28: 1–21.

Gumperz, J. (1982) *Discourse Strategies*. Cambridge: Cambridge University Press.

Gumperz, J. (1992) 'Interviewing in intercultural situations', in P. Drew and J. Heritage (eds), *Talk at Work: Interaction in Institutional Settings*. Cambridge: Cambridge University Press.

Habermas, J. (1984) *Theory of Communicative Action. Vol. 1: Reason and the Rationalization of Society*. London: Heinemann.

Habermas, J. (1987) *The Theory of Communicative Action. Vol. 2: Lifeworld and System*. London: Heinemann.

Habermas J., (1977) 'A Review of Gadamer's *Truth and Method*, in F.R. Dallmayr and T.A. McCarthy, *Understanding and Social Inquiry*. Notre Dame, IN: University of Notre Dame Press.

Hall, D.L. and Ames, R.T. (1995) *Anticipating China: Thinking Through the Narratives of Chinese and Western Culture*. Albany, NY: State University of New York Press.

Halliday, M.K. (1978) *Language as Social Semiotic: The Social Interpretation of Language and Meaning*. Baltimore, MD: Edward Arnold.

Halliday, M.K. (1985) *An Introduction to Functional Grammar*. London: Edward Arnold.

Halliday, M.K. (1993) 'Towards a language-based theory of learning', *Linguistics and Education*, 5(2): 93–101.

Halliday, M.K. and Hasan, R. (1989) *Language, Context, and Text: Aspects of Language in a Social-Semiotic Perspective*. Oxford: Oxford University Press.

Hamilton, P. (1997) 'Rhetorical discourse of local pay', *Organization*, 4(2): 147–57.

Hampshire, S. (1971) *Freedom of Mind*. Princeton: Princeton University Press.

Hannerz, U. (1989) 'Notes on the global ecumene', *Public Culture*, 1(2): 66–75.

Hansen, C.D. and Kahnweiler, W. (1993) 'Storytelling: an instrument for understanding the dynamics of corporate relationships', *Human Relations*, 46(12): 1391–409.

Hardy, J. (1987) *A Psychology with a Soul*. London: Routledge and Kegan Paul.

Harré, R. (1986) *The Social Construction of Emotions*. Oxford: Blackwell.

Harré, R. and Gillett, G. (1994) *The Discursive Mind*. Thousand Oaks, CA: Sage.

Harris, R. and Timms, N. (1993) *Secure Accommodation in Child Care: Between Hospital and Prison or Thereabouts*. London: Routledge.

Hassard, J. (1993) 'Postmodernism and organizational analysis: an overview', in J. Hassard and M. Parker (eds), *Postmodernism and Organizations*. London: Sage.

Hassard, J. (1994) 'Postmodern organisational analysis: toward a conceptual framework', *Journal of Management Studies*, 31(3): 303–24.

Hassard, J. and Parker, M. (eds) (1993) *Postmodernism and Organizations*. London: Sage.

Hay, C. (1996) 'Narrating crisis: the discursive construction of the winter of discontent', *Sociology*, 30(2): 253–77.

Hazen, M.A. (1993) 'Towards polyphonic organization', *Journal of Organizational Change Management*, 6(5): 15–26.

Hedberg, B., Nystrom, C. and Starbuck, W. (1976) 'Camping on seesaws: prescriptions for a self-designing organization', *Administrative Science Quarterly*, 21(1): 41–63.

Heilbron, J. (1995) *The Rise of Social Theory*. Cambridge: Polity.

Helmer, J. (1993) 'Story telling in the creation and maintenance of organizational tension and stratification', *The Southern Communication Journal*, 59(1): 34–44.

Hewitt, J. and Hall, P. (1973) 'Social problems, problematic situations, and quasi-theories', *American Sociological Review*, 38: 367–74.

Hochschild, A. (1983) *The Managed Heart: Commercialization of Human Feeling*. Berkeley, CA: University of California Press.

Hodge, R. and Kress, G. (1988) *Social Semiotics*. Cambridge: Polity.

Hodge, R. and Kress, G. (1993) *Language as Ideology*. London: Routledge.

Hoggett, P. (1991) 'A new management in the public sector?', *Policy and Politics*, 19(4): 243–56.

Hopfl, H. and Linstead, S. (1997) 'Learning to feel and feeling to learn: emotion and learning in organizations', *Management Learning*, 28(1): 5–12.

Hoskin, K. and McLean, C. (1997) 'The Form', paper presented at conference on 'Modes of Organizing', University of Warwick, April.

Hymes, D. (1974) *Foundations in Sociolinguistics: An Ethnographic Approach*. Philadelphia: University of Pennsylvania Press.

Ikea (1984) *The Future is Filled with Opportunities*. Internal booklet, Ikea.

Inns, D. and Jones, P. (1996) 'Metaphor in organization theory: following in the footsteps of the poet?', in D. Grant and C. Oswick (eds), *Metaphor and Organizations*. London: Sage.

Isaacs, W.N. (1993a) 'Taking flight: dialogue, collective thinking and organization learning', *Organizational Dynamics*, 2(3): 24–39.

Isaacs, W.N. (1993b) 'Dialogue: the power of collective thinking', *The Systems Thinker*, 4(3): 1–4.

Jackson, N. and Willmott, H. (1987) 'Beyond epistemology and reflective conversation: towards human relations', *Human Relations*, 40(6): 361–80.

Jackson, P. (1995) 'Organising in time and space: a theoretical framework for the study of worker dispersal'. Working paper, Brunel University.

Jacques, R. (1996) *Manufacturing the Employee: Management Knowledge from the 19th to 21st Centuries*. London: Sage.

Jaworski, A. (1993) *The Power of Silence: Social and Pragmatic Perspectives*. Newbury Park, CA: Sage.

Jay, M. (1994) *Downcast Eyes*. Los Angeles: University of California Press.

Jeffcut, P. (1993) 'From interpretation to representation', in J. Hassard and M. Parker (eds), *Postmodernism and Organizations*. London: Sage.

Johnson, M. (1987) *The Body in the Mind: The Bodily Basis of Meaning, Imagination, and Reason*. Chicago: University of Chicago Press.

Kahane, H. (1973) *Logic and Philosophy: A Modern Introduction*. Belmont, CA: Wadsworth

Kallinikos, J. (1994) 'The architecture of the invisible: technology is representation', *Organization*, 2(1): 117–40.

Kauffman, S.A. (1993) *The Origins of Order: Self-organization and Selection in Evolution*. Oxford: Oxford University Press.

Keenoy, T. and Anthony, P.D. (1992) 'HRM: metaphor, meaning and morality', in P. Blyton and P. Turnbull (eds), *Reassessing Human Resource Management*. London: Sage.

Keenoy, T., Oswick, C. and Grant, D. (1997) 'Organizational discourses: text and context', *Organization*, 4(2): 147–57.

Kelly, K. (1994) *Out of Control: The New Biology of Machines, Social Systems and the Economic World*. Reading, MA: Addison-Wesley.

Knights, D. and Morgan, G. (1991) 'Strategic discourse and subjectivity: towards a critical analysis of corporate strategy in organizations', *Organization Studies*, 12(2): 251–73.

Knights, D. and Willmott, H. (1989) 'Power and subjectivity at work: from degradation to subjugation in social relations', *Sociology*, 23(4): 535–58.

Knights, D. and Vurdubakis, T. (1994) 'Foucault, power, resistance and all that', in J.M. Jermier, D. Knights and W. Nord (eds), *Resistance and Power in Organizations*. London: Routledge.

Knorr-Cetina, K. (1981) 'The micro-sociological challenge of macro-sociology: towards a reconstruction of social theory and methodology', in K. Knorr-Cetina and A.V. Cicourel (eds), *Advances in Social Theory and Methodology*. Boston: Routledge and Kegan Paul.

Knorr-Cetina, K. and Cicourel, A.V. (eds) (1981) *Advances in Social Theory and Methodology*. Boston: Routledge & Kegan Paul.

Koch, S. and Deetz, S. (1984) 'The extent and effects of the sexual harassment of working women', *Sociological Focus*, 17: 31–43.

Kondo, D. (1990) *Crafting Selves: Power, Gender and Discourses of Identity in a Japanese Workplace*. Chicago: University of Chicago Press.

Koontz, H., O'Donnell, C. and Weihrich, H. (1955) *Management*. New York: McGraw-Hill.

Kotter, J.P. and Heskett, J.L. (1992) *Corporate Culture and Performance*. New York: Free Press.

Kress, G. and van Leeuwen, T. (1990) *Reading Images*. Geelon, Vic.: Deakin University Press.

Kress, G. and Threadgold, T. (1988) 'Towards a social theory of genre', *Southern Review*, 21: 215–43.

Krippendorff, K. (1991) 'Reconstructing (some) communication research methods', in F. Steier (ed.), *Research and Reflexivity*. London: Sage.

Kunda, G. (1992) *Engineering Culture: Control and Commitment in a High-Tech Company*. Philadelphia: Temple University Press.

Lacan, J. (1977) *Écrits: A Selection*. London: Routledge.

Laclau, E. and Mouffe, C. (1987) *Hegemony and Socialist Strategy: Towards a Radical Democratic Politics*. London: Verso.

Lakoff, G. (1987) *Women, Fire, and Dangerous Things: What Categories Reveal About the Mind*. Chicago: University of Chicago Press.

Lakoff, G. and Johnson, M. (1980) *Metaphors We Live By*. Chicago: University of Chicago Press.

Langton, C.G. (ed.) (1989) *Artificial Life*. Vol. VI. Reading, MA: Addison-Wesley.

Langton, C.G. (ed) (1992) *Artificial Life II*. Vol. X. Reading, MA: Addison-Wesley.

Laughlin, C.D., McManus, J., and d'Aguili, E.G. (1992) *Brain, Symbol and Experience: Toward a Neurophenomenology of Human Consciousness*. New York: Columbia University Press.

Lawrence, T.B., Phillips, N. and Hardy, C. (1998) 'A relational theory of organizational collaboration', in S. Clegg, E. Ibarra and L. Bueno (eds), *Collective Remembering: Universal Theories and Local Realities*. London: Sage.

Layder, D. (1997) *Modern Social Theory: Key Debates and New Directions*. London: University College London Press.

Leach, E. (1972) 'Anthropological aspects of language: animal categories and verbal abuse', in P. Maranda (ed), *Mythology*. Harmondsworth: Penguin.

Leary, D.E. (ed) (1990) *Metaphors in the History of Psychology*. Cambridge: Cambridge University Press.

Legge, K. (1995) *Human Resource Management: Rhetorics and Realities*. London: Macmillan.

Lemaire, A. (1977) *Jacques Lacan*. London: Routledge and Kegan Paul.

Levin, D. (ed.) (1993) *Modernity and the Hegemony of Vision*. Los Angeles: University of California Press.

Levinson, S. (1983) *Pragmatics*. Cambridge: Cambridge University Press.

Lévi-Strauss, C. (1964) 'Structural analysis in linguistics and anthropology', in D. Hymes (ed), *Language in Culture and Society*. New York: Harper & Row.

Lévi-Strauss, C. (1976) 'The story of Asdiwal', in C. Lévi-Strauss (ed.), *Structural Anthropology*. Vol. 2. Harmondsworth: Penguin.

Lévi-Strauss, C. (1978) *Myth and Meaning: The 1977 Massey Lectures*. London: Routledge.

Lévy, P. (1990) *Les Technologies de l'intelligence – L'avenir de la pensée à l'ère informatique*. Paris: La Découverte.

Lewin, R. (1992) *Complexity: Life at the Edge of Chaos*. New York: Macmillan.

Linde, C. (1993) *Life Stories: The Creation of Coherence*. New York: Oxford University Press.

Linstead, S. (1994) 'Objectivity, reflexivity, and fiction: humanity, inhumanity, and the science of the social', *Human Relations*, 47(11): 1321–46.

Louis, M.R. (1983) 'Organizations as culture-bearing milieux', in L.R. Pondy, P.J. Frost, G. Morgan and T. Dandridge (eds), *Organizational Symbolism*. Greenwich, CT: JAI Press.

Lovejoy, A.O. (1936) *The Great Chain of Being*. Cambridge, MA: Harvard University Press.

Luhman, N. (1986) 'The autopoiesis of social systems', in F. Geyer and J. van der Zouwen (eds), *Sociocybernetic Paradoxes*. London: Sage.

Lyon, D. (1994) *The Electronic Eye: The Rise of Surveillance Society*. Cambridge: Polity.

Lyotard, J.-F. (1984) *The Postmodern Condition: A Report on Knowledge*. Manchester: Manchester University Press.

McCulloch, G. (1994) *Using Sartre: An Analytical Introduction to Early Sartrean Themes*. London: Routledge.

MacIntyre, A. (1981) *After Virtue*. London: Duckworth.

Mackie, J.L. (1973) *Truth, Probability and Paradox: Studies in Philosophical Logic*. Oxford: Clarendon Press.

McLuhan, M. (1962) *The Gutenberg Galaxy: The Making of Typographic Man*. London: Routledge & Kegan Paul.

Mahler, J. (1988) 'The quest for organizational meaning: identifying and interpreting the symbolism in organisational stories', *Administration and Society*, 20(3): 344–68.

Malinowski, B. (1923) 'The problem of meaning in primitive languages', in C. Ogden and I. Richards (eds), *The Meaning of Meaning*. London: Routledge and Kegan Paul.

Mangham, I.L. (1986) *Power and Performance in Organizations*. Oxford: Blackwell.

Mangham, I.L. (1995) 'Scripts, talk and double talk', *Management Learning*, 26(4): 493–511.

Mangham, I.L. (1997) 'Transcripts of interactions in a company'. Unpublished paper. Bath University.

Mangham, I.L., and Overington, M.A. (1987) *Organizations as Theatre: A Social Psychology of Dramatic Appearances*. Chichester: Wiley.

Manguel, A. (1996) *A History of Reading*. London: HarperCollins.

Marshak, R.J. (1993a) 'Managing the metaphors of change', *Organizational Dynamics*, 22(1): 44–56.

Marshak, R.J. (1993b) 'Lewin meets Confucius: a review of the OD model of change', *Journal of Applied Behavioral Science*, 29(4): 393–415.

Marshak, R.J. (1994) 'The tao of change', *OD Practitioner*, 26(2): 18–26.

Marshak, R.J. (1995) 'Managing in chaotic times', in R.A. Ritvo, A.H. Litwin and L. Butler (eds), *Managing in the Age of Change*. Alexandria, VA: Irwin Professional Publishing.

Marshak, R.J. (1996) 'Metaphors, metaphoric fields, and organizational change', in D. Grant and C. Oswick (eds), *Metaphor and Organizations*. London: Sage.

Marshak, R.J. and Katz, J.H. (1997) 'Diagnosing covert processes in groups and organizations', *OD Practitioner*, 29(1): 33–42.

Martin, J. (1982) 'Stories and scripts in organizational settings', in A. Hastorf and A. Isen (eds), *Cognitive and Social Psychology*, New York: Elsevier-North Holland.

Martin, J. (1990) 'Deconstructing organizational taboos: the suppression of gender conflict in organizations', *Organization Science*, 1(4): 339–59.

Martin, J. (1992) *Cultures in Organizations: Three Perspectives*. New York: Oxford University Press.

Martin, J. and Meyerson, D. (1988) 'Organizational cultures and the denial, channeling and acknowledgement of ambiguity', in L.R. Pondy, R.J. Boland, Jr, and H. Thomas (eds), *Managing Ambiguity and Change*. New York: Wiley.

Martin, J. and Powers, M. (1983) 'Truth or corporate propaganda? The value of a good war story', in L.R. Pondy, P.J. Frost, G. Morgan and T. Dandridge (eds), *Organizational Symbolism*. Greenwich, CT: JAI Press.

Martin, J., Feldman, M.S., Hatch, M.J. and Sitkin, S.B. (1983) 'The uniqueness paradox in organizational stories', *Administrative Science Quarterly*, 28: 438–53.

Martin, J., Knopoff, K. and Beckman, C. (1996) 'Seeking an alternative to bureaucratic impersonality and emotional labour at the Body Shop'. Paper presented at the Academy of Management, Cincinnati.

Maturana, H. and Varela, F. (1987) *The Tree of Knowledge*. Boston: Shambhala.

Maturana, H. and Varela, F. (1980) *Autopoiesis and Cognition: The Realization of the Living*. London: Reidel.

Mauws, M. and Phillips, N. (1995) 'Understanding language games', *Organization Science*, 6(3): 322–34.

Meek, V.L. (1988). 'Organizational culture: origins and weaknesses', *Organization Studies*, 9(4): 453–73.

Merleau-Ponty, M. (1962) *Phenomenology of Perception*. London: Routledge & Kegan Paul.

Merleau-Ponty, M. (1964) *L'œil et l'esprit*. Paris: Gallimard.

Merleau-Ponty, M. (1989) *Le Primat de la perception et ses conséquences philosophiques*. Grenoble: Cynara.

Michael, M. (1996) *Constructing Identities*. London: Sage.

Miles, M.A. and Huberman, A.M. (1994) *Qualitative Data Analysis: An Expanded Sourcebook*. Thousand Oaks, CA: Sage.

Miles, R.E. and Snow, C.C. (1978) *Organizational Strategy, Structure, and Process.* New York: McGraw-Hill.

Miller, P. and Rose, N. (1988) 'The Tavistock programme: the government of subjectivity and social life', *Sociology*, 22(2): 171–92.

Miller, P. and Rose, N. (1990) 'Governing economic life', *Economy and Society*, 19(1): 1–31.

Mingers, J. (1995) *Self-Producing Systems: Implications and Applications of Auto-poiesis.* New York: Plenum Press.

Mingers, J. (1996) 'A comparison of Maturana's autopoietic social theory and Giddens' theory of structuration', *Systems Research*, 13(4): 469–82.

Mintzberg, H. (1973) *The Nature of Managerial Work.* New York: Harper & Row.

Moerman, M. (1988) *Talking Culture: Ethnography and Conversation Analysis.* Philadelphia: University of Pennsylvania Press.

Morgan, G. (1980) 'Paradigms, metaphors and puzzle-solving in organization theory', *Administrative Science Quarterly*, 25: 605–22.

Morgan, G. (1983) 'More on metaphor: why we cannot control tropes in administrative science', *Administrative Science Quarterly*, 28(4): 601–7.

Morgan, G. (1986) *Images of Organization.* 1st edn. London: Sage.

Morgan, G. (1988) 'Teaching MBAs transformational thinking', in R. Quinn and K. Cameron (eds), *Paradox and Transformation.* Cambridge, MA: Ballinger.

Morgan, G. (1993) *Imaginization.* Newbury Park, CA: Sage.

Morgan, G. (1996) 'An afterword: is there anything more to be said about metaphor?', in D. Grant and C. Oswick (eds), *Metaphor and Organizations.* London: Sage.

Morgan, G. (1997) *Images of Organization.* 2nd edn. London: Sage.

Morin, E. (1971) *Rumor in Orléans.* New York: Pantheon.

Morouney, K. (1995) 'Kenneth and Joan: difference and the analysis of qualitative data'. Paper presented at the Women in Management Division, Academy of Management Meetings, Vancouver, BC, Canada.

Mullins, L.J. (1985) *Management and Organisational Behaviour.* London: Pitman.

Mumby, D. (1987) 'The political function of narrative in organizations', *Communication Monographs*, 54(2): 113–27.

Mumby, D.K. (1998) 'Power, politics and organizational communication: theoretical perspectives', in F. Jablin and L. Putnam (eds), *The New Handbook of Organizational Communication.* London: Sage.

Mumby, D.K. and Clair, R. (1997) 'Organizational discourse', in T.A. van Dijk (ed.), *Discourse as Structure and Process*, Vol. 2. London: Sage.

Mumby, D.K. and Putnam, L. (1992) 'The politics of emotion: a feminist reading of bounded rationality', *Academy of Management Review*, 17(3): 465–85.

Mumby, D.K. and Stohl, C. (1991) 'Power and discourse in organization studies: absence and the dialectic of control', *Discourse and Society*, 2(3): 313–32.

Munro, D.J. (1988) *Images of Human Nature: A Sung Portrait.* Princeton, NJ: Princeton University Press.

Nevis, E.C. (1987) *Organizational Consulting: A Gestalt Approach.* New York: Gardner Press.

Newall, V. (1980) 'Tell us a story', in J. Cherfas and R. Lewin (eds), *Not Work Alone.* London: Temple Mead.

Newton, T. (1994) 'Discourse and agency: the example of personnel psychology and assessment centres', *Organization Studies*, 15(6): 879–902.

Nielsen, R.P. (1993) 'Woolman's "I am we" triple loop action-learning: origin and application in organization ethics', *Journal of Applied Behavioral Science*, 29(1): 117–38.

Nierenberg, G.I. and Calero, H.H. (1973) *Meta-Talk: The Guide to Hidden Meanings in Conversation.* New York: Cornerstone Library.

Nietzsche, F. (1977) *A Nietzsche Reader* (ed. R.J. Hollingdale). Harmondsworth: Penguin.

Noble, D. (1994) *World without Women*. Oxford: Oxford University Press.

Nohria, N. and Berkley, J. (1994) 'The virtual organization: bureaucracy, technology and the imposition of control', in C. Heckscher and A. Donnellon (eds), *The Post-Bureaucratic Organization: New Perspectives on Organizational Change*. Thousand Oaks, CA: Sage.

Nonaka, I. and Takeuchi, H. (1995) *The Knowledge-Creating Company: How Japanese Companies Create the Dynamics of Innovation*. Oxford: Oxford University Press.

Norton, D.F. (1993) *The Cambridge Companion to Hume*. Cambridge: Cambridge University Press.

Nussbaum, M.C. (1990) *Love's Knowledge: Essays on Philosophy and Literature*. Oxford: Oxford University Press.

Oakley, J. (1991) *Morality and the Emotions*. London: Routledge.

Ochs, E. (1979) 'Transcription as theory', in E. Ochs and B.B. Schieffelin (eds), *Developmental Pragmatics*. New York: Academic Press.

O'Connor, E. (1995) 'Paradoxes of participation: textual analysis and organizational change', *Organization Studies*, 16(5): 769–803.

Okuyama, M. (1996) 'General theory and local knowing in therapy'. Unpublished paper. Ohmiya Child Health Center, Ohmiya-shi, Japan.

O'Neil, J. (1986) 'The disciplinary society', *British Journal of Sociology*, 37(1): 42–60.

Ong, W. (1958) *Ramus, Method and the Decay of Dialogue*. Cambridge: Polity.

Orr, J. (1990) 'Sharing knowledge, celebrating identity: war stories and community memoiry in a service culture', in D.S. Middleton and D. Edwards (eds), *Collective Remembering: Memory in Society*. Beverly Hills, CA: Sage.

Ortony, A. (ed.) (1993) *Metaphor and Thought*, 2nd edn. Cambridge: Cambridge University Press.

Oswick, C. and Grant, D. (eds) (1996) *Organization Development: Metaphorical Explorations*. London: Pitman.

Oswick, C., Keenoy, T. and Grant, D. (1997) 'Managerial discourses: words speak louder than actions?', *Journal of Applied Management Studies*, 6(1): 5–12.

Palmer, I. and Dunford, R. (1995) 'Reframing and organizational action: the unexplored link'. Paper presented at the 6th International Colloquium of the APROS (Asian-Pacific Researchers on Organization Studies), Cuernavaca, Mexico.

Palmer, I. and Dunford, R. (1996) 'Conflicting use of metaphors: reconceptualizing their use in the field of organizational change', *Academy of Management Review*, 21(3): 691–717.

Parker, I. (1992) *Discourse Dynamics*. London: Routledge.

Passeron, J.C. (1991) *Le Raisonnement sociologique: L'espace non-popperien du raisonnement naturel*. Paris: Nathan.

Perinbanayagam, R.S (1991) *Discursive Acts*. New York: Aldine de Gruyter.

Perren, L. and Atkin, R. (1997) 'Owner-manager's discourse: the metaphors-in-use', *Journal of Applied Management Studies*, 6(1): 45–62.

Peters, T.J. and Waterman, R.H. (1982) *In Search of Excellence: Lessons from America's Best-Run Companies*. New York: Harper and Row.

Pfeffer, J. (1993) 'Barriers to the advance of organizational science', *Academy of Management Review*, 18(4): 599–620.

Phillips, N. (1995) 'Telling organizational tales: on the role of narrative fiction in the study of organizations', *Organization Studies*, 16(4): 625–49.

Phillips, N. and Hardy, C. (1997) 'Managing multiple identities: discourse legitimacy and resources in the UK refugee system', *Organization*, 4(2): 159–85.

Pinder, C.C. and Bourgeois, V.W. (1982) 'Controlling tropes in administrative science', *Administrative Science Quarterly*, 27: 641–52.

Plant, S. (1992) *The Most Radical Gesture*, London: Routledge.

Polanyi, M. (1966) *The Tacit Dimension*. London: Routledge.

Pondy, L. (1978) 'Leadership is a language game', in M. McCall and K. Lombardo (eds), *Leadership: Where Else Can We Go?* Durham, NC: Duke University Press.

Poole, M.S. and Van de Ven, A.H. (1989) 'Using paradox to build management and organization theories', *Academy of Management Review*, 14(4): 562–78.

Potter, J. and Wetherell, M. (1987) *Discourse and Social Psychology*. London: Sage.

Power, M. (1990) 'Modernism, postmodernism and organization', in J. Hassard and D. Pym (eds), *The Theory and Philosophy of Organizations*. London: Routledge.

Propp, V. (1984) *Theory and History of Folklore*. Manchester: Manchester University Press.

Putnam, L. (1992) 'Language and meaning: Discourse approaches to the study of organizations'. Paper presented at the 42nd Annual Conference of the International Communication Association, Miami, FL.

Ragland-Sullivan, E. (1986) *Jacques Lacan and the Philosophy of Psychoanalysis*. London: Croom Helm.

Ramanantsoa, B. and Battaglia, V. (1991) 'The autobiography of the firm'. Paper presented at the 8th International SCOS Conference, Copenhagen, Denmark.

Rapport, N. (1994) *The Prose and the Passion: Anthropology, Literature and the Writing of E.M. Forster*. Manchester: Manchester University Press.

Reed, M. (1995) 'Managing quality and organisational politics: TQM as a governmental technology', in I. Kirkpatrick and M. Martinez Lucio (eds), *The Politics of Quality in the Public Sector*. London: Routledge.

Reed, M. (1996) 'Expert power and control in late modernity: an empirical review and theoretical synthesis', *Organization Studies*, 17(4): 573–97.

Reed, M. (1997) 'In praise of duality and dualism: rethinking agency and structure in organizational analysis', *Organization Studies*, 18(1): 21–42.

Reed, M (1998) 'From the cage to the gaze? The dynamics of organizational control in high modernity', in G. Morgan and L. Engwall (eds), *Corporate Regulation and Risks: International Perspectives*. London: Routledge.

Ricoeur, P. (1978) *The Rule of Metaphor: Multi-disciplinary Studies of the Creation of Meaning in Language*. London: Routledge & Kegan Paul.

Roberts, C., Davies, E. and Jupp, T. (1992) *Language and Discrimination: A Study of Communication in Multicultural Workplaces*. New York: Longman.

Roberts, M. (1979) *The New Barbarism*. Oxford: Oxford University Press.

Roe, E. (1994) *Narrative Policy Analysis: Theory and Practice*. Durham, NC: Duke University Press.

Rorty, R. (1980) *Philosophy and the Mirror of Nature*. New Haven, CT: Princeton University Press.

Rosaldo, R. (1993) *Culture and Truth: The Remaking of Social Analysis*. Boston: Beacon Press.

Rose, N. (1990) *Governing the Soul: The Shaping of the Private Self*. London: Routledge.

Rose, N. (1996) 'Governing advanced liberal democracies', in A. Barry, T. Osborne and N.S. Rose (eds), *Foucault and Political Reasoning: Liberalism, Neo-Liberalism and Rationalities of Government*. London: University College London Press.

Rosen, M. (1984) 'Myth and reproduction: the conceptualization of management theory, method and practice', *Journal of Management*, 21(3): 303–22.

Rosen, M. (1985a) 'Breakfast at Spiro's: dramaturgy and dominance', *Journal of Management Studies*, 11(2): 31–48.

Rosen, M. (1985b) 'The reproduction of hegemony: an analysis of bureaucratic control', *Research in Political Economy*, 8: 257–89.

Rosenau, P. (1992) *Post-Modernism and the Social Sciences: Insights, Inroads and Intrusions*. Princeton, CT: Princeton University Press.

Ryle, G. (1949) *The Concept of Mind*. London: Hutchinson.

Sackmann, S. (1992) 'Culture and subcultures: an analysis of organizational knowledge', *Administrative Science Quarterly*, 37(1): 140–61.

Sacks, H., Schegloff, E.A. and Jefferson, G. (1974) 'A simplest systematics for the organization of turn-taking for conversation', *Language*, 40: 696–735.

Salzer, M. (1994) 'Identity across borders: a study in the Ikea-World'. Doctoral dissertation, Department of Management and Economics, Linköping University, Sweden.

Salzer-Mörling, M. (1997) 'The empty space – a crowded place'. Paper presented at the 15th International SCOS Conference, Warsaw.

Sandelands, L.E. and Buckner, G.C. (1989) 'Of art and work: aesthetic experience and the psychology of work feelings', *Research in Organizational Behaviour*, 11: 105–33.

Sapir, E. (1921) *Language: An Introduction to the Study of Speech*. New York: Harcourt Brace.

Sarbin, T. (1987) 'Emotion and act: roles and rhetoric', in R. Harré (ed.), *The Social Construction of Emotions*. Oxford: Blackwell.

Sartre, J.-P. (1962) *Sketch for a Theory of Emotions*. London: Methuen.

Sartre, J.-P. (1972) 'Why write?', in D. Lodge (ed.), *20th Century Literary Criticism: A Reader*. London: Longman.

Sarup, M. (1993) *An Introductory Guide to Post-Structuralism and Postmodernism*. Hemel Hempstead: Harvester Wheatsheaf.

Saussure, F. de (1960) *Course in General Linguistics*. London: Peter Owen.

Sayer, A. (1997) 'Essentialism, social constructionism and beyond', *Sociological Review*, 45(3): 453–87.

Schegloff, E.A. (1988/9) 'From interview to confrontation: observations of the Bush/ Rather encounter', *Research on Language and Social Interaction*, 22: 215–40.

Schegloff, E.A. (1991) 'Conversation analysis and socially shared cognition', in L. Resnick, J. Levine and S. Teasley (eds), *Perspectives on Socially Shared Cognition*. Washington, DC: American Psychological Association.

Schegloff, E.A. and Sacks, H. (1973) 'Opening up closings', *Semiotica*, 7: 289–327.

Schein, E.H. (1993) 'On dialogue, culture, and organizational learning', *Organizational Dynamics*, 2(3): 40–51.

Schenkein, J. (1978) 'Identity negotiations in conversation', in J. Schenkein (ed.), *Studies in the Organization of Conversational Interaction*. New York: Academic Press.

Schiffrin, D. (1987) *Discourse Markers*. Cambridge: Cambridge University Press.

Schlanger, J. (1971) *Les Métaphores de l'organisme*. Paris: Vrin.

Schlanger, J. (1983) *L'Invention intellectuelle*. Paris: Fayard.

Schlanger, J. (1988) 'La pensée inventive', in I. Stengers and J. Schlanger (eds), *Les Concepts scientifiques*. Paris: La Découverte.

Schön, D.A. (1983) *The Reflective Practitioner*. New York: Basic Books.

Schön, D.A. (1993) 'Generative metaphor: a perspective on problem-solving in social policy', in A. Ortony (ed.), *Metaphor and Thought*, 2nd edn. Cambridge: Cambridge University Press.

Schutz, A. (1967) *Collected Papers*. Den Haag: Nijhoff.

Schwartzman, H. (1989) *The Meeting: Gatherings in Organizations and Communities*. New York: Plenum Press.

Scott-Morgan, P. (1994) *The Unwritten Rules of the Game*. New York: McGraw-Hill.

Searle, J.R. (1969) *Speech Acts: An Essay in the Philosophy of Language*. London: Cambridge University Press.

Searle, J.R. (1995) *The Construction of Social Reality*. London: Allen Lane.

Senge, P.M. (1990) *The Fifth Discipline: The Art and Practice of the Learning Organization*. New York: Doubleday.

Sewell, G. (1996) 'Be seeing you: a rejoinder to Webster and Robins and to Jenkins', *Sociology*, 30: 785–97.

Sewell, G. and Wilkinson, B. (1992) 'Someone to watch over me: surveillance, discipline and Just-in-Time labour process', *Sociology*, 26: 271–89.

Silverman, D. (1993) *Interpreting Qualitative Data: Methods for Analysing Talk, Text and Interaction*. London: Sage.

Simon, H.A. (1962) 'The architecture of complexity', *Proceedings of the American Philosophical Society*, 106: 467–82.

Sims, D. (1992) 'Information systems and constructing problems', *Management Decision*, 30(5): 21–7.

Sims, D. (1995a) 'A narrative approach to agenda shaping'. Paper presented to the Third International Workshop on Managerial and Organizational Cognition, Strathclyde University, June.

Sims, D. (1995b) 'Building individual agendas in an organization: a participatory action research project?' Paper presented to the European Group of Organization Studies (EGOS) Colloquium, Istanbul, July.

Sims, D. and Doyle, J. (1995) 'Cognitive sculpting as a means of working with managers' metaphors', *Omega*, 23: 117–24.

Sims, D., Fineman, S. and Gabriel, Y. (1993) *Organizing and Organizations*. London: Sage.

Sinclair, J. and Coulthard, R.M. (1975) *Towards an Analysis of Discourse: The English Used by Teachers and Pupils*. London: Oxford University Press.

Smircich, L. and Morgan, G. (1982) 'Leadership: the management of meaning', *Journal of Applied Behavioural Science*, 18(3): 257–73.

Smith, D. (1991) *The Rise of Historical Sociology*. Cambridge: Polity.

Sobel, D. (1996) *Longitude*. London: Fourth Estate.

Solomon, R.C (1976) *The Passions: The Myth and Nature of Human Emotion*. New York: Anchor Press/Doubleday.

Soyland, A.J. (1994) *Psychology as Metaphor*. London: Sage.

Spence, D.P. and Owens, K.C. (1990) 'Lexical co-occurrence and association strength', *Journal of Psycholinguistic Research*, 19(1): 317–30.

Srivastva, S. and Barrett, F. (1988) 'The transforming nature of metaphors in group development: a study in group theory', *Human Relations*, 41(1): 31–64.

Starbuck, W.H. (1985) 'Acting first and thinking later', in J.M. Pennings (ed.), *Organizational Strategy and Change*. San Francisco: Jossey-Bass.

Stein, H.F. (1994) 'Workplace organizations and culture theory: a psychoanalytic approach'. Paper presented to the Symposium of the International Society for the Psychoanalytic Study of Organizations, Chicago, 2–4 June.

Stewart, R. (1963) *The Reality of Management*. London: Heinemann.

Stocker, M. (1996) 'How emotions reveal value', in E. Crisp, (ed.), *How Should One Live? Essays on Virtues*. Oxford: Clarendon Press.

Strawson, P.F. (1974) *Freedom and Resentment*. London: Methuen.

Stroh, P. and Miller, W.W. (1994) 'Learning to thrive on paradox', *Training and Development*, 48(9): 28–34.

Strombach, W. (1983) 'Wholeness, Gestalt, system: on the meaning of these concepts in German language', *International Journal of General Systems*, 9: 65–72.

Swidler, A. (1986) 'Culture in action: symbols and strategies', *American Sociological Review*, 51(2): 273–86.

Tannen, D. (1986) *That's Not What I Meant*. New York: Ballantine Books.

Tannen, D. (1989) *Talking Voices: Repetition, Dialogue and Imagery in Conversational Discourse*. New York: Cambridge University Press.

Tannen, D. (1990) *You Just Don't Understand*. New York: William Morrow.

Tannen, D. (1994a) *Gender and Discourse*. New York: Oxford University Press.

Tannen, D. (1994b) *Talking from 9–5*. New York: William Morrow.

Tannen, D. (1995) 'The power of talk: who gets heard and why', *Harvard Business Review*, 74(5): 138–48.

Tannen, D. and Saville-Troike, M. (1985) *Perspectives on Silence*. Norwood, NJ: Ablex.

Taylor, A.J.P. (1979) *How Wars Begin*. London: Hamish Hamilton.

Taylor, C. (1985) *Human Agency and Language, Philosophical Papers*, Vol. I Cambridge: Cambridge University Press.

Thibault, P. (1991) *Social Semiotics as Praxis*. Minnesota, MN: University of Minnesota Press.

Thompson, J.D. (1967) *Organizations in Action*. New York: McGraw-Hill.

Thompson, P. and Ackroyd, S. (1995) 'All quiet on the workplace front?: A critique of recent trends in British industrial sociology', *Sociology* 29(4): 615–34.

Townley, B. (1994) *Reframing Human Resource Management: Power, Ethics and the Subject at Work*. London: Sage.

Tregoe, B.B., Zimmerman, J.W., Smith, R.A. and Tobia, P.M. (1989) *Vision in Action*. New York: Simon and Schuster.

Trice, H.M. and Beyer, J.M. (1984) 'Studying organizational cultures through rites and ceremonials', *Academy of Management Review*, 9(4): 653–69.

Tsoukas, H. (1991) 'The missing link: a transformational view of metaphors in organizational science', *Academy of Management Review*, 16(3): 566–85.

Tsoukas, H. (1992) 'Postmodernism, reflexive rationalism and organizational studies: a reply to Martin Parker', *Organization Studies*, 13(4): 643–9.

Turner, B. (1996) *For Weber: Essays on the Sociology of Fate*. London: Sage.

Unger, R.M. (1987) *False Necessity*. Cambridge: Cambridge University Press.

van Dijk, T.A. (1981) *Studies in the Pragmatics of Discourse*. The Hague: Mouton Publishers.

van Dijk, T.A. (ed.) (1997a) *Discourse as Structure and Process*, Vols 1 and 2. London: Sage.

van Dijk, T.A. (1997b) 'The study of discourse', in T.A. van Dijk (ed.), *Discourse as Structure and Process*, Vol. 1. London: Sage.

Varela, F.J. (1979) *Principles of Biological Autonomy*. New York: North Holland.

Vermorel, F. (1997) *Fashion Perversity*. London: Bloomsbury.

Vetlesen, A.J. (1994) *Perception, Empathy, and Judgement: An Inquiry into the Preconditons of Moral Performance*. Pennsylvania: Pennsylvania State University Press.

Volkema, R. and Niederman, F. (1995) 'Organizational meetings: formats and information requirements', *Small Group Research*, 26(1): 3–24.

Volosinov, V.N. (1973) *Marxism and the Philosophy of Language*. Cambridge, MA: Harvard University Press.

von Foerster, H. (1979) 'Cybernetics of cybernetics', in K. Krippendorff (ed.), *Communication and Control in Society*. New York: Gordon & Breach.

von Foerster, H. (1993) 'Über das konstruieren von Wirklichkeiten', in H. von Foerster, *Wissen und Gewissen: Versuch einer Brücke*. Frankfurt: Suhrkamp Verlag.

von Krogh, G. and Roos, J. (1996) 'Conversation management for knowledge development', in G. von Krogh and J. Roos (eds), *Managing Knowledge: Perspectives on Cooperation and Competition*. London: Sage.

Waldrop, M.M. (1992) *Complexity: The Emerging Science at the Edge of Order and Chaos*. New York: Simon and Schuster.

Wasson, C. (1995) 'The production of consensus: theorizing politeness in organizational life'. Paper presented at the Academy of Management 1995 National Meeting, Vancouver, Canada.

Watson, G. and Seiler, R. (eds) (1992) *Text in Context: Contributions to Ethnomethodology*. Newbury Park, CA: Sage.

Watson, T.J. (1994) *In Search of Management: Culture, Chaos and Control in Managerial Work*. London: Routledge.

Watson, T.J. (1995) 'Rhetoric, discourse and argument in organizational sense making: a reflexive tale', *Organization Studies*, 16(5): 805–21.

Watzlawick, P. (1976) *How Real is Real? Confusion, Disinformation, Communication*. New York: Random House.

Watzlawick, P., Beavin, J.H. and Jackson, D.D. (1967) *Pragmatics of Human Communication*. New York: Norton.

Waugh, L.R. and Monville-Burston, M. (eds) (1990) *On Language: Roman Jakobson*. Cambridge, MA: Harvard University Press.

Weber, R. (1990) *Basic Content Analysis*. London: Sage.

Webster, F. (1995) *Theories of the Information Society*. London: Routledge.

Weick, K.E. (1979) *The Social Psychology of Organizing*. Reading, MA: Addison-Wesley.

Weick, K.E. (1984) 'Managerial thought in the context of action', in: S. Srivastva (ed.), *The Executive Mind*. San Francisco: Jossey-Bass.

Weick, K.E. (1985) 'Cosmos vs chaos: sense and nonsense in electronic contexts', *Organizational Dynamics*, 14(2): 50–64.

Weick, K.E. (1993) 'Sensemaking in organizations: small structures with large consequences', in J. Murnighan (ed.) *Social Psychology in Organizations: Advances in Theory and Research*. Englewood Cliffs, NJ: Prentice Hall.

Weick, K.E. (1995) *Sensemaking in Organizations*. Thousand Oaks, CA: Sage.

Weick, K.E. and Westley, F. (1996) 'Organizational learning: reaffirming an oxymoron', in S. Clegg, C. Hardy and W. Nord (eds), *Handbook of Organization Studies*. London: Sage.

West, C. (1996) 'Ethnography and orthography: a (modest) methodological proposal', *Journal of Contemporary Ethnography*, 25(3): 327–52.

West, C. and Zimmerman, D. (1985) 'Gender, language and discourse', in T.A. van Dijk (ed.), *Handbook of Discourse Analysis: Vol. 4. Discourse Analysis in Society*, London: Academic Press.

Westley, F. (1990) 'Middle managers and strategy: the microdynamics of inclusion', *Strategic Management Journal*, 11(5): 337–51.

Wharton, A.S. (1993) 'The affective consequences of service work: managing emotions on the job', *Work and Occupations*, 20(2): 205–32.

Whorf, B.L. (1956) *Language, Thought and Reality*. New York: Wiley.

Widdershoven, G.A.M. (1993). 'The story of life: hermeneutic perspectives on the relationship between narrative and life history', in R. Josselson and A. Lieblich (eds), *The Narrative Study of Lives*. Newbury Park, CA: Sage.

Wiener, N. (1961) *Cybernetics or Control and Communication in the Animal and the Machine*. 2nd edn. Cambridge, MA: MIT Press.

Wilkins A.L. (1983) 'Organizational stories as symbols which control the organization', in L.R. Pondy, P.J. Frost, G. Morgan and T.C. Dandridge (eds), *Organizational Symbolism*. Greenwich, CT: JAI Press.

Willmott, H. (1990) 'Subjectivity and the dialectics of praxis: opening-up the core of labour process analysis', in D. Knights and H. Willmott (eds), *Labour Process Theory*. London: Macmillan.

Willmott, H. (1994) 'Bringing agency (back) into organizational analysis: responding to the crisis of (post)modernity', in J. Hassard and M. Parker (eds), *Towards a New Theory of Organizations*. London: Sage.

Wittgenstein, L. (1968) *Philosophical Investigations*. 3rd edn. New York: Macmillan.

Yeung, L. (1997) 'Confrontation or resolution: discourse strategies for dealing with conflicts in participative decision-making', *Journal of Applied Management Studies*, 6(1): 63–75.

Zadeh, L. (1965) 'Fuzzy sets', *Informational Control*, 8: 338–53.

Zuboff, S. (1988) *In the Age of the Smart Machine: The Future of Work and Power*. London: Macmillan.

Zukov, G. (1980) *The Dancing Wu Li Masters*. London: Fontana.

Index